D1557493

JUSTIN MARTYR AND THE MOSAIC LAW

JUSTIN MARTYR AND THE MOSAIC LAW

by

Theodore Stylianopoulos

Published by

SOCIETY OF BIBLICAL LITERATURE

and

SCHOLARS PRESS

DISSERTATION SERIES, NUMBER 20

1975

Distributed by

SCHOLARS PRESS
University of Montana
Missoula, Montana 59801

JUSTIN MARTYR AND THE MOSAIC LAW

by

Theodore Stylianopoulos
Hellenic College
Holy Cross Greek Orthodox School of Theology
Brookline, Massachusetts   02146

Th.D., 1974   Advisers:
Harvard Divinity School $2\mathcal{g}/ \cdot 3$ Helmut Koester
                                                    John Strugnell

$$J985Yst$$

200981

Library of Congress Cataloging in Publication Data

Stylianopoulos, Theodore.
    Justin Martyr and the Mosaic law.

    (Dissertation series ; no. 20)
    Originally presented as the author's thesis, Harvard
Divinity School, 1974.
    Bibliography: p.
    1. Justinus Martyr, Saint. 2. Christianity and
other religions--Judaism. 3. Judaism--Relations--
Christianity. 4. Jewish law. I. Title. II. Series:
Society of Biblical Literature. Dissertation series ;
no. 20.
BR1720.J8S79 1975   296.1'8   75-22445
ISBN 0-89130-018-X

Printed in the United States of America

Printing Department
University of Montana
Missoula, Montana 59801

TABLE OF CONTENTS

PREFACE

The Mosaic Law became a decisive problem for the ancient Church during two periods. The first was at the time of the initial great expansion of the Christian faith (35-55 AD), when the remarkable success of the gentile mission in Syria, Asia Minor and Greece raised the question of the necessity and legitimacy of the practice of the Mosaic Law in Christian life. The second was about one hundred years later when the role of the Mosaic Law in the divine dispensation was debated among gnostics and Christians. This latter debate was conducted on more theoretical terms as part of larger concerns leading to the first development of theological systems. Justin Martyr played a substantive role in this latter debate which centered on the place of the Old Testament in Christian theology.

My aim in this book is to examine Justin Martyr's attempt at a comprehensive theological evaluation of the Mosaic Law. In his Dialogue with Trypho, Justin gives a great deal of attention to the Mosaic Law. He writes for Jews and Christians, but his concept of the Law is partly determined by the gnostic hermeneutic of Scripture. Justin is a figure of considerable magnitude in ancient Christianity. His attempt at a systematic interpretation of the Mosaic Law, probably pre-dating that of Ptolemy (Letter to Flora), is of great interest to Christian theology and particularly to the history of Jewish-Christian relations.

I wish to express my gratitude to Professor Helmut Koester, my adviser, who guided me throughout this dissertation. His incisive criticisms helped give acceptable shape especially to the early chapters of this work. I am also indebted to Professor John Strugnell who read most of the manuscript and made valuable comments.

In addition, I wish to thank my colleagues at Holy Cross Greek Orthodox School of Theology for their interest in my work

vii

and their moral support. I am also pleased that the Society of Biblical Literature accepted my work for publication in its dissertation series.

Most of all I am indebted to my wife for her devoted support and for typing and retyping the manuscript.

Theodore Stylianopoulos

TO FOTINI

ABBREVIATIONS

AKG	Arbeiten zur Kirchengeschichte
BEvTh	Beiträge zur evangelischen Theologie
BFChTh	Beiträge zur Förderung christlicher Theologie
BHTh	Beiträge zur historischen Theologie
BJRL	Bulletin of the John Rylands Library
EThL	Ephemerides Theologicae Lovanienses
FRLANT	Forschungen zur Religion und Literatur des Alten und Neuen Testaments
Gn	Gnomon
GOTR	Greek Orthodox Theological Review
HE	Historia Ecclesiastica (Eusebius)
HTR	Harvard Theological Review
JBL	Journal of Biblical Literature
JThS	Journal of Theological Studies
KT	Kleine Texte
LXX	Septuagint
RB	Revue Biblique
PG	Patrologia Graeca
RechSR	Recherches de Science Religieuse
SAB	Sitzungsberichte der Berliner Akademie der Wissenschaften
SC	Sources Chrétiennes
Schol.	Scholastik
SJTh	The Scottish Journal of Theology
StTh	Studia Theologica
ThJ	Theologische Jahrbücher
ThW	Theologisches Wörterbuch (Kittel)
TU	Texte und Untersuchungen
VigChr	Vigiliae Christianae
VT	Vetus Testamentum
ZKG	Zeitschrift für Kirchengeschichte
ZNW	Zeitschrift für die neutestamentliche Wissenschaft
ZWTh	Zeitschrift für wissenschaftliche Theologie

INTRODUCTION

Justin Martyr is a crucial figure for the study of the struggle over the Old Testament in the second century. He uses the Old Testament far more extensively than any of his Christian predecessors while vigorously engaged in the defense of Christianity against paganism, Judaism and gnosticism. In his Dialogue with Trypho he deals almost exclusively with the interpretation of the Old Testament. In this same work he also devotes major attention to the Mosaic Law (Dial. 10-30, 40-47, 67, 92-93, and 95), a central problem of Christian theology in the second century.[1] Because Justin is the first Christian author to take into account the gnostic and marcionite critique of Scripture, having written a full-scale work against the second-century heresiarchs,[2] he is also the first to formulate a sharper understanding of the Mosaic Law which is later continued and developed by Irenaeus, Tertullian and others. Two of the most distinctive aspects of Justin's contribution to the ongoing Christian interpretation of the Law, formulated quite probably prior to Ptolemy's Letter to Flora, are his tripartite division of the Law and his historical concept of the purpose of the Law, which are examined in the second and fourth chap-

---

[1] Hans Freiherr von Campenhausen, Die Entstehung der christlichen Bibel, BHTh 39 (Tübingen: J.C.B. Mohr, 1968), p. 99, now in English translation by J. A. Baker, The Formation of the Christian Bible (Philadelphia: Fortress Press, 1972).

[2] The Syntagma Against All Heresies which is mentioned in Ap. 26.8. Marcion apparently is the chief figure against whom Justin writes. Irenaeus' reference to a work of Justin Against Marcion (ἐν τῷ πρὸς Μαρκίωνι συντάγματι, Greek in Eusebius, H.E. 4.18.9 and J. A. Cramer, Catenae Graecorum Patrum, Tomus VIII, pp. 81-82; cf. Adv. Haer. 4.11.2, Harvey) is probably to the same work. Pierre Prigent in Justin et l'Ancien Testament (Paris: Gabalda, 1964) has recently attempted to reconstruct this lost work of Justin on the basis of the Dialogue and the Apology. See also E. Barnikol, "Verfasste oder benutzte Justin das um 140 enstandene, erste antimarcionitische Syntagma gegen die Häresien?" ThJ 6 (1938), 17-19.

ters of this work.[3]

Justin's treatment of the Mosaic Law has, however, received little attention in secondary literature. The older monographs of Karl Semisch[4] and of Moritz von Engelhardt[5] offer brief summaries of Justin's views on the Law. Adolf von Harnack[6] and Erwin Goodenough[7] in their studies on Justin have little or nothing to say about the problem of the Law in the Apologist's thought. The same is true of the more recent literature which has as focus either the exegesis of Justin[8]

---

[3]For an excellent description of the landscape of the problem, and Justin's contribution, see most recently von Campenhausen, Die Entstehung, pp. 76-122. The wider literature on the problem of the Old Testament in the ancient Church is voluminous. See especially Rudolf Bultmann, Theologie des Neuen Testaments (Tübingen: J.C.B. Mohr, 1965), pp. 109ff.; E. Flesseman-Van Leer, Tradition and Scripture in the Early Church (Assen, 1954); Gregory T. Armstrong, Die Genesis in der Alten Kirchen, BGH 4 (Tübingen: J.C.B. Mohr, 1962); Walter Bauer, Orthodoxy and Heresy in Earliest Christianity, ed. R. A. Kraft and G. Krodel (Philadelphia: Fortress Press, 1971), pp. 195-202; R. M. Grant, The Letter and the Spirit (London: S.P.C.K., 1957); M. F. Wiles, "The Old Testament in Controversy with the Jews," SJTh 8 (1955), 113-26; Leonard Goppelt, Christentum und Judentum im ersten und zweiten Jahrhundert, BFChTh 55 (Gütersloh, 1954); Marcel Simon, Verus Israel (Paris, 1964); Arthur Freiherr von Ungern-Sternberg, Der traditionelle alttestamentliche Schriftbeweis 'de Christo' und 'de Evangelio' in der Alten Kirche (Halle, 1913); Victor Ernst Hasler, Gesetz und Evangelium in der Alten Kirche (Zürich, 1953); A. Harnack, Marcion: Das Evangelium vom fremden Gott, TU 45 (Leipzig, 1942); E. C. Blackman, Marcion and His Influence (London, 1948), pp. 113ff., and P. G. Verweijs, Evangelium und neues Gesetz in der ältesten Christenheit bis auf Marcion (Utrecht, 1960).

[4]Justin des Märtyrer, Vols. I-II (Breslau, 1840-1841), especially, II, pp. 58-70.

[5]Das Christentum Justins des Märtyrers (Erlangen, 1878), pp. 241-70. This work sets the basis for the modern study of Justin. For a discussion of the research on Justin up to and including von Engelhardt see Adolf Stählin, Justin der Märtyrer und sein neuester Beurtheiler (Leipzig, 1880). For a review of the more recent literature see Niels Hyldahl, Philosophie und Christentum (Copenhagen, 1966), pp. 30-85).

[6]Judentum und Judenschristentum in Justins Dialog mit Trypho, TU 39 (Leipzig, 1913), pp. 47-92.

[7]E. Goodenough, The Theology of Justin Martyr (Jena, 1923), especially pp. 117-22.

[8]W. A. Shotwell, The Biblical Exegesis of Justin Martyr

, or Septuagintal problems.[9] The recent monograph of L. W.
Barnard,[10] supplementing and updating Goodenough's fine study,
contains a chapter on Justin's relationship to Judaism but
nothing on Justin's interpretation of the Law. Only Pierre
Prigent offers a brief analysis of Dial. chaps. 10-29 and of
other chapters dealing with the Mosaic Law.[11] This analysis is
here taken into consideration. Prigent's main purpose, however,
is not a study of Justin's interpretation of the Law but rather
the discovery of a basic document, the lost Syntagma, behind
Justin's extant works, the Dialogue and the Apology, according
to Prigent's hypothesis. The most penetrating assessment of
Justin's view of the Old Testament and the Law is that by von
Campenhausen in his book Die Entstehung der christlichen
Bibel,[12] to which I am greatly indebted for several insights.

The purpose of this present work, therefore, is to
offer a complete examination of Justin's treatment of the Mosaic
Law against the background of the problem of the Law and the Old
Testament in the second century. This task calls for a close
study of several sections of the Dialogue, especially chaps. 10-
30, and an analysis of Justin's interpretation of the Mosaic Law
in the light of the sources and/or traditions he is using, as
well as in view of the fronts against which he formulates his
arguments. It is our intention to attempt to answer the fol-

(London: S.P.C.K., 1965) and C. L. Franklin, Justin's Concept
of Deliberate Concealment in the Old Testament (Dissertation,
Harvard, 1961).

[9]H. Koester, Septuaginta und Synoptischer Erzählungsstoff im Schriftbeweis Justins des Märtyrers (Habilitations-
schrift, Heidelberg, 1956); D. Barthélemy, "Redécouverte d'un
chaînon manquant de l'histoire de la Septante," RB 60 (1953),
18-29, and Les Devanciers d'Aquila, Supplements to VT 10 (Leiden, 1963); J. S. Sibinga, The Old Testament Text of Justin
Martyr, Vol. I: The Pentateuch (Leiden: Brill, 1963). See the
review of Sibinga's book by R. A. Kraft, Gn 36 (1964), 572-77.

[10]Justin Martyr: His Life and Thought (Cambridge: The
University Press, 1967), pp. 39-52. See also his article "The
Old Testament and Judaism in the Writings of Justin Martyr,"
VT 19 (1965), 86-98.

[11]Prigent, especially pp. 234-85.

[12]Von Campenhausen, pp. 106-22.

lowing questions: why is the Mosaic Law in the first place a problem for Justin? Chapter One deals with this matter involving the historical setting of the Dialogue and the relevance of various fronts with which Justin is engaged when evaluating the Law. Secondly, what is Justin's concept of the Mosaic Law? Chapter Two is devoted to this issue centering on Justin's terminology of the Law and his understanding of the tripartite division of the Law. Finally, what arguments does Justin marshall to demonstrate the invalidity of the Law, on the one hand, and its purpose, on the other? Chapters Three and Four take up these two issues which form the foci of Justin's argumentation on the Law.[13]

The present work offers an analysis of Justin's theological and scriptural interpretation of the Mosaic Law. It is not a study of the scriptural exegesis of Justin nor of his use of the Old Testament as such, although it hopefully contributes something to both of these areas.[14]

Justin deals with the Mosaic Law only in the Dialogue. It is with this massive document that we are chiefly concerned. However, Justin's First and Second Apology[15] are also taken into consideration. These works are the only extant writings of Justin. They are preserved in Codex Regius Parisinus CDL (AD 1364) and Codex Claromontanus LXXXII (AD 1541).[16] The latter codex is a copy of the former, according to Otto,[17]

---

[13]By Law, unless otherwise qualified, we mean the written Law of Moses in its ritual prescriptions.

[14]Much less is this a study of the Old Testament text of Justin. Textual questions are taken up only as they may be relevant for our argument.

[15]Most critics regard the Second Apology as an appendix or post-script to the First, written because of a subsequent incident (App. 2.1ff.). See Goodenough's discussion of this problem, pp. 84-87.

[16]Johannes Karl Theodor von Otto, Justini Philosophi et Martyris Opera (3rd ed.; Jena, 1876), I, Part I, pp. xxi-xxvii. Sibinga, p. 13, gives AD 1363 as the date of the first Codex without explanation as to the difference with Otto.

[17]Otto, pp. xxiii-xxvii.

or perhaps both codices depend on the same earlier lost proto-
type, according to Goodspeed.[18] The text and citations are
Goodspeed's, since they are convenient and more or less established. The text of Otto, which is the best critical text,
and also that of Archambault,[19] are, however, consulted for
significant textual variations or possible emendations. Following Goodspeed, the First Apology is abbreviated by Ap. and
the Second by App. Throughout this work, numerous Greek passages are quoted from the Dialogue for the convenience of the
reader. The English translation of these passages has been added in the published version of this dissertation for those who
may not be proficient in Greek. The translation is that by
A. Lukyn Williams.[20]

---

[18]Edgar J. Goodspeed, Die ältesten Apologeten
(Göttingen, 1914), p. 142.

[19]Georges Archambault, Justin: Dialogue avec Tryphon
(2 vols.; Paris, 1909).

[20]Justin Martyr: The Dialogue with Trypho (London,
1930).

CHAPTER ONE

THE PROBLEM OF THE LAW IN JUSTIN'S DIALOGUE

Justin's Dialogue with Trypho is the most comprehensive
Christian document prior to the writings of Irenaeus and
Tertullian,[1] and the first lengthy exposition of the Christian
faith.[2] Apart from the Prologue (chaps. 1-9), the Dialogue
consists of three main sections: (1) chapters 10-30 dealing
with the Mosaic Law; (2) chapters 31-118 dealing with Christology and (3) chapters 119-142 dealing with the true Israel.[3]
The Mosaic Law is thus the first main theme of the Dialogue.
It is also treated in subsequent sections of this work, chaps.
40-47, 67, 92-93, and 95. The first issue therefore before us
is this: why is so much attention given to the Law in the
Dialogue? Why is the Law a problem for Justin? How is Justin's

---

[1] Harnack, p. 47, estimates that the Dialogue is longer
than Matthew, Luke and John combined, and that in its original
form it was probably not essentially shorter than all four
Gospels. The Dialogue has a serious lacuna at the end of Dial.
74.3 and it may also have been shortened by the loss of the
opening dedication and by the cutting of Old Testament citations as, for example, in Dial. 30.2ff.; 31.1 and 56.18-19,
either inadvertently or deliberately by a lazy scribe. So
Goodenough, p. 97.

[2] Hyldahl, p. 294. Hyldahl, however, seems to overesti-
mate Justin's intentions in the Dialogue when he thinks that
this document is written as "an exposition of Christian philosophy" for pagans (ibid.). See below, pp. 189ff.

[3] Because of the lack of clear organization in the
Dialogue, no two critics have agreed on the structural divi-
sions of this work. For an overview of the outline of the
Dialogue, see von Ungern-Sternberg, pp. 6-27; W. Bousset,
Jüdisch-Christlicher Schulbetrieb in Alexandria und Rom,
FRLANT 6 (Göttingen, 1915), pp. 283-99; and especially
Prigent, pp. 14-17 and 320ff. I adopt the above division,
taking chap. 30 within the unit of chaps. 10-30, since chap.
31 clearly begins a new theme, the Christological proof, and
taking chap. 118 as concluding this theme, because Dial.

treatment of the Law related to his larger concerns in the
Dialogue? These are the questions which will concern us in
this chapter.

A. The Problem

The immediate reasons why the Law is a problem for
Justin are evident in Dial. chaps. 8-10. When Justin recounts
to Trypho his search for truth through various philosophical
schools and his final conversion to Christianity, he closes
his story with a bid for Trypho's conversion to the true way of
Christ (Dial. 8.2). Trypho, however, not only rejects the in-
vitation, but also offers a counter claim as the basis of salvation, the Law of Moses, to which he in his own turn invites
Justin's allegiance:

εἰ οὖν καὶ ἐμοῦ θέλεις ἀκοῦσαι, φίλον γάρ σε ἤδη νενό-
μικα, πρῶτον μὲν περιτεμοῦ, εἶτα φύλαξον, ὡς νενόμισται,
τὸ σάββατον καὶ τὰς ἑορτὰς καὶ τὰς νουμηνίας τοῦ θεοῦ,
καὶ ἀπλῶς τὰ ἐν τῷ νόμῳ γεγραμμένα πάντα ποίει, καὶ
τότε σοι ἴσως[4] ἔλεος ἔσται παρὰ θεοῦ (Dial. 8.4).

If therefore you are willing to listen also to me (for
I already reckon you as a friend), first be circumcised, then (as is commanded in the Law) keep the Sabbath and the Feasts and God's New Moons, and, in short,
do all the things that are written in the Law, and
then perchance you will find mercy from God.

118.3 seems to strike rounding-off echoes of what Justin promises concerning the Christological argument earlier (Dial. 9.1).
Chapter 10 more self-evidently is, as all critics agree, the
beginning of the first section of the Dialogue.

[4]The use of ἴσως is odd here, if we are to follow
Williams' translation ("perchance"), for this would minimize
the power of Trypho's claim. If this is the correct translation, then we have in this adverb a reflection more of
Justin's than of Trypho's doubt regarding the certitude of
salvation through the Law. Trypho is not portrayed in the
Dialogue as having second thoughts about his faith, and he
parts company with Justin politely, yet with no signs of
change of heart (Dial. 142.1ff.). But the problem may have
an entirely different solution if Otto is right, as I think he
is, in translating "haud dubie." He follows a rare usage of
ἴσως meaning "indeed," "truly," "no doubt," and the like, as
in Dial. 85.3 and Ap. 4.7. See Otto, I, Part I, p. 16, n. 12,
and I, Part II, p. 306, n. 11. He is not sure about the adverb in another important passage, Dial. 47.4 (Otto, I, Part
II, p. 159, n. 12). Archambault, p. 45, without comment,
seems to follow Otto and translates "sans aucun doute" at Dial.
8.4. Liddell and Scott do not indicate this rare usage of ἴσως,
but Henricus Stephanus, Thesaurus Graecae Linguae (Paris, 1841),
does, citing among others Aristotle, Plato and Xenophon
Ephesius (II Century AD).

As far as Christ is concerned, continues Trypho, he is really yet to come, an unknown factor, the Christ of Christians being but their own creation in which they foolishly perish (Dial. 8.4b-c).

Trypho's response makes Justin's task two-fold. Above all, Justin must show that Christ is not at all a matter of empty fantasy but, on the contrary, a divinely attested reality (δείξω ὅτι οὐ κενοῖς ἐπιστεύσαμεν μύθοις οὐδὲ ἀναποδείκτοις λόγοις, ἀλλὰ μεστοῖς πνεύματος θείου, Dial. 9.1c). He does this mainly in chaps. 31-118,[5] a discourse which Justin elsewhere calls the Christological proof (τὴν ἀπόδειξιν τὴν περὶ τοῦ Χριστοῦ, Dial. 120.5b), the central and most important theme of the Dialogue. But first he must also show to Trypho's satisfaction why Christians, who say that they revere God and claim to hold a privileged and different place among the gentiles at large, do not observe God's Law, particularly the covenant of circumcision. Trypho's objection is this:

ἐκεῖνο δὲ ἀποροῦμεν μάλιστα, εἰ ὑμεῖς, εὐσεβεῖν λέγοντες, καὶ τῶν ἄλλων οἰόμενοι διαφέρειν, κατ'οὐδὲν αὐτῶν ἀπολείπεσθε, οὐδὲ διαλλάσσετε ἀπὸ τῶν ἐθνῶν τὸν ὑμέτερον βίον, ἐν τῷ μήτε τὰς ἑορτὰς μήτε τὰ σάββατα τηρεῖν μήτε τὴν περιτομὴν ἔχειν. . . ὅμως ἐλπίζετε τεύξεσθαι ἀγαθοῦ τινος παρὰ τοῦ θεοῦ, μὴ ποιοῦντες αὐτοῦ τὰς ἐντολάς· ἢ οὐκ ἀνέγνως, ὅτι ἐξολοθρευθήσεται ἡ ψυχὴ ἐκείνη ἐκ τοῦ γένους αὐτῆς, ἥτις οὐ περιτμηθήσεται τῇ ὀγδόῃ ἡμέρᾳ (Dial. 10.3);

But we are especially at a loss about this, that you, saying you worship God, and thinking yourselves superior to other people, separate from them in no respect, and do not make your life different from the heathen, in that you keep neither the feasts nor the sabbaths, nor have circumcision, . . . you yet hope to obtain some good from God, though you do not do His commandments. Now have you not read: "That soul shall be cut off from his people" which shall not be circumcised on the eighth day?

Trypho is here quoting from Gen. 17:14 (LXX) and, presupposing knowledge of the context of his proof-text, goes on to remind Justin that this covenant (διαθήκη, Dial. 10.4a; cf. Gen.

---

[5]Cf. Dial. 9.1c, the statement of intent regarding the Christological proof, quoted above, and what seems to be the concluding echoes of the Christological discussion in 118.3: οὐ μάτην ἡμεῖς εἰς τοῦτον [τὸν Χριστὸν] πεπιστεύκαμεν οὐδ' ἐπλανήθημεν. See also ματαίαν ἀκοήν, in 8.4c, as well as οὐκ ἀληθεῖ . . . δόξῃ in 10.1d, Trypho's charge. Chaps. 126-29 also deal with Christology, but Justin here seems to be repeating and recapitulating (μὴ νομίζητε . . . ὅτι περιττολογῶν

10

17:13),[6] which the Christians despise, was also intended for
both the strangers among Israel as well as the purchased
slaves (Dial. 10.3c,4a; cf. Gen. 17:12,23,27).[7] The Christians would, therefore, according to Trypho, seem to have
little ground for ignoring circumcision, while claiming that
they obey God. Trypho is willing to discuss the Christology
which is of secondary importance to him (καὶ τὰ ἄλλα, Dial.
10.4b), but Justin must first resolve the problem of the Law.
He must answer the question why Christians hope to receive
any benefit at all from God when they do not in fact observe
God's Law:

εἰ οὖν ἔχεις πρὸς ταῦτα ἀπολογήσασθαι, καὶ ἐπιδεῖ-
ξαι ᾦτινι τρόπῳ ἐλπίζετε ὁτιοῦν, κἄν μὴ φυλάσσοντες
τὸν νόμον, τοῦτό σου ἡδέως ἀκούσαιμεν μάλιστα, καὶ
τὰ ἄλλα δὲ ὁμοίως συνεξετάσωμεν (Dial. 10.4b).

If therefore you have any defence to make with
reference to these points, and can show us how
you have any hope at all, even though you do not
keep the Law, we would very gladly hear from you.
Afterwards let us examine the other points in
the same way.

Trypho thus demands of Justin an apologia for the
non-observance of the Mosaic Law by Christians who claim
obedience to God and to His record of revelation, Scripture
(τὰς γραφάς, Dial. 10.3-4; cf. 9.1), but do not adhere
to the Law. Justin's treatment of the Law in the Dialogue
is therefore to be seen as a theological and scriptural
justification of the Christian rejection of the Mosaic Law,
yet as a preliminary step in order finally to convince
Trypho and his companions of the new life-focus, Jesus
Christ. The larger setting of the Dialogue is accordingly
the Jewish-Christian debate. Justin's work is addressed

ταῦτα λέγω πολλάκις, Dial. 128.2).

[6]In the context of Gen. 17 the covenant of circumcision is called αἰώνιος (Gen. 17:13), but Justin does not allow this element to reinforce Trypho's point because for
Justin only the New Covenant of Christ is eternal (Dial.
11.2ff.; 12.1 et al.).

[7]According to Gen. 17, ἀλλογενεῖς and ἀργυρώνητοι
are not distinguished as they are in Dial. 10.3c, being rather one: οἱ ἀργυρώνητοι ἐξ ἀλλογενῶν (Gen. 17:27; cf.
Gen. 17:12,23). See Sibinga's analysis of the text and its
difficulties, pp. 19-20, 60-61, and 105.

primarily to Jews.

This classic framework of the Dialogue has, however, been challenged in modern times. Karl Hubík[8] was one of the first to deny that the Jews are the actual addressees of the Dialogue and in this he found Goodenough's concurrence.[9] Goodenough himself argued that the Dialogue is addressed not to a Jew, but either to a Christian or to a pagan, probably to a pagan, as a demonstration of the unity and superiority of revelation over against pagan philosophy. Harnack also observed that much of the adversus Judaeos literature involves stock arguments directed to straw men rather than real opponents.[10] In recent times Niels Hyldahl[11] has reaffirmed the view that the Dialogue is addressed to pagans, stating with confidence that the real addressees of this work are part of the Graeco-Roman public which was interested in the question of Judaism as well as in philosophy and religion, and that the Dialogue is essentially a document arising out of the enounter of Christianity with Greek philosophy. On the other hand, Prigent and von Campenhausen have pointed to another front, that of heretical Christianity, particularly Marcionism, as decisive for understanding the content and argument of the Dialogue.[12]

One may thus have to contend with a plurality of fronts when inquiring into the problem of the Law in the Dialogue and Justin's interpretation of it. But a study of Justin's understanding of the Law must begin with a clear picture of the setting in which the Law is a problem for the Apologist. In what follows, Justin's concerns with the Graeco-Roman world, anti-heretical polemics, internal Christian matters, and the Jewish-Christian debate, in connection with his treatment

---

[8] Karl Hubík, Die Apologien des Hl. Justinus des Philosophen und Märtyrers (Vienna, 1912), p. 206.

[9] Goodenough, pp. 96ff.

[10] See Marcel Simon, pp. 167ff. who discusses the point.

[11] Hyldahl, pp. 20 and 294.

[12] But they do not deny that the Dialogue in its present form is addressed to Jews.

of the Mosaic Law, is assessed.

B. Concerns With the Graeco-Roman World

First we shall examine the thesis that philosophical and apologetic concerns over against pagan culture play a significant, even dominant, role in the Dialogue, and therefore in Justin's handling of the problem of the Law. This thesis has been put forward in two forms: (1) that the Dialogue is a document written directly for a pagan or pagan readers, and (2) that the Dialogue is a product of the Jewish-Christian controversy, but that philosophical presuppositions significantly define Justin's view of Christology and the Mosaic Law in this document.

Several authors, notably Goodenough, but also Hyldahl and more recently Reiner Voss,[13] have claimed that the Dialogue is a writing addressed to pagans. This premise requires that Justin's argumentation on the Law, as well as the other themes of the Dialogue, be interpreted as statements formulated for pagan readers. The following evidence has been cited in support of this view:

(1) the name of the stated addressee, Marcus Pompeius (Dial. 141.5), which is strongly Roman, and presumably indicates a pagan, rather than either a Christian or Jewish addressee;[14]

(2) specific references to gentiles who are directly addressed on many occasions throughout the Dialogue (Dial. 23.3; 24.3; 29.1; 32.5 and others;[15]

(3) the philosophical prologue of the Dialogue (chaps. 1-6), as well as Justin's concept of the Christian faith as a philosophy (Dial. 8.1-2),[16] which imply pagan readers, and

---

[13]Reiner Voss, Der Dialog in der frühchristlichen Literatur (Munich, 1970), p. 38.

[14]Goodenough, pp. 98 and 100; Hubík, pp. 206-07.

[15]Theodore Zahn, "Studien zu Justin III: Dichtung und Wahrheit in Justin's Dialog mit dem Juden Trypho," ZKG 8 (1885-1886), 56-61; Hyldahl, pp. 18ff.; Harnack, pp. 51-52, n. 2.

[16]Goodenough, pp. 99-100; Hyldahl, pp. 20ff. and 292ff.

(4) the literary form of the _Dialogue_ which also favors cultured pagan readers.[17]

It would take us too far afield to examine all of the above evidence in detail here. This task is undertaken in the Appendix. Here we may summarize the conclusions reached in the Appendix which show that the hypothesis of a pagan readership of the _Dialogue_ cannot easily be sustained on the basis of the above arguments and the evidence which is adduced to support them.

First of all, the two references to Marcus Pompeius (_Dial._ 8.3 and 141.5), only one of which explicitly mentions him by name (_Dial._ 141.5), are quite isolated in this massive document and are not decisive as clues to the scope of the _Dialogue_.[18] _Dial._ 80.3b, the only passage where Justin takes note of his own intention to commit the discussion to writing, indicates that the "dialogue" between Justin and Trypho is also intended for a wider circle of readers, who are not pagans, but probably gnostics. We must therefore move beyond Marcus Pompeius, a single addressee, and beyond an exclusive or even primary pagan readership for the _Dialogue_ to consideration of multiple addressees or at least multiple fronts with which Justin is engaged.

Secondly, the specific references in the _Dialogue_ which are taken as direct appeals to gentiles, and the presumed pagan readers of this work, are not at all what they first seem. _Dial._ 23.3 is directed to Trypho and his companions, the latter being also Jews, not gentile converts to Judaism as Zahn thought. _Dial._ 24.3 and 29.1 are appeals to gentiles who are already Christians, i.e., the Church which is throughout the _Dialogue_ often designated with the Septuagintal term ἔθνη. _Dial._ 32.5 does contain an allusive reference to pagans who are receptive to Judaism, but in no way suggests that these are the readers of this work.[19] _Dial._ 64.2e is a general reference

---

[17]Voss, p. 38. Voss, however, notes that, though intended for pagans, the _Dialogue_ was read mostly by Christians.

[18]Besides Marcus is a good Jewish name. One cannot discount the possibility that Marcus Pompeius was a Jew, since Jews of Hellenistic times adopted both Greek and Latin names.

[19]Pagans who are receptive to Judaism, and even attached

to all men, including pagans, expressing Justin's universalistic interests, but does not thereby indicate the addressees of the Dialogue. Dial. 80.3b, which we have noted above, points to a wider circle of readers, but the context favors the gnostic opponents of Justin,[20] not, as Harnack conjectured, pagans. Finally, Dial. 119.4 is one of Justin's frequent references to gentiles who are already Christians and drawn from the gentiles at large in fulfilment of prophecy, and has nothing to do with the question of the addressees of the Dialogue.

Thirdly, the arguments that the philosophical prologue of the Dialogue as well as Justin's concept of the Christian faith as a philosophy indicate pagan readers falter because of an erroneous premise. Goodenough sees the Dialogue "as addressed to a man interested in philosophy and not as a record of a controversy, or a text book for controversy, against Judaism."[21] For him the prologue requires a pagan reader, not a Christian, nor certainly a Jew. In similar fashion, Hyldahl

---

to local synagogues as "fearers of God,"--not merely pagans who are, as suggested by Hyldahl, interested in the question of Judaism along with philosophy and religion--could possibly be the addressees of the Dialogue. However, evidence for this is utterly lacking. Justin nowhere is interested in either Jewish proselytes or "fearers of God." On the other hand, there is considerable evidence, especially Justin's view of the eschatological remnant of the Jews to whom he seems to appeal, that the Dialogue is addressed to Jews in general rather than to gentiles who may be closely attached to Judaism in particular. See below, pp. 39ff.

[20] By gnostic opponents are designated throughout this work the second-century heresiarchs and their followers whom Justin mentions and refutes. I refer to them either as "gnostics," or "Justin's gnostic opponents," or sometimes "gnostics and marcionites" to suggest that Marcion and his followers are not uncritically to be identified with the others in one category since in some ways Marcion's views are not "gnostic." See below, pp. 20ff.

[21] Goodenough, p. 99. However, one may note with Merrill Young, The Argument and Meaning of Justin Martyr's Conversion Story (Harvard Dissertation, 1971), that in the Dialogue we have a philosopher (Justin) who deprecates philosophy! Young examines the Dialogue's prologue and finds that, in contrast to the First and Second Apology, the Dialogue expresses Justin's true feelings about philosophy which are sharply critical of the value of philosophy. See below, p. 194. However, Young does not raise the question of the addressees of the Dialogue.

hinks that Justin's view of Christianity as the true philoso-
hy places the Dialogue in the encounter of Christianity with
raeco-Roman culture and that, therefore, the Dialogue is ex-
lusively written for pagans, just as the Apology is also
ritten for pagan readers.

But could not "a man interested in philosophy" be
ither a Jew or a Christian? And does Justin's concept of the
hristian faith as a philosophy necessarily imply only pagan
eaders? On the contrary, the prologue itself and the cultural
ssumptions behind Justin's portrayal of Trypho indicate that
hilosophical interests are not applicable only in the instance
f pagans. Justin himself, wearing the pallium and claiming to
e a philosopher (Dial. 1.2; 8.2), shows that a Christian could
ndeed be keenly interested in philosophy! But Trypho, a Jew,
s also depicted as one who has studied philosophy. The reason
hy he in the first place approaches Justin is to learn some-
hing of philosophical value (Dial. 1.1-3)! Accordingly, philo-
ophical interests in the Dialogue do not necessarily require
agan readers for this work, since such interests equally are
uitable for both Christians and Jews living in the Graeco-Roman
orld. These features indicate the wider cultural setting of
ustin, which includes pagans, Christians, Jews, and others,
ut do not indicate specifically the intended readers of this
ork. The question of the broader milieu of Justin must not be
onfused with the question of the addressees of the Dialogue.

Finally, the view that the literary form of the Dialogue
mplies cultured pagan readers is, as well, based on the same
onfusion of the cultural setting of Justin with the question of
he addressees of the Dialogue. The Dialogue may very well be
 conscious imitation of the Platonic style, as Voss suggests,
ut this hardly indicates pagan readers. Jews and Christians
ho lived in the Graeco-Roman world could also well be expected
o find Greek literary forms attractive, just as much as
agans.[22] Once again, Justin who adopts the literary form of
"dialogue" is a Christian. As far as the Jews are concerned,

---

[22]How unified and self-sustaining the character of
ellenistic culture was, despite its inclusion of many diver-
ent traditions and peoples, is pointed out by Morton Smith,
alestinian Parties and Politics that Shaped the Old Testament
(New York: Columbia University Press, 1971), pp. 76-81.

it is well known that many Hellenistic Jewish authors not only were interested in, but actually made use of, Greek literary forms, including history, poetry and drama, to interpret their tradition, centuries prior to Justin's Dialogue. Voss' point cannot be maintained because the wider cultural setting of the Dialogue is not a clear criterion as to the problem of the intended readers of this work.

We have summarized the evidence cited for the Dialogue as a writing to pagans which is examined in greater detail in the Appendix. The arguments which are based on this evidence do not at all demonstrate the case for the pagan readership of the Dialogue. The evidence can be differently interpreted or, in other instances, is made to yield premises which do not necessarily follow. On the opposite hand, additional evidence may be offered which almost certainly disproves the claim of a pagan readership of the Dialogue. Perhaps the major weakness of the authors who have advocated this hypothesis is the failure seriously to consider the double question of how the Dialogue, which is so different from the Apology, may equally be addressed to pagans, and how the bulk of the content of the Dialogue, which deals with the Mosaic Law, Christology and the new Israel, are relevant for pagan readers. In the Appendix these issues as well are taken up at greater length. Here we may again summarize the findings which indicate that the addressees of the Dialogue cannot be pagans.

First of all, the Dialogue presupposes a familiarity, indeed even intimate knowledge, of both Judaism and Christianity which cannot be presupposed of any wide part of the Graeco-Roman public such as in the case of the Apology. It is telling that in the Apology Justin offers explanatory statements to his pagan readers about matters which they could not be expected to know, for example, as to the origins, character, and translation of the Old Testament (Ap. 31.1-5), as well as with respect to the nature of the words of Jesus which are brief and not extensive as those of a sophist (Ap. 14.5). In the Dialogue, however, no such explanations are to be found. Knowledge of the Old Testament, the Mosaic Law, and also of the Christian Gospel(s) is assumed.

Secondly, the extensive use of Scripture in the Dialogue, and the assumed character of the authority of

Scripture, favor either Christian or Jewish readers, or both, but not pagan readers for the Dialogue. Its range of use in the Dialogue suggests in the first place mutual recognition of its authority by the groups in controversy. The predictive proof from Scripture could, to be sure, be effective with pagans, at least up to a point, as the Apology shows (Ap. chaps. 30ff.). However, Scripture is differently introduced and differently used in the Apology.[23] Furthermore, it may be noted that the Mosaic Law, which occupies considerable attention in the Dialogue and is a central issue of the Jewish-Christian controversy, is not even mentioned in the Apology, which is a writing for pagans.

Finally, important apologetic interests found in the Apology are missing from the Dialogue. Above all, Justin's theory of the Spermatikos Logos and his view of the great philosophers as Christians prior to Christ (Ap. 46.3; cf. App. 8.1-2; 10.8; 13.2-4) are nowhere in evidence in the Dialogue, not even in the prologue where Justin briefly surveys the intellectual horizons of paganism. On the contrary, Justin in the Dialogue concedes nothing to philosophy! He has sharp words of criticism for all philosophical schools and derogatory remarks for the philosophers (Dial. 1.4ff.; 2.2ff.; 3.7; 5.1; 6.1). Even the great Plato and Pythagoras are said to be merely "reputed" philosophers (Dial. 7.1). In the Apology only Crescens, the "pseudo-philosopher" and abhorred opponent of Justin, is called a "reputed" philosopher (App. 9.1; cf. 3.1ff.). These omissions and the sharp difference of attitude concerning philosophy are inexplicable if the Dialogue is conceived of as a writing for pagans, and pagans who are interested in philosophy at that!

The conclusion is that the Dialogue is not addressed to pagans. The thesis that the Dialogue is written for a wider part of the Graeco-Roman public cannot be sustained. Neither direct nor indirect evidence indicates that Justin's argumentation on the Mosaic Law, as well as on the other great themes of

---

[23]For example, in Ap. 31.1ff. Justin explains who the Prophets were and how their writings came into being. In Ap. 32.1, before quoting Moses, he specifies that Moses was "the first of the Prophets." Also, Justin never uses the traditional γέγραπται when he quotes the Old Testament in the Apology, whereas he does so frequently in the Dialogue.

the Dialogue, should be read as written for pagan readers. The
problem of the Law in the Dialogue is not distinctly an apologetic issue over against the higher culture of the Graeco-Roman
world. The Dialogue as we have it adresses its themes to readers other than pagans.

But a caveat is here necessary. The above conclusion
that pagans are not the direct addressees of the Dialogue does
not imply that cultural and philosophical concerns are totally
absent from this document. Justin deports himself as a philosopher, and his thought undoubtedly contains philosophical di-
mensions.[24] The Platonic presuppositions behind Justin's view
of the eternal and universal ethical law are undeniable (Dial.
23.1; 45.4; 93.1-3). Moreover, it is well known that pagans
had long criticized the Hebrew faith and Jewish customs. A-
gainst such criticisms a whole tradition of Jewish apologetics
developed especially in Hellenistic Judaism, a tradition known
and utilized by Christians.[25] Celsus, for example, is a notable pagan intellectual around the time of Justin who pours
scorn on the anthropomorphism of Scripture and the unphiloso-
phical character of the Jewish and Christian faiths.[26] Christians and certainly Justin as a thinker, who was open to "enlightened" concerns of pagan culture, were inevitably faced
with the task of defending and explaining the meaning of Scripture, including that of the Mosaic Law, in terms of such interests. But to what degree is Justin aware of questions of this
nature in the Dialogue?

---

[24]See especially Carl Andresen, "Justin und der
mittlere Platonismus," ZNW 44 (1952-53), 157-95, and his Logos
und Nomos, AKG 30 (Berlin, 1955), where he cites the previous
literature on the subject. More recently see Ragnar Holte,
"Logos Spermatikos: Christianity and Ancient Philosophy
According to St. Justin's Apologies," StTh 12 (1958), 109-68;
J. H. Waszink, "Bemerkungen zu Justins Lehre vom Logos Sperma-
tikos," in Mullus Festschrift Th. Klauser: Jahrbuch für Antike
und Christentum (Münster, 1964), pp. 380-90; H. Chadwick,
Early Christian Thought and the Classical Tradition (New York:
Oxford University Press, 1966), especially pp. 10-22, and N.
Hyldahl's book on Justin.

[25]See among others, J. Bergmann, Jüdische Apologetik
im neutestamentlichen Zeitalter (Berlin, 1908); M. Friedlaender,
Geschichte der jüdischen Apologetik als Vorgeschichte des
Christentums (Zürich, 1903), and P. Krüger, Philo und Josephus
als Apologeten des Judentums (Leipzig, 1906).

[26]Origen, Contra Celsum, 4.36,38,43,52; 6.2,49,54-64.

Von Campenhausen suggests that Justin faced rather acutely the difficulty of the "strangeness" of the Law and, as a "philosopher," had to deal with the problem of the apparent contradiction between the Mosaic Law and the Platonic view of the eternal and immutable character of truth.[27] Von Campenhausen observes that the problem of the Old Testament and the Law was most deeply felt by those circles of Christians who were most receptive to hellenization, i.e., the gnostics. The same proved to be the most willing to relativize the authority of the ancient Scriptures.[28] Is Justin informed by similar concerns?

Justin's main approach to handling the problem of the Law in the Dialogue is not directly determined by such considerations. The alien character of the Law is not the starting point, nor a recurring question, in Justin's exposition on the Law. Nowhere is the Law a problem for Justin because of its "strangeness" from the standpoint of pagan culture. Rather, the Law is a problem for Justin because it is rejected by Christians although it is part of Scripture. This is the key question that controls Justin's interpretation of the Law. To be sure, implicit philosophical presuppositions play a significant role in Justin's understanding of the ethical law, which he conceives of as a universal and eternal norm.[29] Yet his concern with the ethical law in the Dialogue is in the background. There is no question of a discussion of what Justin regards as ethical principles, something that he barely begins in one instance (Dial. 93.1-3). But in contrast it is clear that what is at the forefront is the question of the basis of the Christian rejection of the cultic and ceremonial Law with which Justin time and again deals theologically and exegetically (Dial. 10.3-4; 12.3; 15.1; 16.1 et al.).

This is not of course to say that Justin is totally ignorant of philosophical questionings of the Old Testament. Whether directly through encounters with pagans or indirectly

---

[27]Von Campenhausen, p. 110.

[28]Ibid., pp. 88-91.

[29]See below, pp. 56ff.

through his confrontation with the gnostics, Justin is aware
of philosophical criticisms of Scripture and the Law (<u>Dial</u>.
23.1; 30.1). He is concerned with defending the authority of
Scripture. He understands and apparently grants that, unless
one has the gift of interpretation, a casual reading of the
Old Testament might well show that many things in it are in-
comprehensible and even contemptible (<u>Dial</u>. 92.1). One of his
criticisms against the Jews is that their inadequate exegesis
reinforces such views of Scripture and, by implication, God
(<u>Dial</u>. 112.1). He is also aware of possible apparent inconsistencies in the Old Testament (<u>Dial</u>. 92.1; 94.1), although
he never yields to those who think that these inconsistencies
are real (<u>Dial</u>. 65.2). Moreover, he distinguishes between the
temporary cult of the Mosaic Law which he still defends as
meaningful within the divine dispensation, though superseded,
and, on the other hand, the universal ethical truths in the
Law which are unchanging.[30] To this extent Justin is informed
by cultural and philosophical questions relating to the character of the Law and the nature of the Old Testament in the
<u>Dialogue</u>. We shall see, however, that all of these concerns,
which still do not comprise the central problem of the Law for
him, are expressed as part of Justin's defense against the
gnostic critique of Scripture, and not as part of an apologetic
addressed directly to pagans. If the above concerns are present in the <u>Dialogue</u>, they seem to reach Justin through the
gnostic interpretation of the Old Testament against which he
certainly defends.

C. Anti-gnostic Polemics

If evidence of Justin's direct engagement with pagans
or the pagan world in the <u>Dialogue</u> is lacking, the evidence of
his confrontation with the gnostics and Marcion is abundant.
The gnostics constitute a serious and definite front with which
Justin has to contend both in the <u>Dialogue</u> and the <u>Apology</u>.[31]

---

[30]See below, pp. 55ff. and 77ff.

[31]In the <u>Apology</u> they are presented as examples of the
devil's tools which should, Justin suggests, be punished for
their ethical evils, but in actuality go unpunished, whereas
the orthodox Christians are unjustly persecuted (<u>Ap</u>. 26.1ff.;
56.1ff.; 58.1ff.). His preoccupation with the gnostics in the
<u>Dialogue</u> is greater and more far-reaching, as we shall see. The

In <u>Dial</u>. 35.6, the followers of four major heresiarchs are named, with the list being open-ended. Justin writes:

καὶ εἰσὶν αὐτῶν οἱ μέν τινες καλούμενοι Μαρκιανοί,
οἱ δὲ Οὐαλεντιανοί, οἱ δὲ Βασιλειδιανοί, οἱ δὲ Σα-
τορνιλιανοί, καὶ ἄλλοι ἄλλῳ ὀνόματι, ἀπὸ τοῦ ἀρχηγέ-
του τῆς γνώμης ἕκαστος ὀνομαζόμενος (<u>Dial</u>. 35.6).

And some of them are called Marcianites, and some
Valentinians, and some Basilidians, and some Satorni-
lians, and others by other names, each being named
from the originator of the opinion.

This passage occurs in an extensive digression in the Christological proof (<u>Dial</u>. 35.2-6) where Justin accuses the followers
of the great second-century heresiarchs of blasphemous and impious teachings and actions at the instigation of demons. He
quotes against them several logia of Jesus concerning pseudo-
prophets, schisms and heresies, presumably fulfilled in them.
He states that the Christians of the pure faith have nothing to
do with these ungodly groups (<u>Dial</u>. 35.2-5).

In <u>Dial</u>. chaps. 80-82, where Justin discusses the eschatological hopes of Christians, the gnostics are again polemical-
ly repudiated as unbelievers in these eschatological hopes, especially the hope of resurrection (<u>Dial</u>. 80.4-5; cf. 81.4).
These men may be called Christians by some, but they are really
blasphemous heretics: ὄντας . . . ἀθέους καὶ ἀσεβεῖς αἱρεσιώ-
τας, ὅτι κατὰ πάντα βλάσφημα καὶ ἄθεα καὶ ἀνόητα διδάσκουσιν
(<u>Dial</u>. 80.3).[32] Justin unambiguously distinguishes them from
those whom he considers orthodox Christians: [τοὺς] ὀρθογνώ-
μονας κατὰ πάντα χριστιανούς . . . τῆς καθαρᾶς καὶ εὐσεβοῦς
. . . γνώμης, (<u>Dial</u>. 80.3,5). They are instruments of the devil, the false prophets and false teachers of whom the Lord pro-

---

older literature, e.g., Semisch, I, pp. 42-44; Engelhardt, pp.
216-19, and George Purves, <u>The Testimony of Justin Martyr to
Early Christianity</u> (New York, 1889), pp. 254-57, is aware of
this aspect of Justin's thought. Some of the new literature
curiously is not. Goodenough, Shotwell and Barnard, for example, do not even mention this side of Justin. C. Franklin, in
his dissertation, p. 3, n. 2, writes: "Though Justin does not
in his extant writings, make any reference to Marcion, occasionally one senses a possible consciousness of him." Justin's
contacts with second-century gnosticism are all the more important because Justin was quite probably in Rome at the time Marcion was, as Verweijs, p. 217, observes, and perhaps even Ptolemy. See G. Quispel, <u>Ptolémée: Lettre à Flora</u>, <u>SC</u> 24 (Paris,
1949), p. 9.

[32]The concept of heresy is clearly applied to them by

phesied, and those who teach blasphemous things in his name
(Dial. 82.1-3).

Moreover, these gnostics whom Justin clearly attacks
present an immediate problem. They teach in the very days of
Justin: καὶ διδάσκουσι μέχρι νῦν (Dial. 82.3). The activity
of Marcion is explicitly mentioned: Μαρκίων . . . ὃς καὶ νῦν
ἔτι ἐστὶ διδάσκων τοὺς πειθομένους (Ap. 26.5). In two important passages of the Apology (Ap. 26.5-6 and 58.1-2), Justin explains for pagan readers that Marcion denies the Creator of the
immediate universe, and holds to another greater God and to another Christ, at the instigation of sinister demons. But in both
instances Justin concedes that Marcion is greatly successful,
having gathered around him many followers from all quarters of
the world who think that they possess the truth and deride the
other Christians, e.g.: ᾧ πολλοὶ πεισθέντες ὡς μόνῳ τάληθῆ ἐπι-
σταμένῳ, ἡμῶν καταγελῶσιν, ἀπόδειξιν μηδεμίαν περὶ ὧν λέγουσιν
ἔχοντες, ἀλλὰ ἀλόγως ὡς ὑπὸ λύκου συνηρπασμένοι βορὰ τῶν ἀθέων
δογμάτων καὶ δαιμόνων γίνονται (Dial. 58.2). Marcion and his
followers are naturally repudiated by Justin.

But Justin's concern with the gnostics is not only a
polemical one. Within the scope of the Dialogue the gnostics
and their followers are also the object of missionary concern,
just as are Trypho and the Jews. In Dial. 82.3, Justin says to
Trypho that he strives to persuade the false Christian teachers,
as well as the Jews, from following erroneous doctrines: οὓς
[ψευδοδιδασκάλους] ὁμοίως ὑμῖν μεταπείθειν ἀγωνιζόμεθα. In
Dial. 65.2, he makes a similar claim about those who think that
there are contradictions in Scripture, probably the gnostics:
καὶ τοὺς ἐναντίας τὰς γραφὰς ὑπολαμβάνοντας τὸ αὐτὸ φρονεῖν
μᾶλλον ἐμοὶ πεῖσαι ἀγωνίσομαι. Finally in Dial. 80.3b, where
Justin mentions his intention to write the Dialogue, there is,
as we have noted, the suggestion that this document is in part
also written for these heretical Christians.

It is thus clear that, within the scope of the Dialogue,
Justin is aware of the presence of gnostic opponents whom he
tries both to refute and to convert. But does this fact also

Justin who writes in Dial. 35.5: ὧν οὐδενὶ κοινωνοῦμεν. This
is in distinct contrast to what Justin says about Jewish Christians who live within the catholic Church (Dial. 47.2-3).

imply that Justin's argumentation on the Mosaic Law is formulated from the standpoint of anti-heretical polemics or, as
well, that the Dialogue itself is written for gnostic readers?
To what extent is Justin's argumentation on the Mosaic Law,
and the other themes of the Dialogue, shaped by his anti-
gnostic concerns? These questions need attention.

Prigent has proposed that the heresiological horizon of
Justin's thought and work can be reached through the Dialogue
in massive terms.[33] The Dialogue, according to Prigent, is a
great extract, oftentimes a condensation of Justin's lost
Syntagma Against All Heresies, reworked and addressed to Jews.
We cannot here assess Prigent's hypothesis which is based on
a close study of the content and the order of the whole material in the Dialogue. On the basis of my own studies of the
Dialogue, however, it is my view that Prigent's hypothesis
should be received with caution.[34] Other alternatives can be
cited as explanations of the inconsistencies and ambiguities of
the Dialogue.[35] However, it is certainly possible and even

---

[33]See above, p. 1, n. 2. Prigent's hypothesis is that
in the Dialogue, as well as the First Apology, Justin utilizes
chiefly a single source, his lost Syntagma mentioned in Ap.
26.8. Prigent thinks that the skeletal structure of Justin's
argumentation in the Syntagma was formed by Old Testament texts
most of which are also, according to him, used in the Dialogue.
Prigent's views may be found on pp. 9-12 and 319ff. of his
book. On pp. 332-36 he offers a reconstruction of the hypothetical structure of the Syntagma.

[34]Prigent's painstaking effort has particularly in
view the literary chaos, the repetitions, digressions, and
abrupt transitions of the Dialogue, which Prigent claims to
have resolved or clarified by reference to a single document
used by Justin as his main source. But these anomalies can be
explained in various other ways without recourse each time to
the same source which Justin supposedly reworks unsuccessfully.
See also the reviews of Prigent's book by Daniélou, RechSR 53
(1965), 140ff.; Grant, JBL 84 (1965), 440ff. and JThS 17
(1966), 167ff., as well as by Audet, RB 72 (1965), 469ff.
'Mais qu'est-ce qui nous dit," asks Audet, p. 471, "que le
Syntagma était mieux composé?" And Grant observes, JBL, p.
143, that methodologically Prigent's hypothesis assumes that
Justin proceeded from order (Syntagma) to less order (Apology)
and finally to relative chaos (Dialogue). Dissatisfaction with
the hypothesis, however, does not take away the value of
Prigent's analysis of the Dialogue.

[35]For example, with respect to Dial. chaps. 10ff.,
which Prigent treats on pp. 235ff., he finds that the first

24

quite probable that, just as Tertullian uses material from
his Adversus Marcionem in writing his Adversus Judaeos, so also Justin may in the Dialogue use material contained in his
earlier work, the Syntagma, written against Marcion and the
other gnostic heresiarchs, as Prigent observes.[36]

It is at least clear that certain passages and also
certain lines of thought in Justin's treatment of the Mosaic
Law and elsewhere in the Dialogue have indeed been shaped by
Justin's confrontation with gnostic teaching. Dial. 11.1,
for example, has undoubtedly marcionite teaching in view.
Writes Justin:

οὔτε ἔσται ποτὲ ἄλλος θεός, ὦ Τρύφων, οὔτε ἦν ἀπ'
αἰῶνος . . . πλὴν τοῦ ποιήσαντος καὶ διατάξαντος

---

awkward phrase in Justin's exposition is ταύτης οὖν τῆς διαθήκης εὐθέως καταφρονήσαντες (Dial. 10.4), because in the context "le pronom démonstratif est curieux." Circumcision to
which ταύτης refers has not yet been called διαθήκη and Justin
does not previously quote the whole passage of Gen. 17 which
would make the use of the demonstrative pronoun clear. Prigent goes on to suggest that Justin here presupposes a more
developed argument on the Law which he has before him in the
Syntagma, but does not fully reproduce, leaving the reader
with "le relatif illogisme du démonstratif," p. 236. However,
a much simpler explanation is possible. Justin presupposes not
the Syntagma but simply Gen. 17 from which he is quoting. The
reason why Justin does not quote more fully from Gen. 17 is
probably the fact that in Gen. 17.7 and 17.13 circumcision is
twice called αἰώνιος διαθήκη, a matter which Justin cannot
acknowledge in his argument since for him only the New Covenant
in Christ is eternal (Dial. 11.2ff.). Circumcision and the
other ordinances of the Law are temporary—this is his whole
point about the Mosaic Law in the Dialogue. This example is to
be sure not crucial and Prigent also admits that his suggestion
is somewhat tenuous. Nevertheless, it shows something of Prigent's constant effort to build up his hypothesis on fragile
ground which in the end seems to turn his task into an uncon-
vincing enterprise, as far as the main thesis is concerned.

[36]P. 12. In my own work with Tertullian's two writings
mentioned above, I noted, for example, this striking illustra-
tion of Prigent's point. In Adv. Marc. 2.21, Tertullian has to
defend against a marcionite argument that the Sabbath is not
intrinsically inviolable because, among other things, it was
broken by a contradictory order of God having the Jews march
around Jericho for eight straight days. This was, Tertullian
explains in defense, a special case and according to God's express command. Tertullian, however, uses the same argument
pointedly against the Jews in Adv. Jud. 4, without of course
reference to a possible contradiction here in Scripture, in order to show that the Sabbath is not eternal. In similar fashion
Justin may pose questions and problems of Scripture to Trypho
which in the first place have come to his attention through his
controversies with the gnostics and Marcion.

τόδε τὸ πᾶν. οὐδὲ ἄλλον μὲν ἡμῶν, ἄλλον δὲ ὑμῶν
ἡγούμεθα θεόν, ἀλλ'αὐτὸν ἐκεῖνον τὸν ἐξεγαγόντα
τοὺς πατέρας ὑμῶν ἐκ γῆς Αἰγύπτου . . . οὐδ'εἰς
ἄλλον τινὰ ἠλπίκαμεν, οὐ γὰρ ἔστιν, ἀλλ'εἰς τοῦτον
εἰς ὃν καὶ ὑμεῖς, τὸν θεὸν τοῦ ᾽Αβραὰμ καὶ ᾽Ισαὰκ
καὶ ᾽Ιακώβ (Dial. 11.1).

There will never be any other God, Trypho, and there
never was from all eternity . . . save He who made
and established this universe. Nor do we consider
that we have one God, and you another, but Him only
who brought your fathers out of the land of Egypt
. . . nor have we set our hopes on any other (for
there is none), but only on Him on whom you also have
set yours, the God of Abraham, Isaac and Jacob.

In this passage the emphatic rejection of "another God"
is strikingly out of context. Trypho's earlier remarks in no
way call for Justin's emphatic denial here, nor for the suggestion that the Jews might have a different God from the Christians.
They demand only this, an explanation of why Christians claim
to revere God while not in fact obeying God's commandments
(μὴ ποιοῦντες αὐτοῦ τὰς ἐντολάς . . . τὸν νόμον, Dial. 10.3-4).
Not Trypho, therefore, but Marcion is here in view (cf. Ap. 26.5;
58.1; Dial. 35.5; 56.4,11,16; 80.4).

The same is true of Justin's recurrent reference to the
God of the Old Testament as ὁ ποιητὴς τῶν ὅλων καὶ πατήρ/παντο-
κράτωρ. This cumbersome expression occurs very frequently in
the Dialogue.[37] It is probably an expression of anti-marcionite
polemic,[38] to be read by Christians, Jews, and possibly gnostics
who may by chance take the Dialogue in hand. It affirms the
creation of the entire universe by the one and same God and has
the function of thus affirming the unity of deity.[39] Justin in

----

[37]Dial. 7.3; 16.4; 34.8; 35.5; 38.2; 48.2; 56.1,4,16;
57.3; 58.1; 60.2,3; 67.6; 74.3; 84.2; 116.3.

[38]See also Ap. 26.5 and 58.1-2. Eusebius, H.E. 4.18.9,
preserves a passage from Justin's lost Syntagma quoted by Irenaeus (Adv. Haer. 4.11.2) in which Justin declares that he would
not have believed even Christ, if he had announced any other God
than the Creator. Apparently the gnostics called the Demiurge
πατέρα καὶ ποιητὴν τοῦδε τοῦ παντός. See Ptolemy, Pan. 33.3.2
and 33.6.4.

[39]It might be suggested that this is a captatio benevo-
lentiae argument for Jews to underline monotheism. However, in
the references which follow (and more generally in the Dialogue)
Justin nowhere shows sensitivity to the issue of "monotheism" in
his discussion with Jews, not even where he speaks of Christ as
ἕτερος θεός (Dial. chaps. 55ff.).

several passages explicitly accuses the gnostic heretics of
blaspheming God, the Creator of all things. At the same time
he emphasizes the bond between God and Christ, a bond which Marcion denied: βλασφημεῖν τὸν ποιητὴν τῶν ὅλων καὶ τὸν ὑπ'αὐτοῦ
προφητευόμενον ἐλεύσεσθαι Χριστὸν καὶ τὸν θεὸν 'Αβραὰμ καὶ
'Ισαὰκ καὶ 'Ιακώβ (Dial. 35.5; cf. Ap. 58.1; Dial. 80.4).[40]
Justin has even Trypho saying that he would not listen to Justin
except for the fact that the latter refers everything to Scripture and declares the existence of no god above the Creator of
all things (καὶ μηδένα ὑπὲρ τὸν ποιητὴν τῶν ὅλων εἶναι. θεὸν
ἀποφαίνει, Dial. 56.16). These statements in no way have their
Sitz im Leben in the Jewish-Christian debate, but in the controversies of ancient Christianity against Marcionism.

With respect to the Law, it is well known that although
the Law is a chief issue in the Jewish-Christian debate, the
question of the Law emerged as a central problem in Christian
theology during Justin's times because of the gnostic and marcionite critique of the Old Testament, as Ptolemy's Letter to
Flora amply shows. This brief but elegant treatise on the Mosaic Law, written probably not much later than Justin's Dialogue,
is an eloquent witness to the controversy over the Law as an
inner Christian problem of considerable intensity and breadth.[41]
One is not surprised that Justin, known to later Church Fathers
as an anti-heretical protagonist,[42] took part in this debate
and that some of his views on the Law, directed against the second-century heresiarchs, especially Marcion, may also be reflected in the Dialogue.

---

[40]See also Dial. 48.2; 57.3; 58.1; 60.2-3.

[41]See especially Ptolemy's remarks in Epiphanius, Pan.
33.1-3, who bitingly criticizes both Marcionites and catholic
Christians for "reciting to each other" (διᾴδοντες ἀλλήλοις)
their erroneous views. For an analysis of Ptolemy's treatise
see Quispel. Earlier important treatments of this work are by
A. Hilgenfeld, "Der Brief des Valentinianers Ptolemaeus an die
Flora," ZWTh 24 (1881), 214-30, and by A. Harnack, "Der Brief
des Ptolemaeus an die Flora," SAB 25 (1902), 507-45, which includes the full Greek text and critical apparatus. The text by
Harnack is also in KT 9 (Bonn, 1912).

[42]Prigent, p. 12, notes that writers up to Eusebius view
Justin not as an Apologist to Hellenic culture, nor a specialist
in Jewish-Christian controversy, but as a heresiologist. This
is another reminder of Justin's impact in the ancient Church as
a defender of the faith against gnosticism and Marcionism.

Within the main unit on the Mosaic Law (Dial. chaps. 10-30), certain important passages have in view Justin's gnostic opponents and, as von Campenhausen has pointed out,[43] carry decisive implications for Justin's whole argumentation on the Law. In Dial. 23.1, Justin states that if his interpretation of the Law is not accepted, intolerable premises regarding the consistency of God would follow, namely that one would not be dealing with one and the same God in the case of Enoch and the other Old Testament figures who neither had nor observed the Mosaic legislation. In Dial. 30.1, he repeats the same point. The idea that in the history of the divine dispensation one does not have to do with one and the same God, which is also refuted in Dial. 11.1 by Justin, is gnostic and particularly marcionite. Von Campenhausen has acutely seen that these passages have gnostic teaching in view and that, in addition, Justin's whole argument concerning the Law as historical dispensation for the Jews (Dial. 18.2ff) is an answer originally suited to the gnostics, and especially Marcion, who totally rejected the option of allegorization of the Law.[44]

Passages in the Dialogue about Scripture and the Law which directly or indirectly defend the wisdom, omniscience, unity and perfection of God may also be part of Justin's anti-marcionite polemic. God, says Justin, cannot be charged with ignorance or with wishing to protect Himself from error when ordering that the door posts of Jewish homes be marked with the blood of the passover lamb (Dial. 111.4) or when asking a question of Adam or of Cain (Dial. 99.3). He cannot be charged with lack of foreknowledge when ordering different laws through different leaders, circumcision through Abraham, and the Sabbath, sacrifices and other ordinances through Moses. Much less does such diversity and change of legislations imply that one has to do with a different God (Dial. 92.5). Nor did God institute offerings and sacrifices because He was in need of them (Dial. 22.1,11). Rather, God is one and the same, forever teaching the same truths, a God who possesses all the properly divine attributes, such as that He is the friend of

---

[43]Von Campenhausen, pp. 112ff.

[44]Ibid., especially pp. 112-14. For a more detailed discussion of these issues, see below, pp. 153ff.

man, prescient, without need, just and good: φιλάνθρωπος καὶ
προγνώστης καὶ ἀνενδεῆς καὶ δίκαιος καὶ ἀγαθός (Dial. 23.2).

Of themselves, some of the above passages do not
immediately indicate Justin's anti-marcionite concerns. For
example, that God does not need offerings or anything else human or material is a commonplace in the Hellenistic world.
Justin himself mentions this point in the process of another
argument in the Apology and in another context.[45] Furthermore,
the inner difficulties of Scripture, e.g., the anthropomorphic
depictions of God, improprieties on the part of some biblical
figures, and apparent inconsistencies or contradictions in the
text, were long known to Scriptural interpreters, both Jewish
and Christian. These difficulties were interpreted allegorically in order to yield suitable spiritual meanings. The
Stoics and Platonists interpreted allegorically in a similar
vein problems in the Homeric poems. Christian theologians were
also probably not indifferent to criticisms of the mean expression of Scripture from pagan quarters. Celsus, the Platonist
critic of Judaism and Christianity and the near-contemporary of
Justin, is a notable example of a pagan intellectual who knows
and sharply criticizes the problematic character of the idiom
of Scripture. He also knows and derides attempts at circum-
venting Scriptural difficulties through apologetic allegorization by Christians and Jews.[46]

It is difficult, therefore, to determine in each
instance whether a Justinian passage is part of a broader apologetic over against pagan culture or part of a specifically
anti-marcionite concern. Moreover, Justin's argumentation is
primarily directed to Jews, as we will see. Thus in Dial. 65.2,
where he rejects the notion that there are contradictions in
Scripture, presumably a marcionite teaching,[47] his point quite

---

[45]Ap. 10.1 where the Apologist explains the Christian
conception of God.

[46]c. Celsum, 1.27; 4.38,48-49. However, Celsus himself
allegorizes when he interprets the words of Zeus to Hera in a
Homeric passage as words of the "supreme God" to "matter" (c.
Celsum, 4.42).

[47]So von Campenhausen, p. 111.

naturally arises out of the discussion with Trypho,[48] rather
than out of a polemic against Marcion.

On the other hand, it is abundantly clear that Justin
is seriously concerned with the various heresiological groups
which he mentions. Criticisms of Scripture which he reports
are often linked with the question of the consistency of God
(Dial. 23.1-2; 30.1; 92.1-2), a distinctly marcionite point.[49]
It was Marcion who had an eye for the "contradictions" of
Scripture and who concentrated on the weaknesses and imper-
fections of the Demiurge.[50] Tertullian in his work against
Marcion defends the references to the "passions" of God against
marcionite criticism of them.[51] Irenaeus against the gnostics
repeatedly insists that God does not "need" sacrifices nor does
he take pleasure in sweet-smelling savors.[52] Ptolemy interestingly suggests that the imperfection of the Mosaic Law
necessitates as its author a God other than the perfect God.[53]
Apparently the gnostic and marcionite detractors of the Old
Testament dwelt on these matters. Justin, too, is concerned
with defending Scripture, the Mosaic Law and God against similar charges.

---

[48]Trypho quotes a Scriptural text, suggesting a contradiction, while feigning sincere perplexity about its interpretation. Justin takes him to task and affirms that οὐδεμία γραφῆ
τῇ ἑτέρᾳ ἐναντία ἐστίν . . . καὶ τοὺς ἐναντίας τὰς γραφὰς ὑπολαμβάνοντας τὸ αὐτὸ φρονεῖν μᾶλλον ἐμοῖ πεῖσαι ἀγωνίσομαι (Dial.
65.2).

[49]When Celsus draws attention to "contradictions" between Christ and Moses, Origen suggests that he is indebted to
marcionite teaching, c. Celsum, 8.18. (Celsus knows of the conflicts between the various Christian groups, c. Celsum, 5.54,61).

[50]In Ap. 58.1-2 Justin reports that the Marcionites who
hold to the teaching of another God "deride" the Christians for
their views. Cf. Dial. 30.1; 35.4.

[51]Adv. Marc. 2.11ff. In the same work, 2.25, he states
that Marcion charged the God of the Old Testament with ignorance.
So did also the Valentinians, who equally held that the Demiurge
was imperfect.

[52]Adv. Haer. 4.29.1-5; 31.5. On this and the imperfect
attributes of the Demiurge, according to marcionite teaching,
see also A. Harnack, Marcion, pp. 278-79*.

[53]Pan. 33.3.4.

At times it seems that Justin in fact confronts Trypho
and the Jews with problems of the Law and the Old Testament
derived from the gnostic critique of Scripture. Most clear in
this regard is the case of the "contradiction" of the scriptural
command to make a brazen serpent over against the earlier commandment prohibiting graven images. In <u>Dial</u>. 94.1ff., Justin
poses this problem to Trypho and his companions who are at a
loss for an answer. One of Trypho's companions obligingly admits that even the Jewish teachers also fail to provide adequate
answers to such and other mysteries in Scripture which cause the
teaching of Scripture to be falsely slandered (<u>Dial</u>. 94.4).[54]
But this problem was a well-known "contradiction" in the Old
Testament emphasized by Marcion. It was Marcion who made much
of the inconsistency of the Demiurge in prohibiting graven
images and then ordering Moses to fashion a brazen serpent.[55]

There are other such examples, although not as clear.
The suggestion that the diversity and change in legislation under different leaders, such as Abraham and Moses, implies lack
of foreknowledge or inconsistency on the part of God, which
Justin presents as a problem to Trypho (<u>Dial</u>. 92.2,5), is probably of gnostic, perhaps marcionite, origin. So also perhaps
the suggestion that God ordered the marking of the door posts
with the lamb's blood in order to protect Himself from error and
the like. Such "difficulties" in the Old Testament may well
have come to Justin's attention while dealing with the gnostics,
and especially Marcion, in the <u>Syntagma</u>. In the <u>Dialogue</u> they
are directed as exegetical problems to Trypho and the Jews in
order to point up their inability to interpret the Old Testament
correctly.

Justin, of course, knows the answer to these seemingly
contradictory or imperfect aspects of Scripture. They all
have a deeper purpose and reflect no defect on the part of

---

[54] Ἀληθῶς εἶπας· οὐκ ἔχομεν λόγον διδόναι· καὶ γὰρ ἐγὼ
περὶ τούτου πολλάκις τοὺς διδασκάλους ἠρώτησα, καὶ οὐδείς μοι
λόγον ἀπέδωκεν.

[55] So Tertullian, <u>Adv. Marc</u>. 2.21-22. Tertullian, as
we have seen, also uses marcionite arguments against the Jews.
See above, p. 24, n. 36.

God.[56] They are mysteries which must be examined in sufficient
depth and which require the gift of interpretation (Dial. 92.1).
Indeed, the superficial interpretation of Scripture by the Jews
compromises the perfection of God (ταῦτα ταπεινῶς ἐξηγούμενοι,
πολλὴν ἀσθένειαν καταψηφίζεσθε τοῦ θεοῦ, Dial. 112.1), as well
as the authority of Scripture (εὐκαταφρόνητα . . . συκοφαντητὰ
τὰ διδάγματα τῶν προφητῶν, Dial. 92.1; 94.4). On this basis,
even Moses would be found a violator of the Law (καὶ Μωϋσῆς
οὕτω παράνομος ἂν κριθείη, Dial. 112.1). Justin's whole point
about the Mosaic Law is that, unless correctly interpreted, it
invites blasphemous conclusions regarding God and Scripture,
conclusions which his gnostic opponents had already drawn.

Thus, throughout the Dialogue, Justin seems to defend
the Old Testament, the Law and God against gnostic criticism of
them. It is not of course the case that he addresses the
Dialogue itself to his gnostic opponents, although some of them
might well have been in a position to read the Dialogue. For
Justin had already engaged the various heresiarchs, especially
Marcion, and their followers in his Syntagma Against All
Heresies. Rather, it is the case that arguments developed in
his previous confrontation with the gnostics, he now turns
against the Jews. He poses marcionite-inspired problems of the
Old Testament and the Law to Trypho, and then answers them himself. More importantly, as we shall see in subsequent chapters,
his distinctive insistence on the historical purpose of the Law
as dispensation for the Jews, an argument which in the Dialogue
he addresses to Jews, seems to have been hammered out in his
previous struggle over the Law with the gnostics. In this respect the Dialogue takes us beyond the Jewish-Christian debate
into the controversies of the ancient Church over the Old
Testament with second-century Gnosticism.[57] Justin, earlier

---

[56]Franklin in his dissertation, pp. 166-70, sees that
Justin tries to explain difficulties in Scripture by recourse to
a "deeper" purpose in order to uphold the perfectability of
Scripture. But he does not see that much of this concern is
related to Justin's anti-gnostic polemic.

[57]As we have noted, many scholars, e.g., Flesseman-Van
Leer, pp. 71ff.; Shotwell, pp. 2ff. and others, do not take into
account this aspect of the Apologist's thought. But otherwise
Prigent and von Campenhausen. Verweijs who observes, p. 217,
that Justin knows and combats Marcion in the Dialogue, curiously
treats all of what Justin has to say on the Mosaic Law in terms

than either Irenaeus or Tertullian, is the first major Christian
writer to counter the gnostic critique of Scripture. The lost
Syntagma was a product of his struggle. But the Dialogue, too,
is a witness of Justin's encounter with the gnostics. Signs of
Justin's anti-gnostic thought and anti-gnostic formulations may
be clearly traced in this work. In particular, Justin's handling of the problem of the Law in the Dialogue takes seriously
into account the new hermeneutic of the gnostics and his interpretation of the Law is decisively influenced by it.

D. The Church

At this point another related question must be raised,
namely, whether or not the problem of the Law in the Dialogue
is conceived of only as an intra-Christian problem, apart from
any relationship to the Jewish-Christian controversy in histori
cal terms. The gnostics, as Justin himself attests, fully considered themselves Christians and were so considered also by
others (e.g., Celsus). It was they who raised anew the consciousness of the Church to the problem of the Law and the Old
Testament around the middle of the second century. Ptolemy's
opening remarks in his Letter to Flora attest to the extent of
the controversy over the Law among Christians.[58]

Furthermore, there is evidence in the Dialogue that the
Church at large is unambiguously addressed in liturgical language and in the first person plural hortatory subjunctive
(Dial. 24.3; 29.1).[59] The Dialogue, written by a Christian
author, was of course written within and also for the Christian
community at large, and thus automatically it was directed to
the attention of Christian readers and of all those who claimed
to be Christians. The main themes of the Dialogue, the Mosaic
Law, the Christology and the true Israel, are enduring issues
of Christian theology. Thus, that the Dialogue is a document
written for Christian readers need not be debated, it may be
assumed.

---

of the Jewish-Christian debate, as if Justin had not heard of
Marcion at all.

[58]Pan. 33.1-3.

[59]See below, pp. 177ff. of the Appendix.

The question which remains is whether or not the
Dialogue is intended by its author only for Christian readers,
as a kind of dramatized discussion of internal issues and problems, including of course anti-Jewish polemics, or whether it
can also be viewed as a genuine effort, however inadequate, on
the part of Justin to reach actual Jewish readers. In what
follows, we shall consider this question and present evidence
which indicates that Trypho and the Jews are not a mere foil
in Justin's hands, but rather that they represent a real community or, more precisely, part of a real community, the eschatological remnant, which Justin genuinely hopes and earnestly
strives to convince of what he himself is utterly convinced of:
Christ is the true way of life and no longer the Law which has
been superseded.

E. Jews as Addressees

First one must consider the reasons for which the possibility of Jewish addressees has in the past been denied. Hubík,
one of the first to reject the traditional view that the Dialogue was written for Jews, thought that the Dialogue is a rather free creation written for Christians and pagans, as indicated according to him by the dedication to Marcus Pompeius and
especially the philosophical prologue.[60] However, as we have
noted, neither the isolated references to the otherwise unknown
Marcus Pompeius, nor the philosophical prologue necessarily require pagan readers of the Dialogue,[61] much less decisively
exclude the possibility of Jewish addressees.

---

[60]He deals with the possibility of Jewish addressees
in one sentence: "Der Dialog ist eine freie Schöpfung, mehr
als man bis jetzt angenommen hatte, verfasst nicht bloss um
der Juden willen, sondern, wie schon die Widmung an M.
Pompeius, wie besonders die philosophische Einleitung be-
zeugt, für Christen und Heiden," pp. 206-07. Hubík's chief
interest in this part of his book (which is on Justin's
Apologies) is to show that the Dialogue was written at a time
between the First and Second Apology, reflecting on the one
hand the concern of pagan persecution of Christians found in
the First, but not on the other hand what Hubík calls "der
Philosophenstreit," i.e., with "Crescens und seinen Genossen,"
found in the Second. As regards the dedication, Hubík accepts
Harnack's suggestion (Judentum und Judenschristentum, p. 78)
that the Dialogue originally had one, which is possible.

[61]See our argument above, pp. 13-15, and also in
greater detail in the Appendix.

Goodenough, who also discounts the possibility of Jewish addressees, offers as fundamental reason, apart from his own theory of the purpose of the _Dialogue_, the harshness and unsuitability of the contents of the _Dialogue_ for Jews.[62] In like manner, Hyldahl, who agrees that Jews are not the actual addressees of this work, supposes that the polemical character of the _Dialogue_ makes it inconceivable as a document addressed to Jews, for it could only produce the opposite of Justin's intended purpose.[63]

These concerns of Goodenough and Hyldahl are, however, patently modern. It is doubtful that arguments concerning the suitability or unsuitability of the _Dialogue_ for Jews could settle the issue of whether or not in fact Justin addresses himself to Jews in this document. The _Dialogue_ can readily be conceived of as Justin's candid statement of how things stand without regard for or accommodation to the unpleasantness of the truth as he conceives of it. His confidence of having found the truth, which is evident throughout the _Dialogue_, gives him also the conviction that, as Chadwick puts it, he "must speak without fear or favor as one who has nothing to hide."[64]

More importantly, Justin is a very significant witness for the existence of Jewish Christians who lived within the gentile Church, practicing the Mosaic Law, and who were neverthe-

---

[62] Goodenough, p. 99. Goodenough cites charges of immorality against the Jews by Justin. There are other more prevalent and more severe charges, e.g., _Dial_. 16.2ff.; 17.1ff.; 19.6; 22.1; 27.4 _et al_, pertaining to the Jews as responsible for the death of the Prophets and Christ, and as spiritually incorrigible and blind.

[63] Hyldahl, p. 20.

[64] H. Chadwick, "Justin's Defense of Christianity," _BJRL_ 47 (1964-1965), 278. That he absolutely possesses the truth is one of Justin's most powerful convictions determining his approach both in the _Dialogue_ (3.7; 7.1; 8.1) and the _Apology_ (2.1-2; 23.1; 30.1). Elsewhere Chadwick, in his _Early Christian Thought_, pp. 19-20, makes the point that Justin throughout his writings is so utterly convinced of the self-evident clarity and power of Christian truth that, according to Justin, only a prejudiced or misinformed person would fail to accept it. One might add that for Justin much of this prejudice obstructing clear knowledge is due to demonic influence.

less not spared criticism by fellow Christians (<u>Dial</u>. 47.2-3).[65]
These Jewish Christians obviously had to listen as well to sharp
Christian polemics practiced within Christian circles against unbelieving Jews and unbelieving Judaism in general. Nevertheless
we find them within the gentile Church![66] It is not inconceivable that some of them were contemporary converts to the Christian faith. Nor is it inconceivable that other Jews like them,
probably on a very limited scale, were still open to Christian
missionary activity, and that the kind of missionary appeal
which we find in the <u>Dialogue</u> was to some degree, despite the
polemics, effective among Jews. Certainly, the presence of
Jewish Christians who observed the Mosaic Law within the gentile
Church, and others who probably did not, makes this a reasonable
possibility.

On the other hand, the <u>Dialogue</u> is as well not totally
defined by polemics against the Jews. In the light of the ancient literature of <u>Adversus Judaeos</u> from Barnabas to
Chrysostom's homilies against the Jews, the amazing aspect of
the <u>Dialogue</u> is not its polemical character, which is to be sure
evident, but its distinct effort to be conciliatory; not its
uncompromising spirit, but its attempt to deal with what Justin
views as the weakness, ignorance and even blindness of the Jews.
Justin seems to make an earnest attempt to write a "dialogue,"
not merely to compose a denunciation in the form of an <u>Adversus
Judaeos</u>. In this regard, most eloquent is perhaps the ending of
the <u>Dialogue</u>. Although Trypho and his friends take their leave
without in any way having been persuaded, much less converted,
by Justin's persistent efforts, yet they are not denounced by a
cascade of polemics (<u>Dial</u>. 142.2-3). The fate of the Jews is
not sealed. The door is left open for possible reconciliation.
The ending of the <u>Dialogue</u> is a literary masterpiece which cannot be attributed to Justin's literary talents alone, since
they often fail him in the <u>Dialogue</u>, nor to his irenic disposi-

---

[65]Justin himself took quite a different position, a re-
markably compassionate and enlightened one, declaring that
Jewish Christians living in fellowship with the Church be accepted ὡς ὁμόσπλαχνοι καὶ ἀδελφοί (<u>Dial</u>. 47.3).

[66]Other Jewish Christians refused to accept the fellowship of the gentile Church according to Justin's testimony
(<u>Dial</u>. 47.3).

tion, since it is often broken by polemics, but also to his assumption that the possibility of reaching Trypho and the Jews
indeed exists.[67]

It is not supposed that the _Dialogue_ is a stenographic
account of an actual encounter. Nor do we wish to claim that
the style of the _Dialogue_ is a decisive criterion for demonstrating Justin's intentions in this work. But we do wish to
note that, in view of arguments concerning the polemical and
unsuitable character of the _Dialogue_ for Jews, the _Dialogue_ is
not a book of unrelieved polemics against Judaism. In contrast
to the other extant ancient Christian writings against the Jews,
for example Tertullian's _Adversus Judaeos_, all of which seem to
have been written patently for Christians, and in the service
of inner-Christian polemical refutation of Judaism, there is a
conciliatory tone in the _Dialogue_, an earnestness of appeal, an
irenic spirit, which suggest that the author is writing not only
for the benefit of those who are already on his side, the orthodox Christians, but also of those to whom he seems to appeal,
the Jews.[68]

With respect to the case for the _Dialogue_ as a writing
to Jews there is also the credible argument that this document
adopts as a setting the Jewish-Christian debate and explicitly
sets down the authority of the Old Testament as the criterion of

---

[67]Other evidence of similar import is the following:
Justin and Trypho on many occasions address each other as
"friends," e.g., _Dial._ 8.4; 10.1; 68.2; 72.1; 85.7; 142.1, and
Justin addresses Trypho and his companions even as "brothers"
in _Dial._ 58.3 and 137.1. Justin also earnestly wishes to sus-
tain the "dialogue" with Trypho even at times when the latter
seems to tax Justin's good will by reclaiming points already
conceded or by showing unreasonableness in an open discussion
(_Dial._ 67.7,11; cf. 38.2; 44.1; 64.2, _et al._). In _Dial._ 79.2,
when Trypho is ready to break off the discussion, Justin accom-
modates to his momentary indignation.

[68]The liberality, frankness and irenic character of
Justin's attitude has, of course, long been noted as one
aspect of the _Dialogue_. See Goodenough, p. 122; Williams,
Justin Martyr, p. viii; Williams, _Adversus Judaeos_, p. 24,
and most recently by Peter Richardson, _Israel in the Apostolic
Church_ (Cambridge: The University Press, 1969), pp. 12-14,
who seems to attribute Justin's reasonable tone to his philosophical background.

the discussion.[69] To be sure, the use of the Old Testament in Christian documents against the Jews, as well as the adoption of the genre of Adversus Judaeos, do not of themselves provide sufficient reasons that such writings are directed to Jews. Nevertheless, as Marcel Simon points out,[70] the fact of the existence of the Christian literature of Adversus Judaeos and the fact that, after all, the adversary in such works is sketched as a Jew and not as someone else, imply that Christians were bothered by Jewish questions and that the Jewish community was not totally indifferent to the Jewish-Christian debate as Harnack supposed.

In the case of Justin's Dialogue, two reasons make the above argument stronger. The first is Justin's remarkable acquaintance with post-biblical Judaism. Although Trypho is often a mere tool in Justin's hands, Justin is, as Goodenough puts it, "by no means beating the air in his discussion with Trypho," since he reproduces "with extraordinary accuracy the attitude of many Jews of the time."[71] W. Shotwell has also shown that Justin uses post-biblical haggadic material either through the lips of Trypho or through his own not simply in order to refute it but also as part of his own thought, incorporating it into his argument much in the same was as a rabbinic teacher would.[72] This fact, of course, does not of itself, once again, necessarily imply that Justin wrote the Dialogue for Jews. But it does underscore Justin's unusual proximity to the faith which he as a Christian apologist tries to refute and also indicates a genuine interest on Justin's part at real discussion with his opponents. One may reiterate that the amazing thing is

---

[69] In Dial. 120.5, Justin states that he has made it his concern to quote only from those books of Scripture which the Jews recognize as authoritative.

[70] Verus Israel, pp. 169-70.

[71] Goodenough, pp. 90 and 92.

[72] Shotwell, pp. 88-89. For Justin's knowledge of post-biblical Judaism, see also A. H. Goldfahn, Justinus Märtyr und die Agada (Breslau, 1873) compiled from a series of five articles in Monatschrift für Geschichte und Wissenschaft des Judentums 12 (1873), pp. 49-60, 104-15, 145-53, 192-202 and 257-69; Harnack, Judentum und Judenchristentum; Williams, Justin Martyr, pp. xxx-xxxix, and Barnard, Justin Martyr, pp. 44-52. The latter are dependent on Goldfahn's original study.

not the polemics, but the effort to walk on as much of the opponents' ground as Justin seems to do.

The second reason is Justin's testimony to a varie-
gated Jewish Christian community in his time (<u>Dial</u>. 47.2ff.),
and his suggestive hints that apparently successful missionary
activity was going on between Christians and Jews, and, as well
between Jewish Christians and gentile Christians. The setting
of the <u>Dialogue</u> itself is a proselytistic encounter between a
Christian and a Jew (<u>Dial</u>. 8.2,4). Throughout the <u>Dialogue</u>,
Justin persistently attempts to convert Trypho and his companions to Christianity. Not only Justin, but also Trypho shows
interest in persuading his interlocutor to accept his own
faith (<u>Dial</u>. 8.4). Trypho's attempt at converting Justin to
Judaism is mentioned a second time when Justin begins to talk o
similar attempts by Jewish Christians to convert gentile Christians to the observance of the Mosaic Law (<u>Dial</u>. 47.1). Apparently Justin is aware of both Jewish and Jewish Christian efforts to convince gentile Christians to observe the Mosaic Law.
In <u>Dial</u>. chap. 47, his concern over Jewish Christians inducing
gentile Christians to adhere to the Law is expressed three
times (<u>Dial</u>. 47.1-3). Most interestingly, Justin seems to
assume that some such efforts of Jewish Christians were successful. He states that those gentile Christians who are persuaded to adopt the Mosaic Law, yet who maintain their confession of Christ, have a chance of salvation, but those who have
adopted the Law and have turned their back to Christ are lost
(<u>Dial</u>. 47.4). Thus, in Justin's times, we have traces of actua
proselytizing activity between Jews and Christians, and also
between Jewish and gentile Christians, a crossing of the lines
on several fronts. The setting of the <u>Dialogue</u> as a literary
genre seems to presuppose a concrete situation, where various
kinds of Jews and Christians attempt to proselytize one another
On the basis of this evidence, one can well consider the possibility of the <u>Dialogue</u> as Justin's own contribution to this
mission field, that is, as a writing addressed to Jews, as well
as to Christians.[73]

---

[73]From <u>Dial</u>. chap. 47 one may deduce that Justin's discourse on the Law would find interest among a variety of Jews
and Christians: (a) Jews who were receptive to the Christian
faith, (b) Christians who desired to defend their rejection of
the Mosaic Law, (c) gentile Christians who had second thoughts

The strongest evidence that Justin has indeed Jews in
view when composing the Dialogue is his conviction that a remnant of the Jews, according to God's plan, remains yet to be
saved in Justin's own time. This conviction of Justin, which
finds explicit formulation several times in the Dialogue, is
largely unnoticed by students of Justin, but perfectly explains
Justin's both undaunted persistence in trying to convert Trypho,
as well as his genuine hope of success in such efforts. The
significance which Justin seems to attach to the Scriptural
prophecy of the eschatological remnant may well be the decisive
presupposition behind the writing of the Dialogue and thus possibly the "key" to the purpose of this document for which
Goodenough was looking.[74]

The significant passages are the following:

σὺν ἡμῖν [i.e., the Christians][75] καὶ κληρονομῆσαι
βουλήσονται κἄν ὀλίγον τόπον οὗτοι οἱ δικαιοῦντες
ἑαυτοὺς καὶ λέγοντες εἶναι τέκνα ᾿Αβραάμ, ὡς διὰ τοῦ
᾿Ησαΐου βοᾷ τὸ ἅγιον πνεῦμα (Dial. 25.1).

These who justify themselves and say they are children of Abraham will desire to inherit along with us
even a little place, as the Holy Spirit cries aloud
by Isaiah.

Νῦν δὲ διὰ πάντων τῶν λόγων ἀπὸ τῶν παρ᾿ὑμῖν ἁγίων
καὶ προφητικῶν γραφῶν τὰς πάσας ἀποδείξεις ποιοῦμαι
ἐλπίζων τινὰ ἐξ ὑμῶν δύνασθαι εὑρεθῆναι ἐκ τοῦ κατὰ
χάριν τὴν ἀπὸ τοῦ κυρίου Σαβαὼθ περιλειφθέντος
[σπέρματος] εἰς τὴν αἰώνιον σωτηρίαν (Dial. 32.2c).

But now I am bringing all my proofs by all the words
that I adduce from the passages of Scripture, which
are held by you to be holy and to belong to the
prophets, because I hope that some one of you can be
found to belong to [the seed] which, according to
the grace given by the Lord of Sabaoth is left over
unto eternal salvation.

---

about the legitimacy of rejecting the Law, (d) Jewish Christians
who lived within the gentile Church but practiced the Law, and
(e) Jewish Christians who lived apart from the gentile Church
and tried to induce gentile Christians to observe the Mosaic
Law. However, the Dialogue as a document is primarily addressed
to Jews in general, rather than to Jewish Christians in particular, not only because its setting is a dialogue between a Christian and a Jew, but also because of Justin's view of the Jewish
eschatological remnant which, as we shall now see, pertains to
the Jews as a people rather than to sectarian Jewish Christians
specifically. This is not to deny that Justin has something to
say to all of the groups or fronts mentioned above.

[74]Goodenough, p. 97.

[75]See the Appendix, pp. 177ff.

40

διὰ τὴν ὑμετέραν κακίαν ἀπέκρυψεν ὁ θεὸς ἀφ'ὑμῶν τὸ
δύνασθαι νοεῖν τὴν σοφίαν τὴν ἐν τοῖς λόγοις αὐτοῦ,
πλὴν τινων, οἷς κατὰ χάριν τῆς πολυσπλαχνίας αὐτοῦ,
ὡς ἔφη Ἠσαΐας, ἐγκατέλιπε σπέρμα εἰς σωτηρίαν, ἵνα
μὴ ὡς Σοδομιτῶν καὶ Γομορραίων τέλεον καὶ τὸ ὑμέτερον
γένος ἀπόληται (Dial. 55.3).

God, because of your iniquity, hid from you the ability
to perceive the wisdom that there is in His words--with
the exception of them to whom, after the grace of His
abundant kindness, "He left," as Isaiah said, "a seed"
for salvation, in order that your race should not perish completely, like the men of Sodom and Gomorrah.

Ὦ Τρύφων, εἰ ὁμοίως ὑμῖν φιλέριστος καὶ κενὸς
ὑπῆρχον, οὐκ ἂν ἔτι προσέμενον κοινωνῶν ὑμῖν τῶν λόγων
. . . νῦν δέ, ἐπεὶ κρίσιν θεοῦ δέδοικα, οὐ φθάνω ἀπο-
φαίνεσθαι περὶ οὐδενὸς τῶν ἀπὸ γένους ὑμῶν, εἰ μήτι
ἐστὶν ἀπὸ τῶν κατὰ χάριν ἀπὸ κυρίου Σαβαὼθ σωθῆναι
δυναμένων. διὸ καὶ κἂν ὑμεῖς πονηρεύεσθε, προσμενῶ
. . . ἀποκρινόμενος· . . . ὅτι οὖν καὶ οἱ σωζόμενοι
ἀπὸ τοῦ γένους τοῦ ὑμετέρου διὰ τούτου [τοῦ Χριστοῦ]
σώζονται καὶ ἐν τῇ τούτου μερίδι εἰσί, τοῖς προλελεγ-
μένοις ὑπ'ἐμοῦ ἀπὸ τῶν γραφῶν εἰ προσεσχήκατε, ἐνενοή-
κειτε ἂν ἤδη (Dial. 64.2-3).

Trypho, if I were fond of strife and superficial
like you, I should not continue to join in this discussion with you . . . But now, since I fear the judgment of God, I am in no hurry to express my opinion
about any one of your race, whether he is not of those
who can be saved in accordance with the grace of the
Lord of Sabaoth. Therefore even though you act mali-
ciously I will continue answering . . . That therefore
they from your race who are saved are saved by this
Man, and are in his Portion, you would, if you had
paid attention to the passages from the Scriptures
which I have cited, have already understood.

The first passage is found in the section of the Dialogue in which Justin discusses the Mosaic Law, the first theme
of his work (chaps. 10-30). But the immediate context of the
passage (chaps.24-26) has to do with another theme, that of the
true and false Israel, discussed more fully by Justin elsewhere
in the Dialogue, as we have noted. Justin is here speaking of
the gentile Christians (ἔθνος δίκαιον, Dial. 24.2ff.), the true
Israel, who alone are the heirs of God's promises in the Old
Testament. However, a small number of the Jews are according
to Justin destined to be co-heirs to the promises along with the
gentiles. It is initially not clear that Justin is alluding to
the idea of the eschatological remnant when he states that the
Jews will desire to inherit κἂν ὀλίγον τόπον (Dial. 25.1) along
with gentile Christians. The reference is to Is. 63.18 (ἵνα
μικρὸν κληρονομήσωμεν τοῦ ὄρους τοῦ ἁγίου σου, Dial. 25.3) which
is immediately quoted in the lengthy passage of Isaiah 63:15-

64:12 (Dial. 25.2-5). In addition, the exchange between Justin
and Trypho which follows (Dial. 25.6ff.) seems soon to lose
sight of the idea of the remnant and it might appear that
Justin's point that the Jews will be partial heirs to the new
Jerusalem is made quite in passing without further significance.

However, this is not the case as the second passage indicates. In Dial. 32.2c, we have two very important indications
regarding the purpose and intent of the Dialogue. The purpose
of the Dialogue is to demonstrate the truth of the Christian
claims on the basis of the authority of Scripture which the Jews
accept. And the intent of the work is to convince some of the
Jews as to the truth of these claims. That Justin is here referring to the eschatological remnant of the Prophets is quite
clear. That his repeated appeals for Trypho's conversion are
based on the idea of the remnant and its application by Justin
to the Jews of his time is also explicitly stated in the passage. As Justin sees it, not all Jews will accept the truth of
Scripture as Christians interpret it, but only those Jews who
are according to God's plan included in the eschatological remnant: ἐκ τοῦ κατὰ χάριν τὴν ἀπὸ τοῦ κυρίου Σαβαὼθ περιλειφθέντος [σπέρματος] (Dial. 32.2c).

Even more explicit is Dial. 55.3. God, claims Justin, has
hidden the wisdom of Scripture from the Jews because of their
iniquity. However, a small number of Jews will be granted understanding. They will be the Jews who are according to God's
purpose to constitute the redeemed eschatological remnant from
Judaism, so that old Israel may not be totally lost. In this
passage, the source of Justin's belief is cited, the Book of
Isaiah, which is quoted in the same connection in the Apology.[76]

The final passage, Dial. 64.2-3, summarizes Justin's
intentions in the Dialogue in the clearest fashion. First,
Justin is convinced that Scripture proclaims salvation through
Christ alone, even for the Jews who are to be redeemed.

---

[76]In Ap. 53.6-7 where Justin informs his pagan readers
that the Jews and Samaritans, who had true knowledge of God, in
contrast to the gentiles, nevertheless ignored the Messiah at
his coming, πλὴν ὀλίγων τινῶν οὓς προεῖπε τὸ ἅγιον καὶ προφη-
τικὸν πνεῦμα διὰ Ἡσαΐου σωθήσεσθαι. εἶπε δὲ ὡς ἀπὸ προσώπου
αὐτῶν· εἰ μὴ κύριος ἐγκατέλιπεν ἡμῖν σπέρμα, ὡς Σόδομα καὶ
Γόμορρα ἂν ἐγενήθημεν. The quote is from Isaiah 1:9.

42

Secondly, the process of salvation is not completed, but still
going on, also for the Jews. One may note the present tense of
the participle: οἱ σωζόμενοι ἀπὸ τοῦ γένους ὑμῶν. This is a
process which is still taking place in Justin's time. Thirdly,
Justin does not dare pre-judge who of his contemporary Jews are
or are not to be included in the eschatological remnant, which
is God's mystery: ἐπεὶ κρίσιν θεοῦ δέδοικα, οὐ φθάνω ἀπο-
φαίνεσθαι περὶ οὐδενὸς ἀπὸ γένους ὑμῶν. As far as Justin is
concerned, he cannot seal the fate of any Jew. Trypho and his
companions, or any Jew, may still be drawn into the community
of the Christian faithful by the necessity of God's plan about
the eschatological remnant. Finally, the zealousness and
patience of Justin's efforts to convert Trypho, even in the
face of unreasonableness and contentiousness, is according to
Justin rooted in the same conviction concerning the remnant.
God is in the present day still gathering to Himself the faithful remnant from Judaism and Justin will do his part to fulfil
God's plan.[77]

It may be surprising that a gentile Christian living in
the second century seriously considers that the Jews still have
a part in God's salvation, and moreover, that this is being fulfilled in his own days, given the history of Jewish-Christian
relations. No other Christian writer of the second century
seems to take into account the statements of Scripture concerning the eschatological remnant. But Justin's seriousness
with respect to this matter cannot be doubted. Justin appeals
to Trypho and to the Jews not only out of sincerity and compas-
sion, but also out of a sense of responsibility to the truth
which Justin wants to have fully discharged prior to the coming

---

[77]It is this remnant from Judaism, part of it already
within the Christian community (Dial. 47.2), that Justin thinks
will inherit God's promises along with the believing gentiles
and the Patriarchs, Prophets and Old Testament righteous
(Dial. 26.1; 80.1; 130.2). Richardson, p. 13, writes in a
general way that "Justin, in spite of his exclusive tendencies,
still allows for Jews and Gentiles to be co-heirs in the
Kingdom," giving the obscure reference of Dial. 140.1 as example. But Justin is more specific. About the fate of the unbelieving Jews who may not repent before the judgment he is
uncompromising (Dial. 44.2; 47.4).

judgment.[78] He addresses himself to the Jews with an urgency which is distinctively eschatological: βραχὺς οὗτος ὑμῖν περιλείπεται προσηλύσεως χρόνος· ἐαν φθάσῃ ὁ Χριστὸς ἐλθεῖν, μάτην μετανοήσετε, μάτην κλαύσετε . . . γνῶτε τὸν Χριστόν (Dial. 28.2-3); ἤδη ἐπὶ θύραις ὄντος (Dial. 32.3; cf. 35.8; 38.2; 118.1).[79] One is in fact tempted to view Justin's self-understanding as that of a special witness of God to the Jews in the line of the ancient Prophets whom Justin so greatly admires (Dial. 8.1) and whom he so profusely quotes. Justin's view of the remnant, the kerygmatic tenor of the Dialogue imitating and often continuing the prophetic discourses which he quotes, as well as other features of how he understands his own task,[80] seem to encourage such a supposition. To be sure, Justin does not anywhere claim direct inspiration or the gift of prophecy, although he is highly conscious of spiritual gifts within the Church, δόματα/χαρίσματα, including prophecy (Dial. 39.2,4; 82.1; 87.5-6: 88.1). He only claims the gift of

---

[78]He makes frequent references to this responsibility and to the fact that he will be held accountable for it in the day of judgment (Dial. 38.2; 44.1; 68.1). Justin's profound sense of obligation to witness to the truth, or stand condemned before God, is derived from another Prophet, Ezekiel, whom he quotes in this regard (Dial. 82.3). In the context of Dial. 82.3, Justin has both Jews and the gnostics in view.

[79]In Dial. 35.8 Justin also writes: πιστεύσαντες εἰς αὐτὸν ἐν τῇ πάλιν γενησομένῃ ἐνδόξῳ αὐτοῦ παρουσίᾳ σωθῆτε καὶ μὴ καταδικασθῆτε εἰς τὸ πῦρ ὑπ᾽αὐτοῦ. And in Dial. 118.1: ἐν ᾗ κόπτεσθαι μέλλουσι πάντες οἱ ἀπὸ τῶν φυλῶν ὑμῶν ἐκκεντήσαντες τοῦτον τὸν Χριστόν.

[80]As the Prophets were divinely inspired and fearlessly testified to the truth of God and His Messiah (Dial. 7.1-3), so, too, Justin has received a divine gift to understand and to interpret Scripture (Dial. 58.1; cf. 7.3; 100.2) which is the witness of Christ. As the Prophets castigated the sins of the people and called Israel to repentance (Dial. 12.2ff.; 15.2ff.; 22.2ff.; 27.2ff.), so, too, Justin calls the Jews of his day to repentance while there is still the opportunity (Dial. 12.3ff.; 14.1; 28.2ff.; 44.4; 95.3; 118.1). But as the Jews persisted in their hardness of heart at the time of old, persecuting the Prophets besides, so, too, now, they persist in the same disposition refusing to recognize the Messiah and cursing the Christians since they do not happily have physical power over them (Dial. 14.4; 17.1; 39.1; 44.1; 93.4-5; 95.4; 108.1-3; 133.1,6). Justin comes closest to identifying his task with that of the Prophets in Dial. 39.1 where he mentions Elijah's intercessions with God (echoes of Rm. 11.2ff.?), but he soon moves in a different direction (Dial. 39.2). See also particularly Dial. 108.1-3.

the interpretation of Scripture (<u>Dial</u>. 58.1; cf. 100.1-2; 7.3)
and thinks of himself not as a prophet, but as an exegete of
the Prophets (<u>Dial</u>. 92.1). Nevertheless, his conviction of
knowing the divine truth as well as his distinct sense of obligation to proclaim it to others prior to the coming judgment,
make him not without self-awareness something of a special advocate of God before all men in the end-time, especially the
Jews. Indeed, the <u>Dialogue</u> may have been written by Justin
precisely for this purpose, <u>i.e.</u>, as an expression of his conviction about the eschatological remnant and his desire to do
his part, prior to God's impending judgment, for the rescue of
the remnant of the Jews according to God's will.

It is now time to return to the starting point of our
discussion and ask again what is Justin's chief intention behind
his treatment of the Mosaic Law in the <u>Dialogue</u>. Why is the Law
a problem for Justin? It is true that the problem of the Law
and the Old Testament was in the second century raised chiefly
by the gnostics. Justin himself is one of the first orthodox
Christian theologians who participated in this struggle. Evidence of his confrontation with Gnosticism, as well as evidence
of important lines of argument on the Law developed because of
such confrontation, may be found in the <u>Dialogue</u>.

However, according to all the evidence we have presented
above, the primary setting of the problem of the Law in the
<u>Dialogue</u> is the Jewish-Christian debate. The main reasons
therefore why Justin deals with the Mosaic Law in the <u>Dialogue</u>
are none other than the reasons given in <u>Dial</u>. chaps. 8-10 which
we examined at the beginning of this chapter. Justin wants to
demonstrate that observance of the Mosaic Law, according to
God's will and the testimony of Scripture, is not an indispensable prerequisite to true godliness as Trypho contended (<u>Dial</u>.
10.2ff.). Contrary to Trypho's claims, the Mosaic Law is no
longer a necessary criterion of salvation. The problem of
Justin is to answer the question of why are Christians as Christians not bound by the Mosaic Law, even though they accept the
absolute authority of Scripture. How can Christians claim to
accept the authority of Scripture if they are no longer bound to
observe the Law? In his treatment of the Law in the <u>Dialogue</u>,
Justin attempts to answer these questions for the Jews who are
receptive to the Christian faith as well as for the Christians.

CHAPTER TWO

JUSTIN'S CONCEPT OF THE MOSAIC LAW

What is Justin's understanding of the nature and content of the Mosaic Law? This is the second major question
which calls for our attention. In order properly to answer
this question, one must examine the various ways in which
Justin refers to the Law and, more subtly, to examine the several delineations which he draws with respect to its content.
Finally, one must also inquire into the reasons and presuppositions behind these delineations. Thus our investigation in
this chapter centers on three areas: (A) the terminology which
Justin uses to refer to the Law; (B) Justin's tripartite division of the Law, and (C) the criteria by which Justin divides
the Law into three parts.

A. Terminology

Justin uses the following terms for the Law:

(ὁ) νόμος Dial. 8.4; 10.4; 11.1; 45.3; 89.2; 96.1; 122.3-5.[1]
ὁ νόμος Μωϋσέως Dial. 45.3; 52.3; 95.1.
ὁ νόμος ὁ διαταχθεῖς διὰ Μωϋσέως Dial. 34.1; 45.2; 47.3.
ὁ νόμος θεοῦ Dial. 32.4; 86.6.
τὰ διὰ Μωϋσέως διαταχθέντα Dial. 42.4; 46.1-2.
τὰ ἐν τῷ νόμῳ γεγραμμένα Dial. 8.4.

---

[1]Occurrences of the term νόμος not referring to the Mosaic Law or to Christ as the new Law are extremely rare in the
Dialogue, once designating human laws or customs (Dial. 93.1),
and a second time designating something more philosophical (μετὰ
νόμου καὶ λόγου, Dial. 141.1). In the Apology, where the Mosaic
Law receives no attention at all, the term νόμος is used to refer exclusively to things other than the Mosaic Law: Roman Law
(Ap. 12.3; 15.5; 68.10), human laws and customs (App. 9.3-4),
the law of nature in connection with sexual matters (App. 2.4),
and the law of the universe, i.e., of the heavenly bodies (App.
5.2). It also occurs twice within Old Testament citations sig-
nifying once apparently the Christian gospel (Ap. 39.1-3) and
again, if anything conscious at all, the will of God (Ap. 40.8).

ἔννομος πολιτεία <u>Dial</u>. 47.4.[2]

νομοθεσία <u>Dial</u>. 92.2.

τὰ νόμιμα <u>Dial</u>. 29.3; 52.3; 67.5.

αἱ ἐντολαί <u>Dial</u>. 10.3; 67.4.

τὰ προστάγματα <u>Dial</u>. 21.1-5; 86.6; 124.4.

τὰ ἐντάλματα <u>Dial</u>. 46.5; 67.10.

τὰ δικαιώματα <u>Dial</u>. 21.2-4; 46.2.

Justin also very often refers to the Law by its specific ordinances: περιτομή, σάββατον, ἄζυμα, νηστεῖαι, προσφοραί,
θυσίαι, ἑορταί, ἔμμηνα, τὸ βαπτίζεσθαι, and σποδαί (<u>Dial</u>. 8.4;
10.3; 12.3; 46.2; 92.2, <u>et al</u>.).

The following observations may be made on the above
terms and Justin's use of them in the <u>Dialogue</u>:

(1) By and large the terminology is derived from Christian tradition. Certain terms, however, such as νόμιμα, ἐντάλματα, προστάγματα, and δικαιώματα, are Hellenistic Jewish terms
found in Philo and the Septuagint and are probably derived by
Justin from the Septuagint.[3] This at least seems to be the
case with προστάγματα and δικαιώματα, which are used both in
Old Testament citations and in Justin's own narrative (<u>Dial</u>.
21.1-5; 46.2; 86.6; 124.4). The same is true of σποδαί (<u>Dial</u>.
92.2; cf. 13.1; 15.4). The term νόμιμα is an old Greek legal
term[4] and is perhaps used by Justin to heighten the sense of
antiquity when referring to the Mosaic Law. The terms ἔμμηνα
and τὸ βαπτίζεσθαι, the latter used for ritual washing, have no
occurrence in the Christian tradition prior to Justin. Striking
also is the description of the Jewish way of life as ἔννομος
πολιτεία (<u>Dial</u>. 47.4; cf. 45.3; 67.2,4), echoes of which are

---

[2]Cf. κατὰ τὸν νόμον Μωϋσέως πολιτευσαμένους (<u>Dial</u>. 45.3)
and ἐννόμως πολιτεύεσθαι (<u>Dial</u>. 67.2,4).

[3]The use of the above terms is frequent in the
Septuagint, but not in the New Testament, the Apostolic
Fathers and the other Apologists, with the exception of
particular cases, e.g., Paul (δικαιώματα) and Clement of
Rome (δικαιώματα, νόμιμα and προστάγματα) who are in any
case heavily indebted to septuagintal language.

[4]Many references are given in Liddell and Scott,
p. 1179.

found in Hellenistic Jewish writers and also in later Church
Fathers.[5]

   (2)   Justin frequently refers to the Law with the absolute νόμος and almost always with the article: ὁ νόμος. Sometimes Justin calls the Law ὁ νόμος Μωϋσέως or, more rarely,
ὁ νόμος θεοῦ. This usage also follows the Christian tradition.
But in Justin we find very frequent references to the Law as a
legislation given "through" Moses: ὁ νόμος ὁ διαταχθεῖς διὰ
Μωϋσέως (Dial. 34.1, et al.), τὰ διὰ Μωϋσέως διαταχθέντα (Dial.
42.4, et al.). The ultimate author of the Law, Justin wants to
emphasize, is God. In many instances, Justin mentions God as
the subject: ἐκέλευσεν ὁ θεὸς διὰ Μωϋσέως . . . ὁ θεὸς διὰ
Μωϋσέως ἐντειλάμενος (Dial. 20.4; 46.5). At other times, he
mentions God as the legislator of the Law without reference to
Moses: καὶ τὸ σάββατον ἐντέταλται ὁ θεὸς φυλάσσειν ὑμᾶς καὶ
τὰ ἄλλα προστάγματα προσετετάχει (Dial. 21.1; cf. 22.1,11).
This is a traditional Jewish way of referring to God and Scripture. But the frequency with which Justin speaks of God as the
agent behind both Scripture and the Law may reflect Justin's
anti-marcionite concerns. Justin seems to underline the point
that the ancient Scriptures and the Mosaic Law have ultimately
one and the same author: God Himself.

   (3)   Justin nowhere defines the Law. But the way he
speaks about it indicates that for him the Law is the written
Law of Moses. Just as in the case of Ptolemy, who defines the
Law as ὁ σύμπας ἐκεῖνος νόμος ὁ ἐμπεριεχόμενος τῇ Μωϋσέως
πεντατεύχῳ,[6] so also in the case of Justin, what is at issue is
the written Law of the Pentateuch, although Justin does not use
the term Pentateuch. The first reference to the Law in the
Dialogue, however, quite clearly shows that Trypho's and Justin's
discussion is over the written Law (τὰ ἐν τῷ νόμῳ γεγραμμένα
πάντα, Dial. 8.4).

   But there is a matter in this connection which must be
examined further. The oral tradition, so important to the

---

[5]See especially II and IV Maccabbees and the writings of
Philo. After Justin, such references to the manner of Jewish
life may be found in Eusebius, Demonstr. Evang. 1.2; Hom. Clem.
2.20; Chrysostom, Jud. 4.5 and others.

[6]Pan. 33.4.1.

Judaism of Justin's time,[7] receives some attention in the Dia-logue. Justin explicitly mentions the παράδοσις of the Rabbinic teachers, urging Trypho to pay no heed to it (Dial. 38.2).[8] More often, without using the term παράδοσις, he refers to the Jewish teachers as "your teachers" (οἱ διδάσκαλοι ὑμῶν, Dial. 43.8; 48.2; 62.2: cf. οἱ παρ'ὑμῖν ἐξηγηταί, Dial. 36.2), at-tacking their interpretations of Scripture and charging them with teaching their own doctrines rather than God's. In Dial. 140.2, he quotes Scripture against them (ὡς καὶ ἡ γραφὴ διαρρήδην λέγει, διδάσκοντες διδασκαλίας ἐντάλματα ἀνθρώπων, Is. 29:13).[9] Much like Ptolemy,[10] Justin regards the tradition of the Rabbinic teachers as having nothing to do with God's Law and he completely repudiates it. Unlike Ptolemy, however, he does not think that parts of such a tradition are already con-tained in the Pentateuch, retaining a higher view of the au-thority and revelatory character of the Old Testament. Never-theless, in certain instances Justin seems unconsciously to in-

---

[7]The oral Torah in Rabbinic Judaism, probably in its first stages of codification around the middle of the second century A.D., is not separated from the written Torah, but rath-er traced to the authority of Moses himself (Aboth 1.1). It is part of the whole Torah which is the revelation of God's will and wisdom to Israel: "Turn it and turn it again for everything is in it" (Aboth 5.22). See Birger Gerhardsson, Memory and Manuscript, Acta Seminarii Neotestamentici Upsaliensis (Uppsala: Almquist & Wiksells, 1961), II, 19-21. Sanh. 11.3 places the oral Law above the written Law in importance, since the former is the authentic and living interpretation of the written Law. So Herbert Danby, The Mishnah (London: Oxford University Press, 1964), pp. xvii and 400. See also George Foot Moore, Judaism in the First Centuries of the Christian Era (Cambridge: Harvard University Press, 1927), I, 251-64 and the Encyclopaedia Judaica (Jerusalem: Keter Publishing House, Ltd., 1972), XII, 1439-42.

[8]Throughout the Dialogue Trypho is portrayed as depen-dent on the Jewish teachers, not as a teacher himself (Dial. 38.1; 48.2; 62.2; 137.2). One of the last exhortations of Justin to Trypho is that he should choose Christ rather than his own teachers (Dial. 142.2).

[9]The full quote is given in Dial. 78.11, but there it is applied to all Jews. Cf. Dial. 27.4. But Justin does not quote Jesus' logion against the tradition of the elders.

[10]Pan. 33.4.11-13.

clude practices of the oral Law in his understanding of νόμος.
That the two goats of the Day of Atonement must be alike (Dial.
40.4) is not found in Leviticus but in the Mishnah (Yom. 6.1).
So also with respect to the tassels and the teffilin ("phylacte-
ries," Dial. 46.5) which he treats just as he treats legal precepts of the Pentateuch.[11]

Is Justin tacitly conceding to Trypho the Rabbinic
contention of the identity of the oral with the written Law and
its equal validity with it? Such a possibility seems unlikely.
Justin sharply criticizes the Rabbinic haggadic traditions with
which he disagrees. It is true that in the previous case of the
παράδοσις of the Jewish teachers, which he uncompromisingly rejects, we have to do with interpretations of Psalms,[12] prophetic
passages,[13] and passages from the narrative portions of Genesis,[14] which are not construed as νόμος. But for Justin to recognize any part of the oral Law as having claims equal to those
of Scripture would be, to say the least, exceptional. Both the
gnostics, such as Ptolemy, as we have noted, as well as orthodox
Church Fathers, such as Irenaeus,[15] disparage the oral Law in
its entirety.

An answer to the paradox may perhaps be found in Justin's
so-called "Samaritanisms," Justinian errors regarding post-
biblical Jewish practices which actually entail Samaritan

---

[11]The Rabbinic teachers regarded the tefillin as the
classic example of a biblical law according to the oral tradition, Sanh. 88b. The Samaritans did not wear them (Min. 42b).

[12]Ps. 23(LXX) in Dial. 36.2 and Ps. 109(LXX) in Dial.
83.1.

[13]Is. 7:10-16 in Dial. 43.8; Mic. 4:1-7 in Dial. 110.1,
and Mal. 1:10-12 in Dial. 117.4.

[14]Gen. 1:26-28 and 3:22 in Dial. 62.2-3 and Gen. 49:10
in Dial. 120.5.

[15]Adv. Haer. 4.22.1ff. Irenaeus here defends the Mosaic
Law against the gnostics who regarded it in part as "commandments of men," appealing to the sayings of Jesus. Irenaeus applies Mtt. 15:3 as well as Is. 29:13 and other texts to the oral
pharisaic law alone, not to any part of the Mosaic Law, and
criticizes the oral law as spurious and contrary to the Law of
Moses (aggredientes adulteram legem et contrariam legi . . .
quae usque adhum pharisaica vocatur).

customs.[16] Justin curiously is not sufficiently informed to
know the difference. These errors may indicate that Justin's
partial and unconscious identification of the written and the
oral Law is more by default than by intent.[17] When writing
about the Law, he is fundamentally concerned with the written
Law of Moses, the Law which is part of canonical Scripture.
It is the authority of Scripture which makes the Mosaic Law
theologically problematic for writers such as Justin, Ptolemy
and Irenaeus, whereas the oral Law has for them no standing
whatsoever.

(4) The final observation on Justin's terminology of
the Law is that the Law for him is chiefly the ritual Law of
the Pentateuch. What is at stake is circumcision, the sabbath,
offerings, fasting, ritual washings, and the like, which Christians no longer practice (Dial. 8.4; 10.3; 12.3, et al.). His
treatment of the Law is dominated by his discussion of the
ritual commandments of the Old Testament. This is the νόμος
which is a problem for Christians both as an issue of the
Jewish-Christian debate and as a question among Christians
themselves over the Law.

That the ritual Law is what Justin understands by νόμος
is indicated by the fact that he never uses this term (νόμος)
when he appeals to the moral precepts of the Law and again never
when he refers to the narrative parts of the Pentateuch. When
he quotes from the narrative sections of the Pentateuch he al-

---

[16] Such as, for example, the "scarlet" tassels which in
their Jewish version were blue (Dial. 46.5) and the injunction
not to drink hot water on the sabbath (Dial. 19.3) and others.
See Williams, Justin Martyr, p. xxxiii. P. R. Weis, "Some
Samaritanisms of Justin Martyr," JThS 45 (1944), 199-205, has
shown that we have to do here with practices of the Samaritans
among whom Justin lived as a youth (Ap. 1.1).

[17] Ptolemy, Pan. 33.4.11-13, also seems to do the same
when, quoting from the Corban logion of Jesus, he assigns the
Corban practice to the traditions of the elders which according
to him were already incorporated into the Law of the Pentateuch.
Quispel, p. 22, thinks that perhaps Ptolemy has sufficient
knowledge of Judaeo-Christian traditions to believe that the
Mishnah goes back to the beginning of the Mosaic religion. More
likely, rather, is that he is drawn to this apparent assumption
by his use of the Jesus logion. Justin does not use this logion
nor does he refer to post-biblical Jewish practices as "traditions of the elders."

ways uses the term γραφῆ or γραφαί.[18] On one occasion the title ὁ νόμος καὶ οἱ προφῆται (<u>Dial</u>. 51.3) is used, but this occurs in a direct quotation from the New Testament. When Justin uses his own language in this connection he says: ὁ νομοθέτης καὶ οἱ προφῆται (Dial. 1.3). Without exception, when νόμος designates the Law of Moses, it is always the ritual Law for Justin. This will be confirmed by the Apologist's tripartite division of the Law to which we now turn.[19]

B. The Tripartite Division of the Law

The most important aspect of Justin's understanding of the Mosaic Law is his division of the Law into three parts. Justin, while firmly upholding the authority of Scripture and indirectly defending the Old Testament, the Law and God against marcionite criticisms of them, is nevertheless the first Christian writer explicitly to distinguish different parts within the Law and the Old Testament and consequently the first Christian writer to introduce qualifications into the

---

[18]This is Justin's most frequent reference to Scripture. Justin also quotes Scripture with the words Μωϋσῆς μηνύει, λέγει, φησί, etc. (<u>Dial</u>. 56.1-2; 59.3) or simply ὁ θεὸς κράζει (<u>Dial</u>. 19.2) and not infrequently he mentions the specific book or Prophet from which or whom he quotes, e.g., ἐν τῇ βίβλῳ τῆς γενέσεως (<u>Dial</u>. 20.1; 58.1-2) or Ἡσαΐας βοᾷ (<u>Dial</u>. 12.1). In the <u>Apology</u>, where Justin addresses pagans and is particularly interested in the proof from the fulfilment of Scripture, he always uses βίβλοι τῶν προφητῶν/ προφητειῶν (<u>Ap</u>. 31.2,5,7; 36.3; 44.12) and never γραφῆ or γραφαί.

[19]Verweijs' contention, pp. 228-29, that Justin does not restrict the Law to the ceremonial Law and that the ceremonial Law is not Justin's "vexation" point is very difficult to understand. Verweijs thinks that only much later in the case of the Church Fathers who are actually pre-occupied with Paul does one find the restriction of the Law to the ceremonial Law. But otherwise Goppelt, p. 295, who writes: "Hiernach reduziert sich für Justin das Problem des atl. Gesetzes im wesentlichen auf die Frage nach der Geltung des Zeremonialgesetzes." It is true that Justin does not explicitly isolate and designate a "ceremonial" Law, nor does he distinguish an "ethical" Law. His terminology is not developed. But what he says about the Law and the way in which he treats the problem of the Law indicate that the restriction of the Law (νόμος) to the ritual Law has already occurred in the Christian tradition.

unity of Scripture.[20] This is not totally unique in Justin.
There is evidence from different quarters that, during the second century, the unity of the Old Testament is broken, just as
its authority is also relativized. The Basilidians apparently
ascribed the origins of the Old Testament to a plurality of
lesser gods.[21] Ptolemy, as is well known, not only divided
God's Law into three categories, but also assigned different
authors to the Law contained in the Pentateuch.[22] Heretical
Judaism with its theory of false pericopes which were presumably interpolated into the Old Testament also broke the unity and
authority of Scripture in its own way.[23] Even as orthodox a
Christian writer as Irenaeus, in view of the struggle over the
Old Testament with the gnostics, slightly softens his concept
of Scripture so as to allow at least that some of the precepts
of the Law originated with Moses and not ultimately with

---

[20]Implicit qualifications are already present in Paul
wherever he contrasts Jewish ritual practices with ethical
injunctions, e.g., I Cor. 7:19; Rom. 2:21-26; 13.8-10. Also,
it is clear that the problem of the Law in Galatians has to do
with the ritual Law, circumcision, dietary regulations and
observance of festivals (Gal. 2:3,14b; 4:9-10; 5:2,6; 6:12).
In a similar way, the author of Hebrews views the Law as primarily the cultic Law (Heb. 7:11-12; 10.1ff.).

[21]See Irenaeus, Adv. Haer. 1.19.1-3.

[22]God, Moses and also the Jewish elders, Pan. 33.4.1-6.
The difference between God's Law and the Law of Moses is defined in opposing terms: Moses legislates precepts contrary to
God's Law (ἐναντία τῷ θεῷ νομοθετεῖ). However, explains
Ptolemy, Moses did so because of the necessity of circumstances,
i.e., the elect people's hardness of heart, rather than because
of willful choice. The tradition of the elders is not at all
considered, being deemed by him worthless.

[23]The Kerygmata Petrou where the false pericopes are
said to include those passages of Scripture which speak of God
as having human passions, which speak of many gods, or of sacrifices, the Temple and kingship. See Georg Strecker, "The
Kerygmata Petrou" in Edgar Hennecke, New Testament Apocrypha,
ed. W. Schneemelcher and ET ed. R. McL. Wilson (Philadelphia:
The Westminster Press, 1964), II, pp. 111-14 and also his Das
Judenchristentum in den Pseudoklementinen, TU 70 (Berlin, 1958),
especially pp. 151ff. But this is not in any way relevant for
Justin. According to Strecker, the doctrine of the false pericopes in the Kerygmata Petrou is independent of marcionite dual-
ism and comes from Jewish sources, since it is taught along
with the principle of the eternity of the Law.

God.[24] Justin's own division of the Law and the Old Testament
into different parts is not unrelated to this struggle, as we
shall see.

The tripartite division of the Law has not received
much attention by students of Justin. Whenever occasionally
treated, it is either in passing or in a footnote.[25] The reason is probably that, unlike Ptolemy, Justin does not bring
forward his tripartite division of the Law as the explicit
model of his lengthy treatment of the Law in the Dialogue, but
rather conceals it in a fairly obscure section of the Dialogue
dealing with other interests. Nevertheless, his concept of the
division of the Law into various parts seems actually to determine his treatment of the Law in the Dialogue and constitutes
one of the most decisive aspects of his understanding of the
Law. It is also a landmark in the history of Christian exegesis and deserves careful examination.

Justin's awareness of variegation within the Law is expressed in the following passages of the Dialogue:

καὶ γὰρ ἐν τῷ Μωϋσέως νόμῳ τὰ φύσει καλὰ καὶ εὐσεβῆ καὶ
δίκαια νενομοθέτηται πράττειν τοὺς πειθομένους αὐτοῖς,
καὶ πρὸς σκληροκαρδίαν δὲ τοῦ λαοῦ διαταχθέντα γίνεσθαι
ὁμοίως ἀναγέγραπται, ἃ καὶ ἔπραττον οἱ ὑπὸ τὸν νόμον
(Dial. 45.3).

For in Moses' Law too those things that are by nature
good and pious and just have been laid down for those
that obey and practise it, and such things as were appointed to be done on account of the hardness of the
people's heart are equally recorded, which things also
they that are under the Law used to practice.

διὰ τὸ σκληροκάρδιον τοῦ λαοῦ ὑμῶν διὰ Μωϋσέως τινὲς
τῶν ἐντολῶν τεθειμέναι εἰσίν (Dial. 67.4).

---

[24]Adv. Haer. 4.26.2; 27.1. Irenaeus, like Ptolemy,
bases himself on Jesus' words (Mtt. 19:7-8). He, however, completely rejects any opposition between Moses and God, saying
that one need not wonder that the same God permitted such ac-
commodations for the benefit of the people. God according to
Irenaeus did the same through the Apostles who on their own
took provisions on behalf of Christians. Among other texts,
he cites I Cor. 7:6,12. Moses' allowance of divorce was one
of the "antitheses" Marcion found between the teaching of
Christ and that of Moses, according to Tertullian, Adv. Marc.
4.34.

[25]Only Shotwell, pp. 8-9, attempts a partial analysis
of Justin's division of the Law.

Some of the commandments have been laid down by Moses because of the hardness of the heart of your people.

τί μὲν ὡς αἰώνιον καὶ παντὶ γένει ἁρμόζον καὶ ἔνταλμα καὶ ἔργον ὁ θεὸς ἐπίσταται, τί δὲ πρὸς τὸ σκληροκάρδιον τοῦ λαοῦ ὑμῶν ἁρμοσάμενος . . . ἐνετέταλτο (Dial. 67.10).

What command and work God knows to be everlasting and in harmony with every race, and what He ordered only in harmony with the hardness of your people's heart.

In the context of the first passage, Justin is discussing whether or not the Jews of old who had observed the Mosaic Law will be saved (Dial. 45.1ff.). Justin's answer is yes. His answer is based on a two-fold division of the Law: (1) the commandments which are by nature good (τὰ φύσει καλὰ) and (2) the commandments which were legislated on account of the hardness of the people's heart (πρὸς σκληροκαρδίαν τοῦ λαοῦ διαταχθέντα). Justin says that those who observed the Law will be saved because in this Law, aside from the commandments ordained because of the hard-heartedness of the Jews, there are other commandments of ultimate and universal value.[26]

In the second passage, Justin is responding to Trypho's remark that Jesus, too, lived according to the Law. Justin reminds Trypho that, as they had already agreed, some of the Mosaic commandments were ordained for the hardness of heart of the Jews, implying that others were ordained for other purposes (Dial. 67.4). He does not here immediately indicate what these are.

The third passage occurs within the same context. Justin has asked several questions which compel Trypho again to concede that the Mosaic precepts such as circumcision, sacrifices and offerings are not ultimately essential. Then Justin declares that God had promised another Covenant, now fulfilled, which shows (δεικνύουσαν) (1) what God regards as an eternal and universal precept and deed (αἰώνιον καὶ παντὶ γένει ἁρμόζον καὶ ἔνταλμα καὶ ἔργον) and (2) what God commanded in order to deal with the hardness of heart of the Jews (πρὸς τὸ σκληροκάρδιον τοῦ λαοῦ). He does not say how the promised Covenant indicates this distinction. The two-fold distinction is the same as that of the first passage.

---

[26]He goes on to say explicitly in Dial. 45.4 that those who have observed the eternal and universal principles are pleasing to God and will be saved.

The full classification of the Old Testament and the
Law is offered in another passage, Dial. 44.2. Here we find a
tripartite division of the Law. The passage reads:

τὰ μυστήρια πάντα, λέγω δὲ ὅτι τις μὲν ἐντολῆ εἰς θεοσέβειαν καὶ δικαιοπραξίαν διετέτακτο, τις δὲ ἐντολῆ
καὶ πρᾶξις ὁμοίως εἴρητο ἢ εἰς μυστήριον τοῦ Χριστοῦ
ἢ διὰ τὸ σκληροκάρδιον τοῦ λαοῦ ὑμῶν (Dial. 44.2).

All the mysteries, I mean that one commandment was
appointed for piety and the practice of righteousness,
and another command and action was in the same way
spoken either as referring to the mystery of Christ
or on account of the hardness of your people's heart.

This significant statement occurs in one of Justin's
many digressive critiques of the Jews combined with appeals for
their conversion (Dial. 44.1-4). Although it does not at
first glance determine the arrangement of Justin's discussion
of the Law, it is decisive for his understanding of the Law and
his concept of its tripartite stratification. Like Ptolemy,
but in a different manner and with different presuppositions,[27]
Justin divides the Law and, in some way, all of Scripture into
the following parts: (1) ethics, (2) prophecy and (3) historical dispensation. Justin does not use technical terminology,
but his distinctions are unquestionably discernible. A closer
look at this classification is necessary.

In the foregoing passage Justin speaks fundamentally

---

[27]Ptolemy bases himself on a Valentinian metaphysic
regarding the problem of divine unity and multiplicity in the
universe (πῶς ἀπὸ μιᾶς ἀρχῆς τῶν ὅλων [ἁπλῆς] οὔσης τε καὶ ὁμο-
λογουμένης, τῆς ἀγεννήτου καὶ ἀφθάρτου . . . καὶ αὗται αἱ φύ-
σεις, ἥ τε τῆς φθορᾶς καὶ ἡ τῆς μεσότητος, ἀνομοούσιοι αὗται
καθεστῶσαι, Pan. 33.6.8), even though the speculative elements
of his thought are veiled until the end of his treatise. See
Quispel, pp. 18-19, and also von Campenhausen, pp. 103-05.
One is suprised, however, to read Quispel's comment, p. 23,
that Ptolemy's tripartite division of the Law is "almost identical" with Justin's. Apart from differing metaphysical presuppositions, Ptolemy has nothing of Justin's typological or
prophetic interpretation of the Law and, further, the content
and scope of his divisions, including that which Ptolemy calls
the Law of God, properly speaking, are considerably different.
Ptolemy first divides the Law into three parts according to its
different authors, (1) God, (2) Moses and (3) the elders, a
division totally absent from Justin. Then he divides God's Law
into three more parts, (1) the Decalogue, (2) the law of defense
and retaliation and (3) the ritual practices, a tripartite division which is also different from Justin's. Quispel also conjectures, pp. 23 and 84, that Ptolemy may have known Justin's
Dialogue and that he may have borrowed the tripartite division
from Justin. There is, however, hardly any basis for this.

of "commandments" (τὶς μὲν . . . τὶς δὲ ἐντολή). However, by
the phrase μυστήρια πάντα Justin does not mean only the Mosaic
Law alone, but all of Scripture. He does not finely differentiate between the prophetic aspect of the Law and the prophetic aspect of Scripture as a whole. One is continuous with
the other. But in contrast the first and third divisions of
the Law, the ethical and historical, are more definitely distinguished from the whole of Scripture. They are more closely
related to "Law" (νόμος). Thus, in this respect, Justin is
thinking primarily of a classification of the content of the
Mosaic Law, rather than of all Scripture by his statement of
Dial. 44.2.

First of all, then, Justin distinguishes what may be
designated as the ethical part of the Law (τὶς μὲν ἐντολὴ εἰς
θεοσέβειαν καὶ δικαιοπραξίαν διετέτακτο, Dial. 44.2). What is
here involved is a body of undefined commandments which for
Justin express binding universal principles. This part of the
Law is not at the forefront of Justin's discussion with Trypho.
Both Justin and Trypho seem to assume the validity of a universally binding ethical βίος which is contrasted to the way of
the ritual Law of Judaism.[28] Justin periodically alludes to
the principles of this βίος without naming them. He calls them
τὰ αὐτὰ δίκαια, Dial. 23.1; 30.1; τὰ αἰώνια δίκαια, Dial. 28.4;
τὰ φύσει καλὰ καὶ εὐσεβῆ καὶ δίκαια, Dial. 45.3; τὰ καθόλου
καὶ φύσει καὶ αἰώνια καλά, Dial. 45.4; αἱ αἰώνιαι καὶ φύσει
δικαιοπραξίαι καὶ εὐσέβειαι, Dial. 47.2; or the αἰώνιον καὶ
παντὶ γένει ἁρμόζον ἔνταλμα καὶ ἔργον, Dial. 67.10). These
principles are often contrasted, implicitly or explicitly, to
the Mosaic Law which is temporary and legislated only for the
Jews (Dial. 23.1; 28.4; 30.1 et al.).

What is important is that, although these eternal principles are part of a universal law more ultimate than the Law
of Moses, they are also to be found in the Mosaic Law. Part of

---

[28]In Dial. 10.1 Justin asks Trypho what is the real
Jewish objection to Christians, namely, (1) that they do not
keep the Law (οὐ κατὰ νόμον βιοῦμεν . . . περιτεμνόμεθα . . .
σαββατίζομεν), or (2) also that they have a faulty βίος.
Trypho answers that only the former is in question (Dial.
10.2-4). In Ap. 8.2 Justin states that the Christians follow
the αἰώνιος καὶ καθαρὸς βίος.

the Mosaic Law constitutes or gives expression to these universal ethical principles which are binding upon all men. Justin's
answer to the question of whether or not Jews who lived prior
to Christ, and who observed the Law, will be saved, depends on
his view that the Mosaic Law contains both eternal principles
as well as temporary regulations suited to the hardness of
heart of the Jews (Dial. 45.3).[29] Those who prior to Christ
observed the Law will, according to Justin, be saved not by
virtue of the temporary cultic commandments, but by virtue of
the universal and eternal principles inherent in the Law (τὰ
καθόλου καὶ φύσει καὶ αἰώνια καλά (Dial. 45.4). Justin does
not specifically say what these principles are in this context.

The Apologist explicates his concept of the nature and
content of the ethical law in a single lengthy passage, Dial.
93.1-3, a point in the Dialogue by which his discussion of the
ritual Law has been largely concluded. Part of this passage
reads as follows:

Τὰ γὰρ ἀεὶ καὶ δι᾽ὅλου δίκαια καὶ πᾶσαν δικαιοσύνην
παρέχει ἐν παντὶ γένει ἀνθρώπων, καὶ ἔστι πᾶν γένος
γνωρίζον ὅτι μοιχεία κακὸν καὶ πορνεία καὶ ἀνδροφονία
καὶ ὅσα ἄλλα τοιαῦτα. κἂν πάντες πράττωσιν αὐτά, ἀλλ᾽
οὖν γε τοῦ ἐπίστασθαι ἀδικοῦντες, ὅταν πράττωσι ταῦτα,
οὐκ ἀπηλλαγμένοι εἰσί, πλὴν ὅσοι ὑπὸ ἀκαθάρτου πνεύματος ἐμπεφορημένοι καὶ ἀνατροφῆς καὶ ἐθῶν φαύλων καὶ
νόμων πονηρῶν διαφθαρέντες τὰς φυσικὰς ἐννοίας ἀπώλεσαν,
μᾶλλον δὲ ἔσβεσαν ἢ ἐπεσχημένας ἔχουσιν. ἰδεῖν γὰρ ἔστι
καὶ τοὺς τοιούτους μὴ τὰ αὐτὰ παθεῖν βουλομένους ἅπερ
αὐτοὶ τοὺς ἄλλους διατιθέασι, καὶ ἐν συνειδήσεσιν
ἐχθραῖς ταῦτα ὀνειδίζοντας ἀλλήλοις ἅπερ ἐργάζονται.
ὅθεν μοι δοκεῖ καλῶς εἰρῆσθαι ὑπὸ τοῦ ἡμετέρου κυρίου
καὶ σωτῆρος ᾽Ἰησοῦ Χριστοῦ, ἐν δυσὶν ἐντολαῖς πᾶσαν
δικαιοσύνην καὶ εὐσέβειαν πληροῦσθαι (Dial. 93.1-2).

For He exhibits among every race of men the things
that are righteous at all times and in all places, and
every race is aware that adultery is evil, and fornication, and murder, and all suchlike things. And although all practise them, yet, nevertheless, they are
not set free from knowing they do wrong when they
practice them, with the exception of such as, possessed
by an unclean spirit and corrupted by early education
and bad customs and evil laws, have lost their natural
thoughts, or rather have quenched them or held them down.
For we may see even such persons not wishing to endure
the same sufferings that they inflict on others, and
with a conscience opposed to themselves reproach others

____

[29]καὶ γὰρ ἐν τῷ Μωϋσέως νόμῳ τὰ φύσει καλὰ καὶ εὐσεβῆ
καὶ δίκαια νενομοθέτηται πράττειν τοὺς πειθομένους αὐτοῖς, καὶ
πρὸς σκληροκαρδίαν δὲ τοῦ λαοῦ διαταχθέντα γίνεσθαι ὁμοίως
ἀναγέγραπται (Dial. 45.3).

for the very things that they themselves perform.
Wherefore it seems to me that it was well said by our
Lord and Saviour Jesus Christ, that all righteousness
and piety are fulfilled in two commandments.

In contrast to the temporary precepts of the Law such
as the sabbath, sacrifices, and circumcision (Dial. 92.2-4),
Justin in the above passage explains the eternal and universal
principles of righteousness (τὰ ἀεὶ καὶ δι'ὅλου δίκαια καὶ
πᾶσαν δικαιοσύνην, Dial. 93.1). These principles, says Justin,
are known to all men (παντὶ γένει ἀνθρώπων, Dial. 93.1). According to God's order of creation all men, except those whose
natural insights (φυσικαὶ ἔννοιαι) are corrupted by demonic influence, bad upbringing or evil laws, know that such things as
adultery, fornication and murder are evil, even though they may
themselves commit such things (Dial. 93.1). For even those who
are corrupted cannot bear to endure such wrongs against themselves, but reproach each other for the very things they themselves commit, showing that these deeds are by nature evil
(Dial. 93.2). Thus, says Justin, Christ quite rightly stated
that all righteousness is fulfilled by the double commandment
of love,[30] for he who loves God will honor no other God and he
who loves his neighbor will not wish him evil but good (Dial.
93.2). The Apologist goes on to observe that all righteousness
is divided into two parts (διχῆ . . . τετμημένης), that
involving God and that involving neighbor. Whoever loves God
and neighbor according to the dominical injunction is truly
righteous (Dial. 93.3).

The ethical law for Justin thus involves eternal and
universal principles which find partial expression through the
Mosaic Law. In the Apology, both his interests in the ethical
law and his philosophical presuppositions behind it are more
evident.[31] In the Dialogue, however, the ethical law plays a

---

[30]Justin here quotes the logion of Jesus about love of
God and love of neighbor.

[31]Throughout the Apology Justin strongly upholds the
natural capacity of man to know and to choose the truth, although he recognizes the demonic corruption of this capacity.
See Ap. 2.3; 5.1-4; 10.2,6; 28.3; 46.3; App. 7.5-8; 8.1-3;
13.1-5. His views are grounded in his concept of the
Spermatikos Logos. On this and the philosophical presuppositions of his thought, see Andresen, Holte, Waszink, Chadwick
and Hyldahl, among others. See above, p. 18, n. 24.

minimal role. Justin does not explicitly define the content of
this law.[32] He does not associate the ethical law exclusively
with the Decalogue, as Ptolemy and Irenaeus do.[33] In fact he
does not even mention the Decalogue. Furthermore, Justin never
refers to the ethical part of the Mosaic Law as νόμος and hesitates to apply the terminology of the Mosaic precepts to it.
Very infrequently does he call it even ἐντολή or ἔνταλμα.[34]
He prefers rather such general terminology as τὰ αὐτὰ δίκαια,
τὰ αἰώνια δίκαια, τὰ φύσει καλὰ καὶ εὐσεβῆ καὶ δίκαια and the
like. What he conceives of as being "the Law" (ὁ νόμος), we
may reiterate, is the ritual Law. In the Dialogue, the ethical
part of the Law does not have the same problematic urgency as
the other parts of the Law, but is in the background. Nevertheless, it is clear that Justin assumes that one of the three divisions of the Law is the ethical part, composed of commandments
legislated for the practice of true piety and righteousness
(Dial. 44.2).

The second division of Justin is the predictive aspect
of the Law, i.e., Law as prophecy of Christ (τὶς δὲ ἐντολή καὶ
πρᾶξις ὁμοίως εἴρητο . . . εἰς μυστήριον τοῦ Χριστοῦ, Dial.
44.2). This division is mainly treated by Justin in Dial.
chaps. 40-42, a section of the Dialogue which breaks into the
larger Christological discussion as a parenthesis.[35] However,
these three chapters are not entirely out of context in this
section of the Dialogue because the ongoing argument concerning
the prophecies of Christ in the Old Testament is here continued.
The Passover lamb, writes Justin, is a type (τύπος) prefiguring
Christ (Dial. 40.1). The roasted lamb on crossed spits[36] is a
symbol (σύμβολον) of Christ's passion on the Cross (Dial. 40.3).

---

[32]But one catches occasional glimpses of lists of vir-
tues, e.g., Dial. 110.3. Justin would no doubt also include the
teachings of Christ in the ethical law (Dial. 116.2; 123.9; cf.
Ap. 14.4; chaps. 15-17.

[33]For Ptolemy, see Pan. 33.5.1,3. For Irenaeus, see
Adv. Haer. 4.15.1 and 4.16.3

[34]Dial. 44.2; 67.10; 92.3.

[35]So also Bousset, p. 285; Williams, Justin Martyr, p.
79, n. 4, and Prigent, p. 110.

[36]Another "Samaritanism" of Justin.

60

The two goats of the Great Fast are a foretelling (καταγγελία)
of the two Comings of Christ (Dial. 40.4). The flour offering
is a type of the Eucharistic bread (Dial. 41.1). Circumcision
of the flesh is a type of the true spiritual circumcision (Dial.
41.4). Finally, the twelve bells on the High Priest's robe are
a prophetic symbol of the twelve Apostles (Dial. 42.1ff.).

The series concludes with the statement that all of the
other Mosaic commandments can similarly be interpreted. Says
Justin:

> καὶ τὰ ἄλλα δὲ πάντα ἁπλῶς, ὦ ἄνδρες, ἔφην, τὰ ὑπὸ
> Μωϋσέως διαταχθέντα δύναμαι καταριθμῶν ἀποδεικνύναι
> τύπους καὶ σύμβολα καὶ καταγγελίας τῶν τῷ Χριστῷ
> γίνεσθαι μελλόντων καὶ τῶν εἰς αὐτὸν πιστεύειν προ-
> εγνωσμένων καὶ τῶν ὑπ'αὐτοῦ τοῦ Χριστοῦ ὁμοίως γίνεσθαι
> μελλόντων (Dial. 42.4).

> And in fact all the other things, Gentlemen, I
> said, which were appointed by Moses, I can enumerate
> and prove to be types, and figures, and announcements
> of those persons who were foreknown as about to be-
> lieve in Him, and similarly of those things which
> were to be done by Christ Himself.[37]

The above assertion that all of the other Mosaic precepts can also be interpreted typologically is inconsistent
with Justin's tripartite division of the Law. Is Justin in
Dial. 44.2 drawing perhaps only a two-fold[38] (moral and ceremonial) division of the Law as the conjunctions μὲν and δὲ
(τὰς μὲν . . . τὰς δὲ) might suggest? Does he, then, possibly,
assume that the ethical law is not essentially νόμος, i.e., the
ritual Law, so that therefore in the above passage (καὶ τὰ ἄλλα
δὲ πάντα . . . τὰ ὑπὸ Μωϋσέως διαταχθέντα, Dial. 42.4) he is

---

[37]Williams, Justin Martyr, p. 84, seems to leave out of
his translation τῶν τῷ Χριστῷ γίνεσθαι μελλόντων καί. After
"announcements" the translation should read "of those things
which were to happen to Christ and of those persons who as fore-
known were to believe in him and similarly," etc. Justin is obviously referring to the passover lamb and the two goats of the
Fast as foreshadowing things which were to happen to Christ, to
the flour offering as predicting the Eucharist which Christ commanded the Christians to celebrate (παρέδωκεν ποιεῖν, Dial.
41.1), and to the twelve bells of the High Priest's robe as
foretelling either those who were to believe in him or what was
done by Christ himself gathering the Twelve. On this, Justin
is far more clear later with his exegesis of Gen. 49:8-12 in
Dial. chaps. 52-54. See especially Dial. 52.4; 53.1,4 and also
Ap. 32.5-8.

[38]So Shotwell, p. 8.

thinking of all the ritual commandments in their typological
significance apart from the moral law? Is he, in other words,
merely assigning a double function, one predictive, the other
historical, to the same ritual Law, without thereby distin-
guishing three divisions in the Law?

The evidence from the Dialogue seems to indicate otherwise. While Justin's terminology is undeveloped with respect to
an explicit definition of the tripartite division, the Apologist
seems to be speaking of three rather than two categories. On
the one hand, there can be no doubt about the ethical part of
the Law which is obviously separated by Justin (τὶς μὲν ἐντολῆ
εἰς θεοσέβειαν καὶ δικαιοπραξίαν διετέτακτο, Dial. 44.2). On
the other hand, the historical and prophetic parts of the Law
are also sufficiently distinguished as separate categories for
three reasons. First of all, the emphatic disjunctive in the
second composite clause of Dial. 44.2 (τὶς δὲ ἐντολῆ καὶ πρᾶξις
ὁμοίως εἴρητο ἢ εἰς μυστήριον τοῦ Χριστοῦ ἢ διὰ τὸ σκληροκάρδιον τοῦ λαοῦ ὑμῶν) suggests a strong separation of categories.
A commandment and act (ἐντολῆ καὶ πρᾶξις), says Justin, may
equally refer (ὁμοίως εἴρητο) either (ἢ) to the mystery of
Christ, the prophetic category, or (ἢ) to the matter of the
hardness of heart of the Jews, the historical category, but not
to both. That is to say, some acts and commandments are for
Justin typological and predictive signs of the Christ event,
while other acts and commandments are injunctions or cultic
practices which have a historical function related to the conduct of the Jews. While Justin associates and even blurs the
distinction between ἐντολῆ and πρᾶξις which belong to the same
category of the Law, either the historical or the predictive,
he does not with the adverb ὁμοίως apparently intend to unite
the categories themselves. He does not include the same acts
and same commandments in both the historical and predictive interpretations of the Law.

Secondly, Justin throughout the Dialogue keeps the categories separated. For example, the unit of Dial. chaps. 40-42
is the only place where Justin interprets legal precepts typologically and in this unit he interprets legal precepts only
typologically. On the other hand, in the main unit of Dial.
chaps. 10-30, Justin's interpretation of the Law has to do only
with the historical category, the Law ordained for the σκληρο-

62

κάρδιον τοῦ λαοῦ, and never with the μυστήριον τοῦ Χριστοῦ.[39]
In other sections of the Dialogue (chaps. 45-47 and 67.2-10),
the Law is also interpreted in reference to the historical
category alone, and not to the prophetic one. In the case of
Dial. 92.2-93.3, the first part (Dial. 92.2-5) deals with the
Law ordained for the σκληροκάρδιον τοῦ λαοῦ and the second part
(Dial. 93.1-3) with the ethical law. Dial. 95.1 is a different
case and deals wholistically with the Mosaic Law which confronts
men with the impasse of its curse.[40]

Finally, Justin in no case interprets the same legal
precept or same act as referring both to the mystery of Christ
and to what he calls the hardness of heart of the people.[41] To
be sure, when Justin is not speaking of specific ordinances,
institutions or acts, but rather generalizes about them in the
plural (καὶ τὰ ἄλλα δὲ πάντα . . . τὰ ὑπὸ Μωϋσέως διαταχθέντα,
Dial. 42.4; καὶ θυσίας [ὁ θεός] . . . ἐνετείλατο, Dial. 19.6;
οὐκ ἦν χρεία . . . προσφορῶν, Dial. 23.3; cf. 43.1; 92.2), this
distinction is not consistently preserved, since the general
θυσίαι and προσφοραῖ are related to the hardness of the people's
heart while at the same time the Passover lamb, the two goats of
the Great Fast and the flour offering, which are exclusively interpreted in a typological fashion, are also designated as "sacrifice" or "offering" (τὸ μυστήριον οὖν τοῦ προβάτου, ὃ τὸ πάσχα

_____

[39]The use of the term σύμβολον in Dial. 14.2 is as an
allegorical reference to the timeless moral order rather than as
a typological reference to a future event. In Dial. 24.1, where
Justin seems on the verge of offering a typological interpretation, he quickly stops, thinking of this as a digression (ἵνα
τὰ νῦν μὴ ἐπ᾽ ἄλλους ἐκτρέπεσθαι λόγους δοκῶ).

[40]See below, pp. 103-08.

[41]The only exception is the case of circumcision which
is interpreted in several ways. In Dial. 41.4 Justin interprets
it typologically as the spiritual circumcision through the resurrection of Christ, associating the eighth day of circumcision
with the eighth day of the resurrection. Elsewhere he interprets it allegorically as the spiritual circumcision of the moral order which he associates particularly with baptism (Dial.
18.2; 29.1; 43.2). His most distinctive interpretation of circumcision is as a mark of identity of the Jews, related to their
historical conduct as Justin conceives of it (Dial. 16.2f.;
19.2; 92.2-3). See also his typological interpretation of
Joshua's "second" circumcision of the Israelites as prefiguring
the spiritual circumcision through Christ (Dial. 113.6-7;
114.4).

θύειν ἐντέταλται ὁ θεός, τύπος ἦν τοῦ Χριστοῦ, Dial. 40.1;
ὁ δὲ ἕτερος τῶν τράγων εἰς προσφορὰν [ἐγένετο], Dial. 40.4;
ἡ τῆς σεμιδάλεως προσφορά, Dial. 41.1).[42] Also, more importantly, it is clear that for Justin the Law which he interprets
either historically or predictively has now ceased to be valid.[43] There is, therefore, a material unity between these two
categories which, from this perspective, constitute one ritual
Law having two functions rather than two "divisions."

Nevertheless, the emphatic disjunctive of Dial. 44.2,
the consistent separation of the historical and predictive
interpretations of the Law in various sections of the Dialogue,
as well as the prominence given to the historical interpretation of the Law, all more strongly support a tripartite division of the Law. Greater justice is done to Justin's treatment
of the Law if Dial. 44.2 is read as a tripartite rather than a
bipartite division of the Law and the Old Testament. Thus
Justin's generalization of Dial. 42.4 (καὶ τὰ ἄλλα δὲ πάντα
. . . τὰ ὑπὸ Μωϋσέως διαταχθέντα δύναμαι καταριθμῶν ἀποδεικνύ-
ναι τύπους καὶ σύμβολα καὶ καταγγελίας [εἶναι] must be considered an inaccurate rhetorical exaggeration. The exaggeration
is probably triggered by the lengthy series of typological interpretations which precede it.

With respect to Justin's second division of the Law,
Law as prophecy, an additional point is necessary. Justin remarks that not only a commandment, but also an act (ἐντολὴ καὶ
πρᾶξις) may predictively refer to the mystery of Christ (Dial.
44.2). Thus far we have dealt with "commandments." The ritual
institutions of Dial. chaps. 40-42 which were noted above are
called ἐντολαί (Dial. 40.1; 41.4). But are there also "acts"
described in Scripture which according to the Apologist have a
typological purpose of the same nature? Considerable evidence
shows that this is the case. For Justin, the Old Testament
speaks predictively also through symbolic acts (ἐν συμβόλοις

---

[42]However, Justin never refers to sacrifices, offerings
or feasts in the general plural as having typological significance, but only historical significance. He interprets typologically only the specific ritual practices which he mentions in
Dial. chaps. 40-42 and which he partly repeats in Dial. 111.1-3.

[43]Dial. 23.3; 24.1; 40.1-2; 43.1; 46.2.

64

ἔργων, Dial. 68.6). One needs to interpret not only what has
been spoken but also what has been done by the Prophets (τὰ
εἰρημένα καὶ γεγενημένα ὑπὸ τῶν προφητῶν, Dial. 92.1).[44] The
Holy Spirit foretells future events sometimes through actions
and sometimes through words (Dial. 114.1). What Christ was to
do had been announced in advance through Joshua's miracles and
acts (δυνάμεις καὶ πράξεις, Dial. 115.4).[45]

Justin accordingly does not sharply differentiate between commandments and acts of Scripture which he classifies
in the same prophetic category. Nor does he sharply differentiate between the Mosaic Law and the rest of Scripture in their
predictive significance. Both the Mosaic Law and the Old Testament as a whole constitute for him μυστήρια, παραβολάς, σημεῖα,
σύμβολα, τύπους and καταγγελίας of Christ.[46] In this sense,

_____

[44]Cf. 112.3. Justin is thinking particularly of Moses
and Joshua whom he calls "prophets" (οἱ ἅγιοι ἐκεῖνοι ἄνδρες
καὶ προφῆται, Dial. 111.2).

[45]The whole sections of Dial. chaps. 89-96 and chaps.
111-115 consist of interpretations of symbolic acts by Moses
and Joshua. These acts are: Moses' out-stretched arms at
Joshua's battle with Amalek, foreshadowing the Cross of Christ
(Dial. 90.4; cf. 92.1 and 111.1); Moses' brazen serpent also
prefiguring the Cross (Dial. 94.1-4; cf. 112.1); the change of
Joshua's name and the stopping of the sun which predict aspects
of Christ's ministry (Dial. 111.1; 113.1-5), and others. Among
them, significantly, are again included the offering of the two
goats of the Great Fast as symbolic representations of the two
Comings of Christ (Dial. 111.1; cf. 40.4) and the passover lamb
as a type of the sacrifice of Christ (Dial. 111.3; cf. 40.1-2),
although these are not expressly called πράξεις. However,
Joshua's circumcision of the Israelites (Dial. 113.6-7; 114.4),
which is interpreted by Justin as a foretelling of Christ's
spiritual circumcision of the believers, is certainly understood as a symbolic act (Dial. 115.4; cf. 114.1). So also
later the marriages and other actions of the Patriarchs
(πατριαρχῶν πράξεις, Dial. 134.1) which Justin interprets as
foreshadowing events in the life of Christ (Dial. 134.1-6).

[46]For a study of these terms, see Franklin's dissertation. See also Shotwell, pp. 13-19. Justin's predictive and
typological interpretation of the Old Testament does not add
anything new to the Christian tradition, but places Justin
squarely within it. What Justin seems to contribute is amazing
elaboration of this tradition, applying the typological hermeneutical principle on a grand scale. It may be noted here
that Justin's typological division is quite different from
Ptolemy's. What Ptolemy calls the τυπικόν, i.e., the sabbath,
circumcision, sacrifices, offerings, and the like, he interprets
only allegorically as signs of a spiritual order, not as predictions of future Christian events (Pan. 33.5.8ff.). Quispel,

Justin's tripartite division is applicable both to the Mosaic
Law as well as to Scripture as a whole.

We now turn to the third division of the Law, Law as
historical dispensation. According to the Apologist, the third
division of the Law consists of commandments and acts ordained
by God to deal with the conduct of the Jews: τὶς δὲ ἐντολῇ καὶ
πρᾶξις ὁμοίως εἴρητο . . . διὰ τὸ σκληροκάρδιον τοῦ λαοῦ (Dial.
44.2). This involves Justin's important historical evaluation
of the Law with which he is critically concerned in the Dialogue.

Justin refers to the third part of the Law with the
terms περιτομή, σάββατον, νηστεῖαι, ἑορταί, θυσίαι, προσφοραί,
βρώματα and the like. These are the ritual ordinances which he
discusses in the main unit on the Law (Dial. chaps. 10-30) as
well as in other sections of the Dialogue (chaps. 45-47; 67.2-
10; 92.2-5). They are the ritual "commandments" which he also
calls ἐντολαί, προστάγματα and ἐντάλματα. Because they constitute properly speaking the Mosaic Law which the Christians so
evidently reject, this is the νόμος which Justin has set as his
task to interpret in the Dialogue.

Does Justin conceive of these ordinances also as πράξεις
as Dial. 44.2 (ἐντολῇ καὶ πρᾶξις) might suggest? Justin seems
to think of some ritual institutions, such as the wearing of
the tassels and of the tefillin, which he wrongly assumes to
have been also ordained through Moses, as "acts." He writes in
Dial. 46.5:

---

p. 35, prefers to call this "ethical interpretation." The wider
literature on the predictive and typological interpretations of
the Old Testament in the early Church is immense. See above,
p. 2, n. 3. See also, among others, Krister Stendahl, The
School of St. Matthew and its Use of the Old Testament (Phila-
delphia: Fortress Press, 1968, with a new introduction); S.
Amsler, L'Ancien Testament dans l'Eglise (Neuchâtel, 1960);
A. A. van Ruler, Die christliche Kirche und das Alte Testament,
BEvTh 23 (München, 1955), J. Klevinghaus, Die theologische
Stellung der apostolischen Väter zur alttestamentlichen Offen-
barung, BFChTh 44, No. 1 (Gütersloh, 1948); P. Prigent, Les
Testimonia dans le Christianisme primitif. L'Epître de Barnabé
(1 à 16) et ses sources (Paris, 1961); M. F. Wiles, "The Old
Testament in Controversy with the Jews," SJTh 8 (1955), 113-26;
Henri de Lubac, "Typologie et Allégorisme," RechSR 34 (1947),
180-226; R. P. C. Hanson, Allegory and Event (London: SCM
Press, 1959); Barnabas Lindars, New Testament Apologetic
(London, 1961); Jean Daniélou, From Shadows to Reality (Westminster: The Newman Press, 1960), and Daniélou, Message évangélique et culture hellénistique (Tournai: Desclée & Co.,
1961).

διὰ τὸ σκληροκάρδιον τοῦ λαοῦ ὑμῶν πάντα τὰ τοιαῦτα
ἐντάλματα νοεῖτε τὸν θεὸν διὰ Μωϋσέως ἐντειλάμενον
ὑμῖν, ἵνα διὰ πολλῶν τούτων ἐν πάσῃ τῇ πράξει πρὸ
ὀφθαλμῶν ἀεὶ ἔχητε τὸν θεόν . . . τὸ κόκκινον βάμμα[47]
. . . καὶ φυλακτήριον.

Ye perceive that on account of the hardness of the
heart of your people God enjoined on you by Moses all
such precepts, in order that by these many means you
should always, and in every action, have God before
your eyes . . . the scarlet dye . . . and a phylactery.

The general reference to acts (πάσῃ τῇ πράξει) in the above passage, as well as the similar reference to antecedent precepts
(πάντα τὰ τοιαῦτα ἐντάλματα . . . ἵνα διὰ πολλῶν τούτων), seem
to indicate that Justin conceives of other legal precepts also
as "acts" which he previously mentions within the same context.
In this instance the whole interchange between Justin and Trypho is instructive. Justin speaks first:

Κἀγώ· Τίνα οὖν ἃ δυνατόν ἐστι φυλάσσειν, παρακαλῶ,
λέγε αὐτός· πεισθήσῃ γὰρ ὅτι μὴ φυλάσσων τὰ αἰώνια[48]
δικαιώματά τις ἢ πράξας σωθῆναι ἐκ παντὸς ἔχει.
Κἀκεῖνος· Τὸ σαββατίζειν λέγω καὶ τὸ περιτέμνεσθαι
καὶ τὸ τὰ ἔμμηνα φυλάσσειν καὶ τὸ βαπτίζεσθαι ἀψάμενόν
τινος (Dial. 46.2).

And I said: What the things are therefore which it
is possible to keep, I pray you tell me yourself. For
you will then be persuaded that one can most certainly
be saved without keeping or performing these everlasting
ordinances.
He said: I mean the observance of sabbath, and being
circumcised, and keeping the monthly feasts, and washing,
if one has touched anything.

According to Justin's remarks, one may be found either not observing (φυλάσσων) or also not having performed (πράξας) the
above precepts. The passage seems to presuppose that obser-
vances of the sabbath, circumcision, monthly feasts and ritual

---

[47]Emend to ῥάμμα ("fringe") with Schürer (G.J.V.[4] ii.
566, E.T. II.ii, 112). But why "scarlet"? Williams, Justin
Martyr, p. 92, thinks it is a gloss by a copyist who had his
mind on the scarlet rope of Rahab (Dial. 111.4). More probable
is Weis' explanation that we have here another "Samaritanism"
of Justin. The Samaritan tassels were red, white and black,
red being the most prominent color. See Weis, pp. 202-04.

[48]There is a textual problem here. That Justin would
call the Mosaic ritual ordinances αἰώνια δικαιώματα is impossible, since his whole argument in the Dialogue is that these
ordinances are temporal, not eternal. Otto, p. 153, n. 5, suggests that Justin's words are at this point tinged with irony.
Perhaps better, one may suggest an emendation of αἰώνια to
τοιαῦτα (cf. τοιαῦτα ἐντάλματα, Dial. 46.5).

washings all are regarded by Justin both as commandments and
"acts".

The same is apparently also true of sacrifices, foods
and offerings which, together with many of the above precepts,
are at length discussed by Justin especially in Dial. chaps.
19-22. With regard to the fasting of foods, Justin seems to
emphasize the "action" of the case: καὶ γὰρ βρωμάτων τινῶν ἀπέχεσθαι προσέταξεν ὑμῖν [ὁ θεός], ἵνα καὶ ἐν τῷ ἐσθίειν καὶ πίνειν πρὸ ὀφθαλμῶν ἔχητε τὸν θεόν (Dial. 20.1). It is not clear
to what degree Justin intends to call the cultic precepts and
institutions πράξεις in accordance with his statement of Dial.
44.2 (τίς δὲ ἐντολὴ καὶ πρᾶξις). Such precepts as the sabbath,
circumcision and fasting are certainly not symbolic acts as
those attributed to Moses or Joshua, for example the making of
the brazen serpent or Joshua's circumcision of the Israelites,
which Justin typologically interprets as foreshadowing aspects
of Jesus' ministry.[49] Whether or not all of the ritual practices, besides being ἐντολαί, are also regarded by Justin as
πράξεις, is ambiguous. But he seems to indicate that for him
both acts and commandments can equally be assigned by Scripture
also to the third division of the Law (ἐντολὴ καὶ πρᾶξις ὁμοίως
εἴρητο . . . διὰ τὸ σκληροκάρδιον τοῦ λαοῦ ὑμῶν, Dial. 44.2).
What is clear is that all of these ordinances, the sabbath,
circumcision, fasting, feasts, sacrifices, offerings, washings,
the ashes of purification, tassels and the tefillin, are assigned by Justin to the Law as historical legislation which
pertains to the conduct of the Jews.

This third division of the Law is at the forefront of
Justin's interests. For him the major weight of the Law is
found in its role as historical dispensation. The main unit on
the Law, Dial. chaps. 10-30, as well as nearly all of the other
sections of the Dialogue where Justin discusses the Law, are
exclusively devoted to the Law as historical dispensation for
the Jews. Most decisive in this regard is the fact that Justin
thinks of this interpretation as explaining the "purpose" for
which the Law was ordained, an important consideration in the
Dialogue. In contrast, he never refers to the typological or
predictive interpretations of the Law as constituting the

[49]See above, n. 45.

"purpose" of the Law. Whenever in his lengthy exposition he
brings to the surface the question of why the Law was originally given (διὰ τί . . . προσετάγη, Dial. 12.3; δι'ἣν αἰτίαν
προσετάγη, Dial. 18.2), the answer is always the same: διὰ τὸ
σκληροκάρδιον τοῦ λαοῦ ὑμῶν.[50]

As it will be seen, Justin's historical interpretation
of the Law is derived from his struggles with the gnostics and
Marcion. Whenever Justin insists upon the historical significance of the Law, as von Campenhausen has observed,[51] he alludes
to his gnostic opponents (Dial. 23.1-2; 30.1; 92.5). Justin
confronts Trypho with a new argument forged on the anvil of his
previous confrontation with Marcion. But this is not the place
to pursue this matter further. A separate chapter is devoted
to Justin's interpretation of the purpose of the Law.[52] There
detailed attention is given to the Apologist's view of the Law
as historical dispensation for the Jews.

C. Criteria for the Tripartite Division of the Law

We have examined Justin's division of the Mosaic Law
into (1) ethics, (2) prophecy and (3) historical dispensation.
On what basis does Justin propose his tripartite division of the
Law? Are there discernible criteria to which he appeals? What
presuppositions lie behind his three-fold classification of the
Mosaic Law and Scripture?

Unlike Ptolemy and Marcion, who claim to base their interpretations of the Old Testament and the Mosaic Law on the
teachings of Jesus and the teachings of Paul, Justin invokes the
authority of neither in his evaluation of the Law, despite the
fact that Trypho knows and admires the teachings of Jesus (Dial.
10.2; cf. 18.1).[53] Justin frequently quotes from the sayings of

---

[50]Dial. 18.2; 23.2; 30.1; 46.4-5; 67.8,10; 92.4.

[51]Die Entstehung, p. 112.

[52]See below, Chapter Four.

[53]Appeal to words of Jesus is also found in the Kerygmata Petrou where the true prophet points out the false pericopes
in the Old Testament (Hom. 3.49.2). Strecker, Judenchristentum,
p. 171, n. 1, discounts any direct dependence on Ptolemy. In
the Kerygmata Petrou there is no opposition between Jesus and
Moses. Both proclaim the eternal true Law. Nor is the strati-

Jesus for different purposes,[54] but never as criteria for the
correct interpretation of the Old Testament or the Mosaic Law.
On one occasion, when Trypho reminds Justin of Jesus' own obedience to the Law (Dial. 67.5-6), the person of Jesus is indeed
momentarily suggested as a criterion of the validity of the Law,
but then rather quickly and somewhat curiously[55] he is again
allowed to recede to the background. It would have been illu-
minating to know how Justin interpreted Jesus' words about the
Law and the Prophets (Mtt. 5:17-18; Lk. 16:16), the tradition
of the elders (Mtt. 15.3ff.), Moses' bill of divorce (Mtt. 19:8)
and the like, which were crucial in the conflict over the Law
and the Old Testament during the second century. Many of these
sayings must have been known to Justin. He must have had to
consider them when writing the Syntagma against Marcion and
other gnostics.[56] Nevertheless, neither Justin, nor Trypho,
appeals either to positive or negative sayings of Jesus about
the Mosaic Law. In one instance the logion of Jesus on the
Law and the Prophets is quoted, but even that is cited for ano-

---

fication of the Old Testament there an answer to marcionite
teaching, since a polemic against Marcion's theory of two gods
is absent. So Strecker, pp. 162-67.

[54]For example to reinforce Justin's criticisms of the
Jews (Dial. 17.3-4; 76.4; 120.6), to show Jesus' correct prediction of the Christian heretics (Dial. 35.3; 76.5), to point
to Christian teaching about ethics and doctrine (Dial. 47.5;
81.4; 93.2; 96.3) and others.

[55]According to the context, a fuller discussion of
Jesus' observance of the Law is supposed to have occurred
earlier in the Dialogue, but it has not. In Dial. 67.6 Justin
simply states that Jesus' observance of the Law is part of his
fulfilment of God's plan of salvation, the divine οἰκονομία,
particularly the necessity of his incarnation and his death
by crucifixion, and has nothing to do with whether or not the
Law has intrinsic value for salvation. R. P. C. Hanson, p.
292, interprets οἰκονομία as "accommodation." However, this
term in Justin, as Grant, Letter and Spirit, p. 132, observes,
has to do with Christ's incarnation, birth, life and passion--
the whole plan of salvation.

[56]The "antitheses" between the teaching of Jesus and
those of the God of the Old Testament, as well as the lex
talionis, were favorite examples of the Marcionites to show
the inferiority of the Old Testament God and the opposition
to him by Jesus, as Tertullian, Adv. Marc. 2.18 (cf. 4.16),
and Irenaeus, Adv. Haer. 4.13.1, report.

ther purpose, namely, to show the cessation of John the Baptist as a prophet by Jesus and, with this act, the cessation of all prophecy of the Old Testament.[57]

The case is the same with regard to Paul! Pauline statements certainly figured in the same conflict over the Law and the Old Testament during the second century.[58] Justin could not but have known the Pauline Letters, at least indirectly, through writing against Marcion whom he must have read, or must have known about, before refuting. Indeed, intriguing echoes of Paul are sounded in the Dialogue, such as with respect to the faith of Abraham (Dial. 23.4; 44.2; 92.3; 119.5-6), the curse of the Law (Dial. 95.1), the Passover being the crucified Christ (ἦν γὰρ τὸ πάσχα ὁ Χριστός, ὁ τυθείς, Dial. 111.3; cf. I Cor. 5:7) and others.[59] In one instance, Justin's reading of an Old Testament text, Dt. 27:36, seems to be dependent on Gal. 3:13.[60] But once again, neither Justin, nor of course Trypho, explicitly refers to Paul or to the Pauline Letters. Scriptural citations which may in the first instance have come to Justin's attention through knowledge of the Pauline Letters, just as those citations which may have come to him through knowledge of the

---

[57]Justin's argument is that prophecy among the Jews has ceased with the coming of Christ, but that it continues among Christians (Dial. 52.3-4; 81.4; 82.1; 87.3ff.). The same logion was used by Marcion as proof of the cessation of the Law and the Prophets by the power of another higher God. So Tertullian, Adv. Marc. 4.33. But Justin does not use it in his own argument about the Law's cessation.

[58]Ptolemy uses words of Paul as criteria, quoting I Cor. 5:7, Eph. 2:15 and Rm. 7:12 (Pan. 33.5.15 and 6.6). According to the Marcionites, Paul was the only Apostle who had knowledge of the truth, as Irenaeus, Adv. Haer. 3.13.1, notes. In Book 5 of his Adversus Marcionem, Tertullian tries to "rescue" Paul from Marcion by showing that the Pauline Letters are not at variance but in complete harmony with the Old Testament.

[59]See also Dial. 39.1-2; 41.1; 85.2; 110.2; 112.5; 139.5. A. Thoma, "Justins literarisches Verhältniss zu Paulus und zum Johannes-Evangelium," ZWTh 18 (1875), 385-412 (and pp. 490-544 for the Gospel of John), who examines the parallels, is convinced that Justin knows and uses Paul. But Justin never cites the Apostle. Similarly intriguing are the echoes of the language and ideas of Acts in the Dialogue. On this see Franz Overbeck, "Über das Verhältniss Justins des Märtyrers zur Apostelgeschichte," ZWTh 15 (1872), 305-49.

[60]See below, pp. 105ff.

Gospels, are always directly attributed to the Old Testament.

Two reasons are possible for Justin's failure to use sayings of Jesus as hermeneutical criteria and also for his conspicuous silence regarding Paul. One reason is that Justin simply did not know what to do with either the extremely positive (e.g., Mtt. 5:18; Rm. 7:12) or even negative (e.g., Mtt. 19:8; Lk. 16:16; Gal. 3:11; I Cor. 15:56) pronouncements of Jesus and Paul on the Law. In the case of Paul, Marcion's hero, Justin may have had good reason to be cautious. Nevertheless, he quotes at least the logion of Jesus on the Law and the Prophets, which Marcion also used for his own purposes, and in the Syntagma Justin must have had to deal with other similar pronouncements which did not fail to come to Marcion's attention. With regard to Paul, Justin could offhandedly have altogether dismissed the Apostle's authority. Yet the frequent Pauline echoes in the Dialogue show, however allusively, that Justin by no means harbors a "hostile neglect" of Paul.[61]

Therefore, only the second reason can be true: Justin refrains from quoting Jesus and much less Paul regarding the Law because the Dialogue is addressed to Jews. The mutually accepted authority between the disputants is the Old Testament. The Scriptures of the Old Testament represent the decisive authority by which Justin hopes to prove his case about the Law, Christ and the new Israel to Trypho and his companions. Trypho declares to Justin that no other authority is accepted: καὶ σοῦ λέγοντος οὐκ ἠνειχόμεθα, εἰ μὴ πάντα ἐπὶ τὰς γραφὰς ἀνῆγες, (Dial. 56.16). This is probably the reason why, whereas Ptolemy draws his proofs from the words of Jesus (τὰς ἀποδείξεις ἐκ τῶν τοῦ σωτῆρος ἡμῶν λόγων παριστῶντες, Pan. 33.3.8), Justin draws his own proofs from the Old Testament (ἀποδείξεις ἐκ τῶν γραφῶν, Dial. 28.2).[62] This is also the reason why, when Justin first begins to quote sayings of Jesus, he has to ask for Trypho's in-

---

[61]Discounted by Harnack, Judentum und Judenchristentum, p. 50, who suggests that either Paul's dialectic was unsuitable to Justin or his name was a disgusting hindrance to Jews. The theory of "hostile neglect" had been proposed by F. C. Baur. On the other hand, one can hardly call Paul, as does Shotwell, p. 12, Justin's "mentor."

[62]In Dial. 120.5, Justin tells Trypho that he has taken care even to quote only from the Scriptures which the Jews regard as canonical.

dulgence (Dial. 18.1). Directed to Jews, Justin's argument must be supported and validated by the Old Testament.

Tertullian's works yield the same evidence. While in his Adversus Marcionem sayings of Jesus are often the authoritative subject matter under discussion, in his Adversus Judaeos the Old Testament is exclusively cited. But in both works many of the same issues concerning the Law, its character, purpose, validity and cessation, are inevitably considered. Justin's case is likely similar. While in the Syntagma words of Jesus were quite probably quoted and interpreted against Marcion, in the Dialogue the authority of the Old Testament exclusively prevails.

But this is not the whole story. There are passages in the Dialogue which hint at Justin's ultimate criteria. Although he appeals to the Old Testament in his discussion with Trypho, Justin also makes other indirect appeals which disclose the controlling criteria behind his tripartite classification of the Mosaic Law, namely, Christ and Christian presuppositions. To be sure, Justin does not discuss these matters. In each of the four passages in which he indicates awareness of the division of the Law and the Old Testament, he is usually silent about the reasons for the division. But in two of the passages there are hints which lead to Justin's hermeneutical criteria:

The first passage reads:

'Ετέραν διαθήκην ἔσεσθαι ὁ θεὸς ὑπέσχετο, . . . δεικνύουσαν τί μὲν ὡς αἰώνιον καὶ παντὶ γένει ἁρμόζον καὶ ἔνταλμα καὶ ἔργον ὁ θεὸς ἐπίσταται, τί δὲ πρὸς τὸ σκληροκάρδιον τοῦ λαοῦ ὑμῶν ἁρμοσάμενος . . . ἐνετέταλτο (Dial. 67.10).

God promised that there should be another Covenant, . . . one that shows what command and work God knows to be everlasting and in harmony with every race, and what He ordered only in harmony with the hardness of your people's heart.

According to this passage, the criterion indicating the character and classification of Scripture is the ἑτέρα διαθήκη promised by God. This is the same as the καινὴ διαθήκη which Justin mentions in the same context (Dial. 67.9). For Justin, καινὴ διαθήκη is the historical dispensation of God in Christ

for the universal salvation of man.[63] Justin often identifies
the New Covenant with Christ. In Dial. 51.3 he writes: ἡ πάλαι
κηρυσσομένη ὑπὸ τοῦ θεοῦ καινὴ διαθήκη . . . παρῆν, τουτ'ἔστιν
αὐτὸς ὢν ὁ Χριστός. Similar associations are frequent in the
Dialogue.[64] In the final analysis, as Behm notes,[65] the two
terms are synonymous for Justin. The above passage suggests
that the criterion for the proper classification of the Law is
Christ himself.

The second passage is the statement of Dial. 44.2. According to the passage, those in a position to discern the division of Scripture and the Law are the ones who know all the
mysteries of Scripture (ἐπιγνόντες τὰ μυστήρια πάντα), the
Christians. He who can interpret Scripture correctly has also
the key to the proper identification of its layered contents.

Justin, accordingly, bases his tripartite division of
the Law on the same criteria on which he bases all of his argumentation in the Dialogue, i.e., Scripture and Christ. Scripture is for him the authoritative document. Christ is the
hermeneutical principle. But this does not mean that Justin
appeals to the teaching of Jesus. Justin does not quote sayings of Jesus in his evaluation of the Law. Rather he appeals
to the Christ who grants the spiritual gift of interpretation.
In Dial. 100.1-2 Justin quotes the dominical logion about the
transfer of all authority to the Son and about the Son as the
exclusive way of revelation. He then states that the Son is
the Christians' source of revelation for their understanding of

---

[63]J. Behm, Der Begriff ΔΙΑΘΗΚΗ im Neuen Testament
(Leipzig, 1912), who includes an appendix on Justin, pp. 102-06,
and calls Justin's concept of διαθήκη "heilsgeschichtliche
Gottesverfügung" (this expression occurs only in the table of
contents, p. vi, of Behm's book). According to Behm, p. 106,
Justin has the same understanding of covenant as the New Testament authors. See also E. Lohmeyer, Diatheke (Leipzig,
1912) and W. C. van Unnik, "Ἡ Καινὴ Διαθήκη--A Problem in
the Early History of the Canon," TU 79 (1961), 212-27, especially p. 221.

[64]Dial. 11.2,4; 12.1; 24.1; 34.1; 43.1; 122.5-6. For
Justin, Christ is also the New Law.

[65]Behm, p. 103.

74

Scripture.[66] In <u>Dial</u>. 58.1 Justin explicitly claims to possess this gift of interpretation.[67]

Thus Justin's criteria rest fundamentally on Christian presuppositions about the Old Testament, presuppositions which had been challenged by confrontation with Marcionism.[68] It is difficult to say what exact conceptual development leads Justin to the tripartite division. He does not directly discuss the distinctions within Scripture, nor does he allow the fact of the division of the Law to come to the forefront. His own understanding of the tripartite division has not reached high conceptual clarity. Perhaps also Justin's high regard for the authority of Scripture unconsciously prevented him from working out a bolder and more sharply defined breakdown of the unity of Scripture in the manner of Ptolemy. We find a similar case in Irenaeus and Tertullian both of whom are aware of a certain stratification and differentiation in Scripture, but do not

---

[66] Ἐν τῷ εὐαγγελίῳ γέγραπται . . . πάντα μοι παραδέδο-
ται ὑπὸ τοῦ πατρός, καὶ οὐδεὶς γινώσκει τὸν πατέρα εἰ μὴ ὁ
υἱός, οὐδὲ τὸν υἱὸν εἰ μὴ ὁ πατὴρ καὶ οἷς ἂν ὁ υἱὸς ἀποκαλύψῃ.
Ἀπεκάλυψεν οὖν ἡμῖν πάντα ὅσα καὶ ἀπὸ τῶν γραφῶν διὰ τῆς χάριτος αὐτοῦ νενοήκαμεν (<u>Dial</u>. 100.1-2). This is at the heart
of Justin's hermeneutical presuppositions. For Justin, Christ
is the inspirer of the Prophets and authors of Scripture (<u>Ap</u>.
36.1-2), as well as the true interpreter of Scripture (<u>Dial</u>.
7.3; 76.3,6). He is the interpreter of Scripture both in the
sense of granting the gift of interpretation, as well as in
the sense of explaining to his disciples after the Resurrection
prophecies of the Old Testament which no one could otherwise
have understood (<u>Dial</u>. 53.5; 76.6; <u>Ap</u>. 50.12; 53.5). This apparently is the meaning of Christ as the interpreter of obscure
prophecies (<u>Ap</u>. 32.2). Van Leer is not entirely correct to
think that according to Justin Christ is the interpreter of
these veiled prophecies by his "very coming" (p. 79).

[67] Οὐ κατασκευὴν λόγων ἐν μόνῃ τέχνῃ ἐπιδείκνυσθαι
σπεύδω· οὐδὲ γὰρ δύναμις ἐμοὶ τοιαύτη τίς ἐστιν, ἀλλὰ χάρις
παρὰ θεοῦ μόνη εἰς τὸ συνιέναι τὰς γραφὰς αὐτοῦ ἐδόθη μοι
(<u>Dial</u>. 58.1; cf. 39.2,4-5; 87.4; 88.1). Barnabas (10.12) and
also Ptolemy (<u>Pan</u>. 33.3.6-8) claim to have spiritual gnosis.
Irenaeus reports, <u>Adv. Haer</u>. 1.1.15, that the Valentinians
boasted of having perfect knowledge higher than that of anyone
else. On Justin's view see also Nestor Pucke, "Connaissance
rationelle et connaissance de grâce chez Saint Justin," <u>EThL</u>
37 (1961), 52-85.

[68] See below, pp. 153-63.

proceed to an objective analysis of it,[69] even though they write
considerably later than Justin. In this regard only Ptolemy,
who has few scruples about the authority of Scripture as a
whole, provides a kind of scientifically critical account of
the diversity of the Mosaic Law, parts of which he rejects as
unworthy of God and others as being the work of men.

As far as Justin is concerned, this much is clear:
while firmly maintaining the traditional Christian view of the
Old Testament as prophecy of Christ and as revelation of God's
moral will, he marks at the same time a significant change by
holding a more precise concept of the ethical part of the Law,
and, even more importantly, by viewing part of the Law as historical dispensation. This change occurs no doubt through his
participation in the struggle over the Old Testament against
the gnostics, particularly Marcion. The Church's struggle
against the marcionite critique of the Old Testament is the cat-
alyst of Justin's sharpened understanding of Scripture and his
division of the Mosaic Law. In particular, Justin's historical
view of the Law, developed in defense of the Law, Scripture and
God's perfection over against marcionite teaching, is quite certainly the decisive trigger leading to the tripartite division
of the Law. Justin thus holds to the unity and authority both
of God and Scripture, but he qualifies the unity of Scripture.
His fundamental reply to Marcion, as far as it may be indirectly
gleaned from the Dialogue, seems to be that one should distin-

---

[69]Irenaeus, Adv. Haer. 4.25.3-26.1, says that the Jews
had a law, the Decalogue, implanted in their hearts (as did all
men), and also a prophecy of future things. The Mosaic Law was
received only later as bondage after the worship of the golden
calf. He thus presupposes a tripartite division of the contents
of the Old Testament into ethics, prophecy and historical legislation which is very similar to Justin's. He does not, however,
articulate this division any more clearly than does Justin.
Tertullian, Adv. Jud. 2, also is aware of diversification in
Scripture and the Law, but instead of giving a clear analysis
and division of the contents of Scripture, he is content with a
theory of development which preserves the continuity and unity
of the divine dispensation. According to Tertullian, God begins
with a primordial natural law which He reforms according to circumstances throughout Jewish history with a view to man's salvation. A clearer effort toward a definite classification of
Scripture, although not necessarily a more successful one, may
later be found in Clement of Alexandria, Strom. 1.18, who divides the Pentateuch into four parts, historical, legislative,
cultic and theological (mystical).

76

guish different parts and different purposes in Scripture, not incompatibly different dispensations nor, much less, different Gods. Justin continues to advocate the principle of the absolute authority and consistency of Scripture. But in the process of coming to grips with Marcionism he is compelled to develop an important qualification, the historical interpretation of the Law and his tripartite division of the Law, which is new and far-reaching in the Christian exegetical tradition.

CHAPTER THREE

THE INVALIDITY OF THE LAW

The problem of the Law in the Dialogue is posed in this
fashion by Trypho: How can the Christians claim to observe
true piety and to enjoy a different standing among other peoples
before God when they do in fact not separate themselves from the
gentiles and do not observe God's commandments? How can they
justifiably ground their hope in God if they do not obey God's
Law according to the express commands of Scripture (Dial. 10.
3-4)? As a Christian apologist Justin, whenever dealing with
the Mosaic Law, tries to resolve this problem by recourse to
two theses: (1) the invalidity of the Law as an eternal and
universal criterion of salvation, and (2) the historical purpose
of the Law as legislation for the Jews. These theses are the
two anchors of Justin's whole argumentation on the Law. Both of
them Justin tries to base on the authority of Scripture in order
to demonstrate that Christians rightfully reject the Mosaic Law
while yet holding to the authority of the Old Testament as a
whole. In this chapter we will be concerned with the first of
these theses.

Justin uses many arguments in different sections of the
Dialogue to demonstrate the invalidity of the Law. One argument
deals directly with the cessation of the Law with the coming of
Christ. Other arguments underscore the thesis by showing that
the Law is temporal rather than eternal, limited rather than
universal, or that the Law has no intrinsic value before God.
Another argument points to the unfulfilability of the Law in its
entirety and to the consequent impasse of its attendant curse.
All of these arguments are intended by Justin to demonstrate the
valid cessation of the Mosaic Law as a Scriptural norm of life.

An examination of these arguments has to face the problem of their classification. The following analysis divides
Justin's arguments into two categories: (A) arguments from

Scripture and (B) arguments from reality. This classification
is based on Justin's own claim to deal with the problem of the
Law on the basis of Scripture and reason (ἀπό τε τῶν γραφῶν καὶ
τῶν πραγμάτων, Dial. 28.2). Arguments from Scripture are those
developed on the basis of citations from the Old Testament.
These are for the most part at the forefront of Justin's argumentation and represent the most decisive proofs in Justin's
case about the Law. Arguments from reality (τὰ πράγματα) are
arguments drawn from the history of salvation, creation, and
the phenomena of nature or the cosmos, based on observations and
inferences of reason. These arguments are secondary in Justin's
argumentation and play a supportive role to the thesis of the
invalidity of the Law.

A. Arguments from Scripture

There are three Scriptural arguments in the Dialogue pertaining to the invalidity of the Mosaic Law. The first is that
a New Covenant and a New Law, Jesus Christ, has abolished both
the Old Covenant and the Old Law according to the predictions of
the Old Testament. The second is that God, as demonstrated from
the words of the Prophets, does not truly desire observance of
the cultic Law of Moses, but spiritual obedience to a higher
moral law. This argument is reinforced with partial allegorization of the Law. The third argument is that observance of the
Law leads to an impasse because no man is able to observe the
whole Law and failure to do so incurs a curse according to the
Book of Deuteronomy.

(1) The first argument, the cessation of the Law
through the coming of Christ, appears to be the most decisive
one for Justin in his attempt to state the case for the invalidity of the Law. Trypho contends that the Mosaic Law is an
indispensable prerequisite to salvation (Dial. 8.4) and that
obedience to God and Sacred Scripture necessarily implies obedience to the Law (Dial. 10.3-4). Justin's first response, giv-
en in Dial. 11-13, is that the Mosaic Covenant and the Mosaic
Law have according to Scripture been abrogated by another Covenant and another Law, and are therefore no longer valid. He
constructs his argument on four texts, Is. 51:4-5, Jer. 38:31-
32(LXX), Is. 55:3-5 and Is. 52:10-54:6. The fourth text is, as
we shall see, not directly connected with the other three, but
occurs in a slightly different context in Justin's exposition.

While emphasizing that the Christians believe in the
same, not another, God as do the Jews, Justin insists that
Christians nevertheless do not adhere either to Moses or to the
Law because this would essentially identify them with the Jews
(<u>Dial</u>. 11.1).[1] His thesis regarding the abrogation of the Old
Law then runs as follows:

> νυνὶ δὲ ἀνέγνων γάρ, ὦ Τρύφων, ὅτι ἔσοιτο καὶ τελευ-
> ταῖος νόμος καὶ διαθήκη κυριωτάτη πασῶν, ἣν νῦν δέον
> φυλάσσειν πάντας ἀνθρώπους, ὅσοι τῆς τοῦ θεοῦ κληρο-
> νομίας ἀντιποιοῦνται. ὁ γὰρ ἐν Χωρὴβ παλαιὸς ἤδη νόμος
> καὶ ὑμῶν μόνων, ὁ δὲ πάντων ἁπλῶς· νόμος δὲ κατὰ νόμου
> τεθεὶς τὸν πρὸ αὐτοῦ ἔπαυσε, καὶ διαθήκη μετέπειτα γε-
> νομένη τὴν προτέραν ὁμοίως ἔστησεν. αἰώνιός τε ἡμῖν νό-
> μος καὶ τελευταῖος ὁ Χριστὸς ἐδόθη καὶ ἡ διαθήκη πιστή,
> μεθ'ἣν οὐ νόμος, οὐ πρόσταγμα, οὐκ ἐντολή (<u>Dial</u>. 11.2).

> For in fact I have read, Trypho, that there is to be
> both a final Law and a Disposition that is superior to
> all others, which must now be observed by all those
> who lay claim to the inheritance of God. For the Law
> given at Horeb is already antiquated and belongs to
> you alone, but that other belongs to all men absolute-
> ly. And a Law set over against a Law has made the one
> before it to cease, and a Disposition coming into ex-
> istence afterwards has in like manner limited any for-
> mer one. And as an eternal and final Law was Christ
> given to us, and this Disposition is sure, after which
> there is no law, or ordinance, or command.

This declaration is validated by the citation of Is. 51:4-5 and
Jer. 38:31-32(<u>LXX</u>), which immediately follow (<u>Dial</u>. 11.3), and
also of Is. 55:3-5, which comes a little later (<u>Dial</u>. 12.1).
Justin's words anticipate this latter text as well.[2] But prior
to this text, Justin breaks the continuity of his argument by
announcing the third major theme of the <u>Dialogue</u> (<u>Dial</u>. 11.4-5),
the true and false Israel, which he takes up time and again
throughout his work.

The first text, Is. 51:4-5, is cited by Justin from the
Septuagint without significant variations. This text occurs up

---

[1] ἢ γὰρ ἂν τὸ αὐτὸ ὑμῖν ἐποιοῦμεν, <u>Dial</u>. 11.1. Justin
wants to affirm Christian acceptance of the God of the Old Testament, yet also to distinguish the difference between the
Christians and the Jews. Perhaps the Marcionites accused Christians who adhered to the authority of the Old Testament of being
one with the Jews.

[2] Thus Prigent, p. 236, writes: "Cette formulation n'est
certes pas totalement inadéquate pour annoncer les citations
d'Is. 51,4-5 et Jér. 31,31s., mais il est évident qu'elle fait
bien plus directement allusion à Is. 55,3."

to the time of Tertullian only in Justin.[3] The second text,
Jer. 38:31-32(LXX), is allusively used in the Gospel tradition,
namely, in the pericope of the Lord's Supper, which Justin undoubtedly knows. It is also extensively quoted in the Epistle
to the Hebrews (Heb. 8:8-12) with which Justin may be familiar.[4]
Nevertheless, this text, too, is very closely quoted by Justin
from the Septuagint.[5] The case is the same with regard to the
third text, Is. 55:3-5, which has insignificant occurrences in
writers prior to Justin.[6]

These texts do not come to Justin as part of a testimonia tradition but are cited by him directly from the Septuagint. Thus Justin seems to work independently with the Old
Testament, making a serious attempt to construct a theological
argument concerning the cessation of the validity of the Law on
the basis of prophetic texts which he selects. Whether or not
he has in some way also influenced Tertullian and Irenaeus in

---

[3]Tertullian uses part of the text (Is. 51:4) against
Marcion, Adv. Marc. 4.1.5. Since Jer. 31:31-32 is also quoted
by Tertullian within the same context (Adv. Marc. 4.1.6), we
may here have a dependence on Justin.

[4]See below, p. 85 and n. 18. But the peculiarities of
the text show that without question the citation is not taken
from Hebrews.

[5]For a close study of the variants, see Prigent, pp.
237-39. This text is quoted by Irenaeus, Tertullian and others,
and appears to be a common proof-text in the Christian tradition, especially after the time of Justin. But the author of
Barnabas, who has much to say about διαθήκη does not quote it.

[6]It is partially quoted in Acts 13:34. Of the writers
after Justin, only Tertullian, Adv. Marc. 3.20.5, and Cyprian,
Ad. Quir. 1.21, quote parts of this text, but nothing significant can be surmised from this. More interesting is that
Justin himself quotes the text with some variations in Dial. 14.
4-7 (Is. 55:3-13). Prigent, p. 240, conjectures that the first
citation is not directly from the Septuagint but from an un-
specified collection of texts on the Law and the Covenant in
Justin's lost Syntagma beyond which Prigent programmatically
does not want to explore (p. 13). But there is not the
slightest evidence of Justin's use of such a collection of
texts in this instance.

this regard, as Prigent seems to think, must remain uncertain.[7]

From the first text Justin takes the term νόμος (νόμος παρ'ἐμοῦ ἐξελεύσεται, Is. 51:4) and applies it to Christ (τελευταῖος νόμος, Dial. 11.2). Justin often calls Christ νόμος in contrast to the Law of Moses.[8] He derives this term from Old Testament texts, that is, prophetic rather than legal texts. In addition to Is. 51:4-5, he also knows Mic. 4:1-7 which speaks of the coming νόμος of God (ἐκ Σιὼν ἐξελεύσεται νόμος καὶ λόγος, Dial. 109.2f.).[9] In Dial. 34.1, evidently having Ps. 18:8(LXX) in view, he also suggests that the reference to the spotless Law of the Lord signifies Christ.[10] The future Law predicted by Scripture is for Justin Christ himself.

From the second text, Jer. 38:31-32(LXX), Justin takes the adjective καινός which he freely applies both to the promised Law and the promised Covenant (Dial. 11.3-4; 12.3; 14.3; 43.1 et al.). As we have noted, Justin identifies the New Covenant and the New Law with Christ.[11] His numerous references to καινὸς νόμος, καινὴ διαθήκη or καινὸς νομοθέτης ultimately derive from this proof-text from the Book of Jeremiah. By contrast, the former Law is called παλαιὸς νόμος (Dial.

---

[7]Tertullian quotes Jer. 38:31-32(LXX), and parts of the above Isaianic texts, together with a great many other citations from the Old Testament, in Adv. Marc. 4.1. Prigent sees a possible influence of Justin on Tertullian and Irenaeus through the use by both of Justin's Syntagma.

[8]The author of Barnabas is the first Christian writer indirectly to apply the term νόμος to Christ (Barn. 2.6.

[9]Cf. Dial. 110.2; 24.1 and also Ap. 39.1 where Is. 2:3-4 (ἐκ γὰρ Σιὼν ἐξελεύσεται νόμος καὶ λόγος κυρίου) is quoted.

[10]Christ is further called νομοθέτης on several occasions in vague parallelism to Moses. The term νομοθέτης is applied to Moses in Dial. 1.3; 112.3, and 127.1, whereas in Dial. 12.2; 14.3, and 18.3 it is applied to Christ. The parallelism is never explicit.

[11]See above, p. 73, n. 63. In Dial. 11.4 Justin states: οὗτός ἐστιν ὁ καινὸς νόμος καὶ ἡ καινὴ διαθήκη.

11.2; 125.5) and the former Covenant παλαιά διαθήκη (Dial. 67.9).[12]

From the third text, Is. 55:3-5, Justin draws the term αἰώνιος and to a lesser extent the term πιστή (διαθήσομαι ὑμῖν διαθήκην αἰώνιον, τὰ ὅσια Δαυεὶδ τὰ πιστά, Is. 55:3/Dial. 12.1). Justin's declaration about the abrogation of the Law in Dial. 11.2 accents the eternal character as well as the finality of the New Law: αἰώνιός τε ἡμῖν νόμος καὶ τελευταῖος ὁ Χριστὸς ἐδόθη καὶ ἡ διαθήκη πιστή, μεθ᾽ἣν οὐ νόμος, οὐ πρόσταγμα, οὐκ ἐντολή. The eternal character of the New Law and of the New Covenant is frequently affirmed in the Dialogue. According to Justin Christ is the αἰώνιος νόμος (Dial. 11.2; 43.1; 122.5), the αἰωνία διαθήκη (Dial. 12.1; 118.3) as well as the αἰώνιος βασιλεὺς καὶ ἱερεύς (Dial. 36.1; 96.1; 118.2), the bearer of the αἰωνία βασιλεία (Dial. 31.7; 32.1; 39.7 et al.). In contrast, the Old Law with its ritual commandments is temporal (πρόσκαιρος, Dial. 40.1).

There is an additional element in Justin's thesis about the abrogation of the Law, that is, the contrast between the particularity of the Mosaic Law and the universality of the New Law. Justin's statement of Dial. 11.2 contains in part also this idea:

> ἔσοιτο καὶ τελευταῖος νόμος καὶ διαθήκη κυριωτάτη πα-
> σῶν, ἣν νῦν δέον φυλάσσειν πάντας ἀνθρώπους . . . ὁ
> γὰρ ἐν Χωρῆβ παλαιὸς ἤδη νόμος καὶ ὑμῶν μόνον, ὁ δὲ
> πάντων ἀπλῶς.

> There is to be both a final Law and a Disposition that
> is superior to all others, which must now be observed
> by all . . . For the Law given at Horeb is already
> antiquated and belongs to you alone, but that other
> to all men absolutely.

---

[12]Justin emphasizes that it is the Old Law of Horeb (Dial. 11.2) and that the Old Covenant was commanded with fear, trembling and lightning (Dial. 67.9-10). The reference to Horeb instead of to Sinai is the first in Christian literature. Prigent, pp. 237-38, thinks that Justin's quotation from Jeremiah may have originally contained the reference to Horeb, too, but that a later scribe may have corrected the text to conform to the Septuagint. With respect to the "fear, trembling and lightning," we may have to do with marcionite language emphasizing the negative circumstance in which the Old Covenant was ordained. Harnack, Marcion, p. 278*, cites a passage of similar import from Clem. Hom. 2.43 which he thinks comes from Marcion's Antitheses. It describes the manner in which the Old Testament God exists and manifests Himself: ἐν γνόφῳ καὶ σκότῳ καὶ θυέλλῃ καὶ καπνῷ σύνεστιν, διὰ σαλπίγγων καὶ ὀλολυγμῶν καὶ βολίδων καὶ τοξευμάτων προσέρχεται.

It is not without significance that two of his proof-texts
speak favorably of the gentiles as recipients of God's promises (ἡ κρίσις μου εἰς φῶς ἐθνῶν . . . καὶ εἰς τὸν βραχίονά μου
ἔθνη ἐλπιοῦσι, Is. 51:4-5/Dial. 11.3; ἰδοῦ μάρτυρα αὐτὸν ἔθνεσι
δέδωκα, ἔθνη, ἃ οὐκ οἴδασί σε, ἐπικαλέσονταί σε, λαοῖ οἳ οὐκ
ἐπίστανταί σε καταφεύξονται ἐπὶ σέ, Is. 55:4-5/Dial. 12.1).
Justin is highly conscious of such passages in Scripture and of
the fact that the New Covenant is according to him proclaimed
for the gentiles (ὁ θεὸς διαθήκην καινὴν ἐκήρυξε μέλλουσαν
διαταχθήσεσθαι καὶ ταύτην εἰς φῶς ἐθνῶν, Dial. 11.4).[13] His
whole point which rings throughout the Dialogue is that Christ,
the New Law and New Covenant, is the focus of great expectation
of the believing gentiles: οὗτος [ὁ Χριστὸς] ἐστὶν ὁ καινὸς
νόμος καὶ ἡ καινὴ διαθήκη καὶ ἡ προσδοκία τῶν ἀπὸ πάντων τῶν
ἐθνῶν ἀναμενόντων τὰ παρὰ τοῦ θεοῦ ἀγαθά (Dial. 11.4).

Thus Justin is able to show from his proof-texts the
eternity and universality of the New Law promised by God. However, he is not able to show on the basis of the same texts the
abolishment of the Old Law, which is Justin's main point in his
declaration of Dial. 11.2. According to him, the New Law abro-
gates the Old and the New Covenant annuls the former (ἔπαυσε
. . . ἔστησεν, Dial. 11.2). It is true that the cessation of
the Mosaic Law may be inferred from God's promise of the New
Law. Much later in the Dialogue Justin in fact argues that if
the Mosaic Law possessed effective power, there would be no need
of a New Covenant and an Eternal Law.[14] This, however, is not
a necessary inference. The Jews had no problem harmonizing the
teaching of the eternity of the Mosaic Law with the concept of
the Age to Come and the promise of Scripture about a New Covenant.[15] Rather, Justin's inference that the Mosaic Law has

[13] In Dial. 43.1, he writes: [ὁ Χριστὸς] καὶ αἰώνιος νόμος καὶ καινὴ διαθήκη τῷ παντὶ κόσμῳ ἐκηρύσσετο προελευσόμενος.

[14] ἐπεὶ εἰ νόμος εἶχε τὸ φωτίζειν τὰ ἔθνη καὶ τοὺς ἔ-
χοντας αὐτόν, τίς χρεία καινῆς διαθήκης (Dial. 122.5). Cf. 34.
1. One is reminded of a similar point by Paul in Gal. 3:21.

[15] While it is true that, as J. Behm observes, the prophecy of Jeremiah is infrequently noted in Rabbinic literature,
when it is, emphasis is laid on the future Torah written on the
heart as distinct from the ineffective Torah which one learns
and forgets. See Behm's article on "διατίθημι, διαθήκη" in
Kittel's ThW, ET, II, 129. More widely among the Rabbinic

ceased to be valid with the coming of Christ is a theological principle derived from the Christian tradition and is not directly supported by the above texts. Justin however insists on a sharp displacement of the one Law by the other. We shall return to this point after our examination of the final text.

Is. 52:10-54:6, cited in _Dial_. 13.2-9, is not directly connected with the previous texts. Justin's exposition unfortunately suffers here because of the polemical aside of _Dial_. 12.2. Moreover, in _Dial_. 12.3 Justin begins a different type of argument about the Law, namely, an allegorical interpretation of the Law, which continues in _Dial_. 14.1b-2 after the lengthy Isaianic text. In this sense, the quote from Isaiah is "secondarily"[16] introduced in this context. However, Justin's use of this text adds an important point to his argument about the abrogation of the Law.

The context is set by λουσάσθω in _Dial_. 12.3. Then Justin, alluding to Is. 1:16 (λούσασθε, καθαροὶ γίνεσθε),[17] states that it was not to a bath that Isaiah pointed for ritual washing, which is completely useless for obtaining forgiveness, but to the σωτήριον λουτρὸν which for Justin is identified with Christian baptism (_Dial_. 13.1; cf. 14.1). What the Apologist does is to contrast cleansing through the Mosaic ritual, through sacrifices of goats and sheep, as well as the ashes of a heifer and the flour offering, with cleansing through the sacrifice of

---

teachers, the eternity and perpetuity of the Law is firmly held also for the New Age when the Law will be better studied and better observed than ever before, apart from certain precepts which may no longer be practicable in the Age to Come. See G. F. Moore, _Judaism_, I, 269-73; W. D. Davies, _Torah in the Messianic Age_ (Philadelphia, 1952), pp. 84ff. and also the _Encyclopaedia Judaica_, Vol. XV, col. 1244. For another view, see H. J. Schoeps who, writing on Paul's teaching of the end of the Law, emphasizes the Rabbinic references to the cessation of the Law with the coming of the Messiah and the inbreaking of the Age to Come. See his book _Paul: The Theology of the Apostle in the Light of Jewish Religious History_, trans. Harold Knight (Philadelphia: The Westminster Press, 1961), pp. 171ff.

[16]So Prigent, _Justin_, p. 247. Prigent also suspects that the text may have been amplified by a scribe. But the quote suits Justin's purposes too well here for such a possibility.

[17]The text is cited by Justin in _Dial_. 18.2.

Christic, his death.[18] It was for this reason, Justin says, that
Christ died. He then cites Is. 52:10-54:6 as a proof-text.

This classic text has two connections with Justin's argument about the cessation of the Law and the previous texts
cited in support of this thesis. First, it calls attention to
the promise of God's salvation directed universally to the gentiles. The text opens with Is. 52:10 which states: ἀποκαλύψει
κύριος τὸν βραχίονα αὐτοῦ τὸν ἅγιον ἐνώπιον πάντων τῶν ἐθνῶν,
καὶ ὄψονται πάντα τὰ ἔθνη καὶ τὰ ἄκρα τῆς γῆς τὴν σωτηρίαν τὴν
παρὰ τοῦ θεοῦ. This is surely not by chance but by Justin's
initiative. The text is a widely known testimonium.[19] But
where Justin begins to quote from it is unusual and no doubt
due to his deliberate choice. His purpose is to bring forward
once again what he has affirmed earlier about the universality
of the New Law (Dial. 11.2-4; 12.1). Two of the previous texts,
as we have noted, make the same point.[20] The same interest is
expressed by Justin's comment at the end of the citation of Is.
52:10-54:6. He repeats the phrase of the text τῶν ἀνομιῶν τοῦ
λαοῦ μου (Is. 53:8/Dial. 13.6), but changes and universalizes
it for his purposes (τῆς ἀνομίας τῶν λαῶν τοῦ θεοῦ, Dial. 14.1).

---

[18]We may have in Dial. 13.1 distant echoes of the Epistle to the Hebrews. Heb. 9:13 reads αἷμα τράγων καὶ ταύρων καὶ
σποδὸς δαμάλεως, whereas Justin reads αἵμασι τράγων καὶ προβάτων ἢ σποδῷ δαμάλεως and adds ἢ σεμιδάλεως προσφοραῖς. Justin
may vaguely be alluding here to Is. 1:11-13 (στέαρ ἀρνῶν καὶ
αἷμα ταύρων . . . σεμίδαλιν) which is used in Ap. 37.7 (κἂν
φέρητε σεμίδαλιν . . . βδέλυγμά μοί ἐστι· στέαρ ἀρνῶν καὶ αἷμα
ταύρων οὐ βούλομαι). This would explain the προβάτων in Dial.
13.1 for ἀρνῶν in Is. 1:11 and also the reference to σεμίδαλις,
but not the σποδὸς δαμάλεως which occurs only in the reading of
Hebrews. Justin has also much to say about Christ as the αἰώνιος ἱερεὺς appointed by God μεθ'ὅρκου (Dial. 33.2; cf. Heb.
6:16-17; 7:20-21, 28). However, we find no definite evidence
for Justin's possible knowledge of the Epistle to the Hebrews.

[19]E.g., Mtt. 8:17; Acts 8:32-33; I Pe. 2:22; I Clem.
16.3-13; Barn. 5.2. The length of it in Justin easily indicates that the Apologist is working with the Septuagint.

[20]Is. 51:4-5/Dial. 11.3 reads: νόμος παρ'ἐμοῦ ἐξελεύσεται . . . εἰς φῶς ἐθνῶν . . . εἰς τὸν βραχίονά μου ἔθνη
ἐλπιοῦσι. Is. 55:4/Dial. 12.1 reads: ἰδοὺ μάρτυρα αὐτὸν
ἔθνεσι δέδωκα. In Dial. 11.4, Justin specifically notes that
a New Covenant was not only promised, but promised for the
gentiles (εἰς φῶς ἐθνῶν). He often dwells on this point
throughout the Dialogue. In Ap. 53.3-12 he explains this
claim for pagan readers.

The second connection, which is more important for the
argument, concerns the abrogation of the Law itself. According
to Justin, the Mosaic ritual is completely ineffective, whereas
the death of Christ is fully efficacious (Dial. 13.1). The purpose for which the above Isaianic text is cited is to demonstrate that forgiveness of sins is granted to all the nations
through the death of Christ. It is the death of Christ as the
new criterion of salvation which renders the Mosaic Law obso-
lete. Here one may note that, when Justin speaks of Christ as
the New Law, he neither means Christ as the legislator of a new
body of commandments nor Christ as a universal ethical principle, but the crucified Christ. God's σωτήριον/σωτηρία (Dial.
11.3; 13.2) which goes forth to all the nations and reaches
the ends of the earth is none other than the σωτήριον μυστήριον, the passion of Christ.[21] This is why Justin can say that
the New Law has abolished the Old. In Dial. 24.1, he indicates
that the ritual act of circumcision has been abolished by the
establishment of a New Covenant based on the saving blood of
Christ (τὸ αἷμα τῆς περιτομῆς ἐκείνης κατήργηται καὶ αἵματι σω-
τηρίῳ πεπιστεύκαμεν· ἄλλη διαθήκη νῦν, καὶ ἄλλος ἐξῆλθεν ἐκ
Σιὼν νόμος).[22]

It is now appropriate to return to Justin's main point
about the abrogation of the Law. With language reminiscent of

---

[21]This point is very clearly expressed in Dial. 74.2-3
where Justin, interpreting Ps. 95.1(LXX), identifies the saving
mystery with the passion of Christ: ὡς τῷ θεῷ καὶ πατρὶ τῶν
ὅλων ᾄδοντας καὶ ψάλλοντας τοὺς ἀπὸ πάσης τῆς γῆς γνόντας τὸ
σωτήριον τοῦτο μυστήριον, τοῦτ'ἔστι τὸ πάθος τοῦ Χριστοῦ, δι'
οὗ τούτους ἔσωσεν . . . ὁ τοῦτο τὸ σωτήριον ὑπὲρ τοῦ ἀνθρωπείου
γένους ποιήσας. Verweijs is quite correct to stress that for
Justin the ground of salvation is the Gospel, pp. 220ff., 224.
Although Justin calls Christ νόμος, the Apologist cannot be
accused of "legal thinking" or "work-righteousness" as
Engelhardt, p. 243, and Goppelt, p. 296, charge.

[22]Justin also associates baptism very closely with the
death of Christ (σωτήριον λουτρόν . . . τὸ βάπτισμα, Dial.
13.1 and 14.1). In Dial. 14.1b-c and 19.2b-c, he contrasts
the uselessness of ritual washings with the value of baptism,
citing Jer. 2:13. In both cases Justin passes quickly to other
arguments. See also Dial. 29.1e for a similar contrast. The
text of Jeremiah follows closely the Septuagint and has little
to do with the citation of Jer. 2:12-13 in Barn. 11.2 which is
both longer and markedly different.

Hebrews, Justin opts for a radical displacement of the one Law by the other and of the former Covenant by the new one. In his statement of <u>Dial</u>. 11.2, he writes: νόμος δὲ κατὰ νόμου τεθεὶς τὸν πρὸ αὐτοῦ ἔπαυσε, καὶ διαθήκη μετέπειτα γενομένη τὴν προτέραν ὁμοίως ἔστησεν. Here the verb ἔπαυσε should be translated "put to an end" and the verb ἔστησεν "annulled," as suggested by Justin's opposition of the Old and New Law in the context.[23] In the passage of <u>Dial</u>. 24.1 quoted above, Justin uses the verb καταργεῖν "to abolish" (τὸ αἷμα τῆς περιτομῆς ἐκείνης κατήργηται, <u>Dial</u>. 24.1), and elsewhere again the verb παύειν "to cease" (παύσασθαι ἔδει, <u>Dial</u>. 43.1). In the same connection, one may also note Justin's rather harsh statement of the cessation of Old Testament prophecy by Christ when the Messiah comes to John the Baptist and "stops" him from prophesying and baptizing: καὶ Χριστὸς ἔτι αὐτοῦ [<u>i.e</u>., τοῦ 'Ιωάννου] καθεζομένου ἐπὶ τοῦ 'Ιορδάνου ποταμοῦ ἐπελθὼν ἔπαυσέ τε αὐτὸν τοῦ προφητεύειν καὶ βαπτίζειν (<u>Dial</u>. 51.2).

It is interesting that Justin formulates the Christian teaching of the cessation of the Law as sharply as he does. In this respect, he maintains the emphasis of the earlier tradition and does not give evidence of another view which we find in Christian writers after him in reaction to Marcion. Paul earlier used the verb καταργεῖν with regard to the Law and the Old Covenant (Rm. 7:2,6; II Cor. 3:14; cf. Eph. 2:15), but his statements on the cessation of the Law are not as thoroughgoing as Justin's.[24] The author of Hebrews is more firm about the inefficacy, even the intrinsic weakness of the Law, which is

---

[23] νόμος δὲ κατὰ νόμου τεθείς, <u>Dial</u>. 11.2. The use of ἵστημι in the sense of "to bring to a stand-still," "to check" and "to stop" is to be sure rare in classical Greek as Liddell and Scott show. F. Preisigke, <u>Wörterbuch der griechischen Papyrusurkunden mit Einschluss der griechischen Inschriften, Aufschriften, Ostrake, Mumienschilder usw. aus Ägypten</u> (Berlin, 1914-1927), reports instances meaning "to replace" or "to substitute" in the papyri. Sophocles in his Lexicon, however, gives "to stop" or "to check" as the first meaning in later Greek. It is in this sense of stopping and replacing that Justin uses ἵστημι above. Cf. τὸν ἥλιον ἔστησεν ἐκεῖνος about Joshua's stopping of the sun (<u>Dial</u>. 113.4). Williams, <u>Justin Martyr</u>, weakly translates "limited" for ἔστησεν, while Otto rightly translates "finem imponit." But Archambault has "annule." "Annuls" in the sense of "cause validly to cease," "checks effectively," or "cancels" best suits the context.

[24] For example, in Rm. 3:31 Paul hesitates to draw the line sharply.

radically replaced by the indestructible new life through the
sacrifice of Christ (Heb. 7:12,16-18; 10:1ff.; 12:27f.).[25] The
author of Barnabas is also uncompromising: sacrifices, offerings, circumcision and the Temple have been abolished by God
(κατήργηται, Barn. 2.6; 9.4; 14.2). Some of the gnostics and
especially the Marcionites fully exploited this tendency of the
Christian tradition. Ptolemy says that the Savior abrogated
(ἀνεῖλεν) the Law of retaliation as alien to his nature and
transformed (μετέθηκεν) the cultic Law (Pan. 33.5.1-2,8-9).[26]
But he at least allows that the pure legislation, the Decalogue,
was fulfilled, not destroyed, by Christ: ὃν [i.e., τὸν κυρίως
νόμον] οὐκ ἦλθε καταλῦσαι ὁ σωτὴρ ἀλλὰ πληρῶσαι (Pan. 33.5.1).[27]
Marcion, however, would have nothing of such a concept of
fulfilment.[28]

In contrast, the writers after Justin begin to construct
a theory of development between the old and new dispensations
and insist that Christ does not abrogate, but rather fulfils,
the Law. This theory of development is a reaction to Marcion.
Against the Marcionites Irenaeus quotes from Mtt. 5 and explains
that these words of the Lord do not imply an opposition to or
abolishment of the precepts of the Law, but a fulfilment and

---

[25]For him it is a case of the "removal" of the Law
because of its "weakness and uselessness" (μετάθεσις νόμου, Heb.
7:12; ἀθέτησις, 7:18). One might note that whereas for Paul
σάρκινος is applied to man, not to the Law which is πνευματικὸς
(Rm. 7:14), for the author of Hebrews σάρκινος is applied to
the Law itself (Heb. 7:16).

[26]The verb μετατίθημι is used by Ptolemy in its softer
sense of "to transpose" or "transform." What Ptolemy has in
mind is the spiritualization of the Law (Pan. 33.5.8ff.).

[27]He is obviously referring to Mtt. 5:17. Later he
also cites Rm. 7:12 (Pan. 33.6.6) which speaks of the Law as
holy and good.

[28]For Marcion, the logion of Jesus about the Law and
the Prophets being fulfilled, not destroyed, by him, was an
interpolation, as Tertullian reports in Adv. Marc. 4.7.4 (Non
ut legem et prophetas dissolueret, sed ut potius adimpleret.
Hoc enim Marcion ut additum erasit). Marcion also substituted
λόγος for νόμος in this logion: ἡ . . . γῆ καὶ ὁ οὐρανὸς πα-
ρελεύσονται, ὁ δὲ λόγος μου μένει εἰς τὸν αἰῶνα. See Harnack,
Marcion, p. 232*.

extension of them.[29]   When Tertullian in a similar way writes
against Marcion, he is particularly attentive the question of
demonstrating the fact that the old dispensation is reformed
rather than destroyed, restored rather than abolished.[30]   M. F.
Wiles correctly observes that the abrogation of the Law in the
patristic tradition is softened in view of the marcionite
threat.[31]

Justin, however, totally avoids any appeals to a theory of development, even though he has had surely to deal with
Marcion's view of the two dispensations. As far as the abrogation of the Mosaic Law is concerned, Justin is apparently one
with Marcion. The Law for the Apologist belongs to the old
dispensation, it was intended for the Jews, and it was completely abolished by Christ. The only important difference is
that for Justin the Mosaic Law was given by the same God and
Father of all. Only once, when Justin briefly expounds on his
concept of the eternal and universal righteousness (Dial. 93.
1-3), does he show a trace of the idea of fulfilment, i.e.,
fulfilment in the sense of bringing to completion or perfection,
not of course typological fulfilment which is very often advocated by Justin. He writes: καλῶς εἰρῆσθαι ὑπὸ τοῦ ἡμετέρου
κυρίου καὶ σωτῆρος Ἰησοῦ Χριστοῦ, ἐν δυσὶν ἐντολαῖς πᾶσαν δικαιοσύνην καὶ εὐσέβειαν πληροῦσθαι (Dial. 93.2).[32]   Justin
uses the verb πληροῦν or πληροῦσθαι on several occasions with
other non-metaphorical meanings (Dial. 7.1; 12.3; 45.1).[33]   He

---

[29]"Omnia enim haec non contrarietatem et dissolutionem
praeteritorum continent, sicut qui a Marcione sunt vociferan-
tur; sed plenitudinem et extensionem," Adv. Haer. 4.24.1.
Irenaeus is here speaking of the ethical precepts of the Law
("naturalia Legis"). However, elsewhere he explains in a similar fashion the violation of the sabbath by Jesus and the disciples (Adv. Haer. 4.16-17), as well as Jesus' logion about the
Law and the Prophets being valid until John (Adv. Haer. 4.6).

[30]"Ita per antithesis facilius ostendi potest ordo
creatoris a Christo reformatus quam repercussus, et redditus
potius quam exclusus," Adv. Marc. 2.29.3. Tertullian tries to
reverse the tables on Marcion.

[31]The Divine Apostle, pp. 58ff.

[32]Justin then quotes the two-fold commandment of love.

[33]Usually in the simple sense of "to make full" or "to
fill" and even "to fulfil" as in performing God's will.

never uses this verb or its derivatives in connection with his typological interpretation of Scripture. The case of Dial. 93.2 is unique in the Dialogue. Here the Apologist evidently means the summation of the ethical righteousness, its coming to fullness or perfection in Christ's double commandment of love. It will be remembered that Ptolemy, on the basis of Mtt. 5:17, also speaks of the "fulfilment" of the ethical Law, the Decalogue, which is his primary concern (Pan. 33.5.1).[34]

One can only conjecture about the reasons behind Justin's uncompromising statement of the cessation of the Law and his apparent agreement with Marcion in this regard. The simplest explanation is that Justin remains within the older tradition, much as the author of Barnabas, and does not yet perceive the marcionite threat as deeply as Irenaeus and Tertullian later do. Perhaps he feels safe in affirming the abrogation of the Law because of his tripartite division of the Law. It is also possible that a concept of fulfilment in the sense of bringing to perfection might well have suggested to Justin imperfection on the part of the Mosaic Law and thus, consequently, also of God, something which Justin could not allow. Ptolemy underlines the fact that the Law was imperfect, given by the imperfect God, and that therefore it was in need of fulfilment by Christ.[35] And Clement of Alexandria clearly combats the notion that the Law was imperfect.[36]

(2) The second argument which Justin develops on the basis of Scriptural citations in support of his thesis of the

---

[34]Irenaeus is inclined to do the same, but not exclusively. See above, n. 29.

[35]Οὔτε γὰρ ὑπὸ τοῦ τελείου θεοῦ καὶ πατρὸς φαίνεται τοῦτον [i.e., τὸν νόμον Μωϋσέως] τεθεῖσθαι (ἑπόμενος γάρ ἐστιν), ἀτελῆ τε ὄντα καὶ τοῦ ὑφ'ἑτέρου πληρωθῆναι ἐνδεῆ, ἔχοντά τε προστάξεις ἀνοικείας τῇ τοῦ τοιούτου θεοῦ φύσει τε καὶ γνώμῃ (Pan. 33.3.4). Ptolemy repeats this later (Pan. 33.5.1,3).

[36]ὁ δὲ κύριος οὐ καταλύειν τὸν νόμον ἀφικνεῖται, ἀλλὰ πληρῶσαι· πληρῶσαι δὲ οὐχ ὡς ἐνδεῆ, ἀλλὰ τῷ τὰς κατὰ νόμον προφητείας ἐπιτελεῖς γενέσθαι κατὰ τὴν αὐτοῦ παρουσίαν (Strom. 3.46.2). Clement is here thinking of prophetic and typological fulfilment.

invalidity of the Law follows the line of the prophetic critique of the Temple cult and is reinforced by partial allegorization of the Law. Similar prophetic texts, but without allegorization of the Law, are also used by Justin in his interpretation of the purpose of the Law, as it will be seen in the following chapter.

This second Scriptural argument is primarily developed
in Dial. chaps. 14-18, though the first sign of it occurs in
Dial. 12.3 and another expression of it later in Dial. 28.2-5.
Because of the long polemical digression of Dial. 16.2-17.4,
and also Justin's generally unpolished exposition, Dial. chaps.
14-18 can by no means be considered a cohesive unit. However,
Dial. 18.2 (λούσασθε . . . καὶ περιτέμνεσθαι τὴν ἀληθινὴν περιτομὴν) shows that Justin is ending here the allegorization of
the Law which he begins in Dial. 12.3 (δευτέρας ἤδη χρεία περιτομῆς . . . λουσάσθω) and from then on he turns primarily to
the purpose of the Law (Dial. 18.2-30.1). The first part of
the polemical digression (Dial. 16.2-3) and an allusion in Dial.
12.3 (διὰ τί ὑμῖν προσετάγη) have also to do with the purpose
of the Law and are examined in the following chapter on the purpose of the Law.

The main point of the second Scriptural argument is to
show that God does not truly desire observance of the ritual
Law, but rather prefers obedience to a higher spiritual order.
With this reasoning drawn from prophetic texts and supported by
allegorization of the Law, Justin hopes to negate the literal
value of the Law and thus to underscore the Law's rightful cessation by Christ. It will become evident that, just as in the
case of Justin's interpretation of the purpose of the Law, so
also here the Apologist exploits the prophetic critique of the
cult drawing an entirely negative inference about the Law which
the Old Testament Prophets themselves did not draw.

A word is necessary about Justin's allegorization of
the Law. As in the parallel case of typological exegesis, the
allegorical interpretation of the Law places Justin within the
Christian exegetical tradition. Another example is the author
of Barnabas. But it sharply differentiates Justin from Marcion,
who, as is well known, totally rejected the allegorization of

the Old Testament.[37] In the case of Justin, however, we find
nothing of the kind of allegorization which one finds in Barnabas and the Epistle of Aristeas,[38] nor of the elaborate allegorization one finds in Philo and in many of the second-century
gnostics. Justin is interested more in predictive and typological interpretations than in allegorizing.[39] His spiritualizing
interpretation of the Law is for the most part closely related
to the prophetic texts which are quoted. The spiritualizing
exegesis has the function of supporting these texts which are
critical of the Mosaic cult.

In Dial. 12.3, after a critical comment against the Jews
for neglecting the New Law and for lack of understanding, Justin
tells Trypho and his friends:

> δευτέρας ἤδη χρεία περιτομῆς, καὶ ὑμεῖς ἐπὶ τῇ σαρκὶ
> μέγα φρονεῖτε. σαββατίζειν ὑμᾶς ὁ καινὸς νόμος διὰ
> παντὸς ἐθέλει, καὶ ὑμεῖς μίαν ἀργοῦντες ἡμέραν εὐσε-
> βεῖν δοκεῖτε, μὴ νοοῦντες διὰ τί ὑμῖν προσετάγη· καὶ
> ἐὰν ἄζυμον ἄρτον φάγητε, πεπληρωκέναι τὸ θέλημα τοῦ
> θεοῦ φατε. οὐκ ἐν τούτοις εὐδοκεῖ κύριος ὁ θεὸς ἡ-
> μῶν. εἴ τις ἐστὶν ἐν ὑμῖν ἐπίορκος ἢ κλέπτης, παυ-
> σάσθω· εἴ τις μοιχός, μετανοησάτω, καὶ σεσαββάτικε
> τὰ τρυφερὰ καὶ ἀληθινὰ σάββατα τοῦ θεοῦ· εἴ τις κα-
> θαρὰς οὐκ ἔχει χεῖρας, λουσάσθω, καὶ καθαρός ἐστιν.

---

[37]Harnack, Marcion, pp. 66 and 260* where he cites Ori-
gen's report (Comm. on Mtt. 15.3) that Μαρκίων φάσκει μὴ δεῖν
ἀλληγορεῖν τήν γραφήν. For the wider allegorical exegetical
tradition, see Prigent, L'Epître de Barnabé; R. A. Kraft, "The
Apostolic Fathers, Vol. III: Barnabas and the Didache, ed. R.
M. Grant (New York: Thomas Nelson & Sons, 1965) and also his
"The Epistle of Barnabas, its Quotations and their Sources"
(Harvard Dissertation, 1961); H. Windisch, Der Barnabasbrief
(Tübingen, 1920); R. M. Grant, Letter and Spirit; R. P. C. Han-
son, Allegory and Event; I. Heinemann, Altjüdische Allegoristic
(Breslau, 1935); I. Heinemann, Philons griechische und jüdische
Bildung (Breslau, 1932); P. Heinisch, Der Einfluss Philos, and
others.

[38]For example that Moses prohibted the eating of pigs to
teach that one should not associate with men who are like pigs.
See Barn. 10 and Aristeas 144-51, 163-67.

[39]Typology serves Justin's purposes very well in the
Dialogue where his chief aim is to ground Christology in the Old
Testament. Allegorizing, however, does not help him very much,
at least in the case of the problem of the Law, since his main
interest in this regard is to show that the Law is a historical
dispensation for the Jews. Typology always contains an element
referring to future fulfilment, whereas allegory always has to
do with the timeless order of true wisdom, piety and morality.
Of course, both assume that a given text means something else,
whether future or timeless, other than the literal meaning.

> A second circumcision is now necessary, and ye are
> making much of your flesh; the new Law wishes you to
> keep sabbath all the time, and you think you are act-
> ing piously by being lazy for one day, not considering
> the reason why it was commanded you; and if ye eat un-
> leavened bread, ye say ye have fulfilled the will of
> God.   It is not in these things that our Lord takes
> pleasure.   If any among you is a false-swearer or a
> thief, let him cease; if any an adulterer, let him re-
> pent; then he has kept the delightsome and true sab-
> baths of God.   If any has not clean hands, let him
> wash; then is he clean.

Justin then proceeds to his point about the atoning death of
Christ and the citation of Is. 53 (<u>Dial</u>. 13.1ff.).

In the above passage we have the first instance of Justin's allegorization of the Law.   Circumcision, the sabbath and
the azymes, suggests Justin, have a deeper significance which
the Jews self-confidently miss, but a significance in which God
truly takes pleasure.   The whole intent of Justin's use of the
prophetic critique of the cult and his allegorizing interpretation of the Law is to show what principles God truly desires:
[τί] εὐδοκεῖ κύριος ὁ θεός(<u>Dial</u>. 12.3).   These are none other
than the principles of the spiritual moral order.   In this instance Justin urges moral correction and repentance on the part
of one who may be either ἐπίορκος ἢ κλέπτης or μοιχός.   Peni-
tent behavior is equivalent to observance of God's true sabbath.

The passage offers few clues as to whether or not Justin
may be working with a previous source or sources.   The designation δευτέρα περιτομή for the spiritual circumcision of the
heart is Justin's own (cf. <u>Dial</u>. 113.6-7; 114.4) and does not
occur prior to him.   The order of the Mosaic ordinances, circumcision, the sabbath and unleavened bread, indicates very little or nothing.   The order of the nouns ἐπίορκος ἢ κλέπτης and
μοιχός is in reverse sequence to the related commandments of the
Decalogue (Ex. 20:13-16 or Dt. 5:17-20), although ἐπίορκος could
be related to the second commandment.   A sequence of the same
commandments occurs in Mk. 10:19 and parallels.[40]   But Justin's
use of the nouns and his order probably derive from a catalogue
of vices rather than from either the Decalogue or the Gospels.

The reference to καινὸς νόμος, which Justin identifies
with Christ (<u>Dial</u>. 11.4), is odd at this point because Justin's

---

[40]Cf. more remotely Rm. 13:9; <u>Did</u>. 2.2f.; <u>Barn</u>. 19.4.

94

argument is based on the authority of the Old Testament, not on
the authority of Christ. Justin states that σαββατίζειν ὑμᾶς
ὁ καινὸς νόμος . . . ἐθέλει probably because his preceding polemical statements present Christ, the New Law, as a figure who
challenges the unresponsive Jews (Dial. 12.2).[41] The same feature occurs again in Dial. 14.3 where the allegorizing of the
Law is directly related to a prophetic text, Is. 55:3-13, also
partially quoted in Dial. 12.1 as has been noted. In Dial. 14.3
Justin writes: καὶ ὅτι τοῦτό ἐστιν ὁ ἀξιοῖ ὑμᾶς οὗτος ὁ καινὸς
νομοθέτης, τοὺς προλελεγμένους ὑπ'ἐμοῦ λόγους πάλιν ἀνιστορήσω
. . . εἴρηνται δὲ ὑπὸ τοῦ 'Ησαΐου οὕτως. Christ is the chal-
lenging figure who calls Jews to observance of the true spiritual principles. In the above passage Christ speaks through
Isaiah and is thus suggested as the inspirer of the Prophets,
which is quite in harmony with Justin's views.[42] This is why
Christ as the New Law is mentioned in Dial. 12.3. The awkward-
ness arises from the fact that this claim is not here directly
acknowledged.

At the end of Dial. 12.3 Justin alludes to Is. 58:13
(τρυφερά . . . σάββατα). This text is also quoted in Dial. 27.1
by Trypho making a different point. Less clearly Justin alludes
as well to Is. 1:16 (λουσάσθω . . . cf. οὐ γὰρ . . . εἰς βαλα-
νεῖον ὑμᾶς ἔπεμπεν ὁ 'Ησαΐας ἀπολουσομένους, Dial. 13.1) which
he cites in Dial. 18.2. We leave these texts for examination
at the appropriate time.

The Scriptural argument continues in Dial. 14.2-3.
Justin continues his allegorical interpretation of the Law as
follows:

βαπτίσθητε τὴν ψυχὴν ἀπὸ ὀργῆς καὶ ἀπὸ πλεονεξίας, ἀπὸ
φθόνου, ἀπὸ μίσους· καὶ ἰδοὺ τὸ σῶμα καθαρόν ἐστι. τοῦ-
τὸ γάρ ἐστι τὸ σύμβολον τῶν ἀζύμων, ἵνα μὴ τὰ παλαιὰ τῆς

---

[41] τοῦτον αὐτὸν ὑμεῖς ἠτιμώσατε τὸν νόμον . . . καὶ οὐδὲ
νῦν παραδέχεσθε . . . πάρεστιν ὁ νομοθέτης, καὶ οὐχ ὁρᾶτε (Dial.
12.2).

[42] Christ as the Divine Logos inspiring the Prophets is
explicitly mentioned only in Ap. 36.1; cf. Ap. 63.4. But Justin's interpretation of the Old Testament theophanies (Dial.
56ff.) and his view of the pre-existence of Christ, imply the
same thing. More often Justin says that Christ is the correct
interpreter of the Old Testament and the one who grants the
gift of interpretation to those who believe in him.

κακῆς ζύμης ἔργα πράττητε. ὑμεῖς δὲ πάντα σαρκικῶς νε-
νοήκατε, καὶ ἡγεῖσθε εὐσέβειαν, ἐὰν τοιαῦτα ποιοῦντες
τὰς ψυχὰς μεμεστωμένοι ἦτε δόλου καὶ πάσης κακίας ἁπλῶς.
διὸ καὶ μετὰ τὰς ἑπτὰ ἡμέρας τῶν ἀζυμοφαγιῶν νέαν ζύμην
φυρᾶσαι ἑαυτοῖς ὁ θεὸς παρήγγειλε, τοῦτ᾽ ἔστιν ἄλλων
ἔργων πρᾶξιν καὶ μὴ τῶν παλαιῶν καὶ φαύλων τὴν μίμησιν.
καὶ ὅτι τοῦτό ἐστιν ὁ ἀξιοῖ ὑμᾶς οὗτος ὁ καινὸς νομοθέτης, τοὺς προλελεγμένους ὑπ᾽ ἐμοῦ λόγους πάλιν ἀνιστορήσω μετὰ καὶ τῶν ἄλλων τῶν παραλειφθέντων. εἴρηνται δὲ
ὑπὸ τοῦ Ἠσαΐου οὕτως (Dial. 14.2-3).

Baptize your soul (free) from anger and from covetous-
ness, from envy, from hatred—and behold your body is
clean. For this is the inner meaning of the unleavened
bread, that ye do not practise the old deeds of the bad
leaven. But you have thought of all things in a carnal
way, and consider it to be piety, even though when ye
do such things, your souls are filled with guile, and,
in fact, evil of every kind. Therefore also after the
seven days of eating unleavened bread God charged you
to knead new leaven for yourselves, that is, the practice of other deeds, and not the imitation of the old
and worthless. And to show that this is what this new
Lawgiver requires of you I will repeat over again the
words that have before been spoken by me, together
with the rest that were omitted. Now they are thus
said by Isaiah.

The lengthy citation of Is. 55:3-13 then follows (Dial. 14.4-7).

The main purpose of the above passage is the allegorical interpretation of the eating of unleavened bread during
the Passover (τὸ σύμβολον τῶν ἀζύμων) which for Justin signifies abstinence from evil deeds (ἵνα μὴ τὰ παλαιὰ τῆς κακῆς
ζύμης ἔργα πράττητε). The eating of unleavened bread, suggests
Justin, should not be interpreted simply in its literal meaning
(σαρκικῶς),[43] as the Jews may interpret it, but in its deeper
meaning, calling for cleansing of the soul from ethical evils:
βαπτίσθητε τὴν ψυχὴν ἀπὸ ὀργῆς καὶ ἀπὸ πλεονεξίας, ἀπὸ φθόνου,
ἀπὸ μίσους. The verb βαπτίσθητε comes to Justin from the preceding reference to ritual washing (τί γὰρ ὄφελος ἐκείνου τοῦ
βαπτίσματος, Dial. 14.1). We have here a continuation of the
argument of Dial. 12.3 where the allegorical interpretation of
Mosaic practices includes that of eating unleavened bread (ἄζυ-
μον ἄρτον).

---

[43]Cf. Barn. 10.2: Μωϋσῆς δὲ ἐν πνεύματι ἐλάλησεν.
For the author of Barnabas, the Mosaic precepts had from the
beginning only a spiritual meaning which the Jews missed
(Barn. 9.4). On the other hand, the Christians have been giv-
en the gnosis to know the true spiritual meaning of the Mosaic commandments (Barn. 9.3; 10.12).

96

The idea of leaven as something evil and corrupting is
found both in Jewish and Graeco-Roman literature.[44] Justin's
reference, however, to the "old" deeds (παλαιά . . . ἔργα, cf.
παλαιά καὶ φαῦλα, Dial. 14.3), as well as to the "new" leaven
(νέαν ζύμην φυρᾶσαι), links him with the Christian tradition.
We may here have the first sign of Justin's indebtedness to
Paul. The original contrast of παλαιά ζύμη/νέον φύραμα occurs
in I Cor. 5:7-8. Ptolemy, in his own allegorizing of the Law,
explicitly appeals to Paul. He says: καὶ τὸ πάσχα δὲ ὁμοίως
καὶ τὰ ἄζυμα, ὅτι εἰκόνες ἦσαν, δηλοῖ καὶ Παῦλος ὁ ἀπόστολος
τὸ πάσχα ἡμῶν, λέγων, ἐτύθη Χριστός, καὶ ἵνα ἦτε, φησίν, ἄζυμοι,
μὴ μετέχοντες ζύμης (ζύμην δὲ νῦν τὴν κακίαν λέγει), ἀλλ'ἦτε
νέον φύραμα (Pan. 33.5.15). Justin does not appeal to Paul.
But his antithesis of the old and new leaven, and his statement
later ἦν γὰρ τὸ πάσχα ὁ Χριστός, ὁ τυθείς (Dial. 111.3), are
quite probably derived from Paul. No writer prior to Justin
uses the image of the leavened and unleavened bread, and those
writers after him who use it usually connect Paul's name with
it.[45] One must assume that Justin was aware of the Pauline
origin of this contrast between the new and old leaven. With
respect to the commandment to knead new leaven after the seven
days of unleavened bread, mentioned in the above passage, we
have apparently another "Samaritanism" of Justin.[46]

The allegorical interpretation of the unleavened bread
is connected to the text of Is. 55:3-13, as has been noted. The
"new leaven" of good works required by the New Lawgiver is
according to Justin announced by Scripture. Is. 55:3-13, however, does not well serve Justin's purposes here. Although it

---

[44]See H. Windisch, "ζύμη," ThW, ET, 904-06. This is
especially true of the Passover prohibition of leavened bread.
The Rabbinic teachers commonly designate the evil inclination
as "leaven." Philo has various interpretations of leavened
bread both positive and negative.

[45]Tertullian, De Pud. 18; Clement of Alexandria, Strom.
3.18; Cyprian, Ad Quir. 3.11. Tertullian, in Adv. Marc. 5.7.3,
cites I Cor. 5:7 against Marcion saying that the unleavened
bread in the Creator's ordinance was a figure of the Christians
(ergo azymi figurae erant nostrae apud creatorem).

[46]Weis, pp. 200-01. No such specific command exists in
the Pentateuch.

contains the reference to the eternal Covenant, which for Justin
is Christ, as well as to God's testimony before all nations
(διαθήκην αἰώνιον . . . ἰδοὺ μαρτύριον αὐτὸν ἔθνεσι δέδωκα,
Dial. 14.4), and also a brief exhortation to repentance from
evil ways and thoughts (ἀπολιπέτω ὁ ἀσεβῆς τὰς ὁδοὺς αὐτοῦ,
Dial. 14.5), the remainder of the quote seems to speak of the
promise of God's eschatological future and ends with the statement: καὶ ἔσται κύριος εἰς ὄνομα καὶ εἰς σημεῖον αἰώνιον καὶ
οὐκ ἐκλείψει (Is. 55:13/Dial. 14.7). This may be the reason why,
even more awkwardly, Justin then digresses into a comment about
the First and Second Coming of Christ (Dial. 14.8), which is
completely out of context here. Apparently the second part of
Is. 55:3-13 reminds him of the bright eschatological future to
be ushered in with the Second Coming of Christ, while the previous lengthy quotation of Is. 52:10-54:6 more clearly suggests
to him the First Coming.[47]

     After this curious aside, Justin resumes his Scriptural
argument based on Old Testament texts with an allegorical interpretation of fasting. Justin tells Trypho: Καὶ τὴν ἀληθινὴν
οὖν τοῦ θεοῦ νηστείαν μάθετε νηστεύειν, ὡς Ἠσαΐας φησίν, ἵνα
θεῷ εὐαρεστῆτε (Dial. 15.1). The true fasting which pleases
God, just as the true sabbath mentioned earlier (Dial. 12.3),
has to do with obedience to the moral order. Justin's proof-
text is now Is. 58:1-11, which contains an example of the prophetic critique of the Mosaic cult. This text serves Justin's
purpose well indeed (οὐχὶ τοιαύτην νηστείαν ἐγὼ ἐξελεξάμην,
λέγει κύριος· ἀλλὰ λῦε πάντα σύνδεσμον ἀδικίας, διάλυε στραγ-
γαλιὰς βιαίων συναλλαγμάτων, Is. 58:6/Dial. 15.4).[48] The text
is a widely used testimonium, cited extensively by the author of
Barnabas (Barn. 3.1-5/Is. 58:4-10), Irenaeus (Adv. Haer. 4.29.3/
Is. 58:6-9), Tertullian (Adv. Marc. 2.19.2/Is. 58:6-7), Clement

---

[47]He writes in Dial. 14.8: Τῶν τε λόγων τούτων καὶ τοιούτων εἰρημένων ὑπὸ τῶν προφητῶν, ἔλεγον, ὦ Τρύφων, οἱ μὲν
εἴρηνται εἰς τὴν πρώτην παρουσίαν τοῦ Χριστοῦ, ἐν ᾗ καὶ ἄτιμος
καὶ ἀειδὴς καὶ θνητὸς φανήσεσθαι κεκηρυγμένος ἐστίν, οἱ δὲ εἰς
τὴν δευτέραν αὐτοῦ παρουσίαν.

[48]It is to this verse that Justin draws attention in two
other instances (Dial. 40.4; Ap. 37.8).

98

(Paedag. 3.12.90/Is. 58:4-9)[49] and also Cyprian (Ad. Quir. 3.1/ Is. 58:1-9). But the text is cited with sufficient variation that one can hardly surmise dependence of any of these authors on another.[50] Justin, who cites the text in its longest reading, follows the Septuagint very closely and does not in any case share the textual variations of Barnabas.[51] He is no doubt working independently, even if the text may well have first been suggested to him by the tradition.

Justin rounds off the above citation with a comment which seems to recapitulate the argument. He exhorts the Jews to practice circumcision of the heart in accordance with the text which he has quoted: περιτέμεσθε οὖν τὴν ἀκροβυστίαν τῆς καρδίας ὑμῶν, ὡς οἱ λόγοι τοῦ θεοῦ διὰ πάντων τούτων τῶν λόγων ἀξιοῦσι (Dial. 15.7). He then continues with an additional argument (καὶ διὰ Μωϋσέως, Dial. 16.1). But the recapitulating comment is inappropriate since the quoted text, Is. 58:1-11, speaks only of fasting, not circumcision. Rather, the comment anticipates what follows and two additional texts which refer to circumcision and continue the same Scriptural argument about what God truly desires.

The first text, Dt. 10:16-17, calls for circumcision of the heart (περιτέμεῖσθε τὴν σκληροκαρδίαν ὑμῶν) and exalts the awesome lordship and strict impartiality of God. The second text, Lev. 26:40-41, which immediately follows, tells of a future judgment of God when the Jews will be shamed because of the uncircumcision of their heart (τότε ἐντραπήσεται ἡ καρδία ἡ ἀπερίτμητος αὐτῶν). The second text dwells distinctly on judgment and is less relevant to the overall argument. It probably ex-

---

[49]Clement divides the text, quoting first vss. 7b-9 as exemplifying true prayer, and then vss. 4-7a as exemplifying true fasting.

[50]Kraft in his dissertation, pp. 103-10, scrutinizes this text together with others cited in Barn. 2-3 and finds no dependence on Barnabas by either Tertullian or Irenaeus. Prigent, Justin, pp. 249-50, on the other hand, sees a definite connection between Justin, Irenaeus and Tertullian on the basis not of Dial. 15, but Ap. 37.8 where Justin combines Is. 1:12 with Is. 58:6-7. The connection, according to Prigent, is provided by the use of a common source, Justin's Syntagma.

[51]But the quote in Barnabas shows significant textual disturbances.

plains the polemical digression which begins with <u>Dial</u>. 16.2ff.,
a long tirade against the Jews. Nevertheless, both of these
texts, as the introductory statement indicates (καὶ διὰ Μωϋσέως
κέκραγεν ὁ θεὸς αὐτός, οὕτως λέγων . . . καὶ ἐν τῷ Λευιτικῷ),
are consecutively cited with the same purpose of emphasizing
circumcision of the heart as the true spiritual principle.

The two texts are quite precisely quoted from the Septuagint. Together they occur only in Justin. The first is partially quoted by the author of <u>Barnabas</u> (<u>Barn</u>. 9.5/Dt. 10:16)
and even in briefer form by Irenaeus and Tertullian.[52] In fuller form it is also cited by Clement of Alexandria (<u>Strom</u>. 6.3.
30.5), though in an entirely different context.[53] The second
text, Lev. 26:40-41, does not occur in any of these writers, including Cyprian. Justin, therefore, works independently and is
not dependent upon any tradition for his use of these texts.

Justin's argumentation at this point takes quite a different turn with the extensive polemical denunciation of the
Jews, <u>Dial</u>. 16.2-17.4. Only the first part of this denunciation
has to do with Justin's argument on the Law, but it also introduces a peculiar non-Scriptural argument which we will examine
later. As far as the Scriptural argument is concerned, we may
move directly to <u>Dial</u>. 18.2[54] which concludes the allegorizing
argument about spiritual circumcision. In <u>Dial</u>. 18.2, Justin
quotes Is. 1:16 and calls for spiritual circumcision: Λούσασθε
οὖν καὶ νῦν καθαροὶ γένεσθε καὶ ἀφέλεσθε τὰς πονηρίας ἀπὸ τῶν
ψυχῶν ἡμῶν, ὡς δὲ λούσασθαι ὑμῖν τοῦτο τὸ λουτρὸν κελεύει ὁ θεὸς
καὶ περιτέμνεσθαι τὴν ἀληθινὴν περιτομήν. He continues with a
statement about the purpose of the Law (<u>Dial</u>. 18.2b-3) which is
also examined later.

The citation of Is. 1:16 and Justin's words look back to
<u>Dial</u>. 12.3 and 14.1. The bath which God commands (τοῦτο τὸ

---

[52]Irenaeus in <u>Adv. Haer</u>. 4.27.1 ("Et propheta ait:
Circumcidite duritiam cordis vestri") and Tertullian in <u>Adv.
Marc</u>. 5.4.10 ("quia et Moyses: circumcidetis duricordiam
uestram"); cf. <u>Adv. Marc</u>. 5.13.7.

[53]He is speaking about miracles and powers and refers to
the text for its description of the awesome magnitude of God (Dt.
10:17).

[54]<u>Dial</u>. 18.1 is transitional and explains the citation
of sayings of Jesus in the last part of the polemical aside.

100

λουτρὸν) is Christian baptism (τοῦτ'ἐκεῖνο, ὃ προηγόρευε
['Ησαΐας], τὸ βάπτισμα, Dial. 14.1). Christian baptism is what
Isaiah predicted with his words of Is. 1:16 (Dial. 13.1; 14.1)
and he also predicted true circumcision of the heart (καὶ περιτέμνεσθαι τὴν ἀληθινὴν περιτομήν, Dial. 18.2). True circumcision is the putting away of the iniquities of the soul (ἀφέλεσθε
τὰς πονηρίας ἀπὸ τῶν ψυχῶν ὑμῶν, Dial. 18.2). Justin here
seems to recapitulate (οὖν) and conclude the second Scriptural
argument. This proof-text, quoted more fully by Justin in Ap.
44.3 and 61.7 (Is. 1:16-20), is a widely known text in the tradition.[55]

A final expression of the second Scriptural argument occurs in Dial. 28.2-5. The key statement is the following:

ὁρᾶτε ὡς οὐ ταύτην τὴν περιτομὴν τὴν εἰς σημεῖον δοθεῖ-
σαν ὁ θεὸς θέλει· οὐδὲ γὰρ Αἰγυπτίοις χρήσιμος οὐδὲ
τοῖς υἱοῖς Μωὰβ οὐδὲ τοῖς υἱοῖς 'Εδώμ. ἀλλὰ κἂν Σκύθης
ᾖ τις ἢ Πέρσης, ἔχει δὲ τὴν τοῦ θεοῦ γνῶσιν καὶ τοῦ
Χριστοῦ αὐτοῦ καὶ φυλάσσει τὰ αἰώνια δίκαια, περιτέτμη-
ται τὴν καλὴν καὶ ὠφέλιμον περιτομήν, καὶ φίλος ἐστὶ τῷ
θεῷ, καὶ ἐπὶ τοῖς δώροις αὐτοῦ καὶ ταῖς προσφοραῖς
χαίρει (Dial. 28.4).

Ye see that God does not wish for this circumcision
which was given for a sign; for it does not advantage
either the Egyptians, or the sons of Moab, or the sons
of Edom. But though a man be even a Scythian or a
Persian, yet has the knowledge of God and of His Christ,
and keeps the eternal acts of righteousness, he is circumcised with the fair and profitable circumcision, and
he is dear to God, and God rejoices over all his gifts
and offerings.

According to the passage, God desires not physical circumcision which Egyptians, Moabites and Edomites also possessed
without much avail, but spiritual circumcision, i.e., knowledge
of God and Christ and observance of deeds of eternal righteous-

---

[55]Especially in connection with baptism, e.g., Cyprian,
Ad. Quir. 1.24(Is. 1:15-20). Origen in his Comm. on John (32.2
on Jn. 13.12f.) quotes Is. 1:16 in connection with the washing
of the disciples' feet by Jesus. Is. 1:16 is not found in
Barnabas, but other parts of the same chapter are. Is. 1 which
speaks of the destruction of Jerusalem and is also generally
critical both of the Jews as a people and of the Mosaic cult is
used in different ways numerous times by Justin, Tertullian,
Irenaeus and other Christian writers. The use of this chapter
by these writers, however, is too diverse and too allusive in
terms of individual verses and very small portions of this chapter for discerning any identifiable patterns in the tradition.
Justin is in any case again quoting from the LXX even if knowledge of Is. 1:16-20 was provided to him by the tradition.

ness (τὰ αἰώνια δίκαια). This is the superior circumcision
which, if one possesses, whether he be a Scythian[56] or a Persian,
makes one the friend of God (φίλος ἐστὶ τῷ θεῷ).[57] The allegorical interpretation of the ritual Law is here associated by Justin with the eternal ethical order (τὰ αἰώνια δίκαια), according
to Justin's concept,[58] although not apart from what he considers
true knowledge of God and Christ.

Justin supports the above statement with three Old Testament texts, Jer. 4:3-4 and 9:25-26, which precede the statement (Dial. 28.2-3), and Mal. 1:10-12 which follows the statement (Dial. 28.5). He smoothly works the first text into one
of his appeals to Trypho (νεώσατε ἑαυτοῖς νεώματα. . . . γνῶτε
τὸν Χριστόν, Dial. 28.2-3). From the second text he takes the
reference to the Egyptians, Moabites and Edomites (Dial. 28.3/
Jer. 9:25). Since other peoples also practiced circumcision,[59]
as the latter text suggests, circumcision is not decisive, reasons Justin. True circumcision is circumcision of the heart,
as the former text states (περιτέμνεσθε τὴν ἀκροβυστίαν τῆς
καρδίας ὑμῶν, Dial. 28.2/Jer. 4:4). Both of these citations occur within a similar context also in Barnabas (Barn. 9.5), but
in Barnabas they are cited in substantially shorter form and are

---

[56]Perhaps an echo of Col. 3:11: βάρβαρος, Σκύθης. The
Scythians were known in antiquity as the barbarians par excel-
lence (Bauer, Lexicon). Justin's reference has no parallel.
For another intriguing echo of Col. 1:15 see πρωτότοκος πάσης
κτίσεως in Dial. 85.2 and 138.2. The phrase is repeated with
variations also in Dial. 84.2; 100.2; 125.3.

[57]In the Christian tradition, Abraham is known as the
"friend of God." Cf. Jm. 2:23; Clem. 10.1 and 17.1. Justin
has much to say about Abraham, but does not call him friend of
God. This title is applied by Philo to Moses (De Sacr. 130),
to Abraham (De Abr. 273) and to any man who practices virtue
and contemplation (Leg. Alleg. 3.71; De Som. 2.219,297; De Ebr.
94).

[58]See above, pp. 56ff.

[59]Cf. Barn. 9.5. Pagans in antiquity knew that circumcision was not exclusively a Jewish custom, e.g., Celsus
(c. Celsum, 5.41). Already Herodotus, Hist. 2.104, reports that
Egyptians practiced circumcision. For more on this, see
Windisch, Der Barnasbasbrief, pp. 354-55.

102

combined with Dt. 10:16.[60] Justin's reading is, as usual, much
closer to the Septuagint. Later writers seem to quote the two
citations separately, and for the most part only Jer. 4:3-4.[61]
Therefore, if we have in this instance evidence of a testimonia
source behind the text of Justin and that of Barnabas, which may
well be the case,[62] such a testimonia source is not much in evidence in the later tradition, not even in Cyprian's Book of
Testimonies. Justin for his own part seems again to work directly with the Septuagint.

The third text, Mal. 1:10-12, is given by Justin without
much exegetical comment. It speaks of God's accepting a pure
sacrifice by gentiles, i.e., the honoring of His Name among them
(θυσία καθαρά, ὅτι τιμᾶται τὸ ὄνομά μου ἐν τοῖς ἔθνεσι), and His
rejection of ritual sacrifices. In the context, Justin simply
suggests that those who have inward circumcision of the heart
are the ones who also offer desirable sacrifices to God. Elsewhere, however, quoting the same text again (Dial. 41.2; cf.
117.1-5), he associates it with the Eucharist. This text is
also widely known in the tradition, usually as a testimonium for
the Eucharist.[63]

---

[60]Μὴ σπείρητε ἐπ'ἀκάνθαις, περιτμήθητε τῷ κυρίῳ ὑμῶν,
(Jer. 4:3-4). Καὶ τί λέγει; περιτμήθητε τὴν σκληροκαρδίαν ὑμῶν,
καὶ τὸν τράχηλον ὑμῶν οὐ σκληρυνεῖτε (Dt. 10:16). λάβε πάλιν·
Ἰδού, λέγει κύριος, πάντα τὰ ἔθνη ἀπερίτμητα ἀκροβυστίᾳ, ὁ δὲ
λαὸς οὗτος ἀπερίτμητος καρδίᾳ (Jer. 19:25-26). For a textual
analysis see Kraft's dissertation, pp. 188-90.

[61]E.g., Tertullian, Adv. Jud. 3.7 and Adv. Marc. 4.1.6;
Cyprian, Ad Quir. 1.8, both of whom cite only Jer. 4:3-4.

[62]As we saw, Justin also uses Dt. 10:16-17 earlier in
Dial. 16.1. The three texts occur together also in Ps.-Greg.
11, as Kraft notes in his dissertation, p. 187. If this is the
case, then Justin breaks the compilation and cites the texts
more fully. Curiously, when Justin quotes Jer. 9:26 in Ap. 53.
11, he attributes it to Isaiah.

[63]Already so, but in a condensed form, in Did. 14.2.
In later writers, the text is cited in a briefer form (Mal. 1:
10-11) than Justin's (Mal. 1:10-12). See Irenaeus, Adv. Haer.
4.29.5 and Greek frag. 16 (Harvey, pp. 500-01); Tertullian,
Adv. Marc. 3.22.6 and 4.1.8, as well as Adv. Jud. 5.4 and 5.7;
Cyprian, Ad Quir. 1.16; Clement of Alexandria, Strom. 5.14.
136.1. Prigent, Justin et l'Ancien Testament, pp. 273-77, who
carefully examines this text in the tradition, is convinced
that we have to do here with "une grande tradition liturgique."

(3) Thus far we have examined two Scriptural arguments
which Justin develops to demonstrate the cessation of the Law,
the first regarding the abolition of the Old Covenant by the
New Covenant and the Mosaic Law by the New Law, and the second
regarding what God truly desires, not observance of the ritual
Law, but conformity to a higher spiritual order. In Dial. 95.1,
Justin briefly develops a third and final Scriptural argument to
point up the futility of the Law as a criterion of salvation and
thus to underscore its invalidity. This argument, based on Dt.
27:26, is one of Justin's last points regarding the Law and oc-
curs as a kind of afterthought in his argumentation on the Law.
It is found in the larger discussion about the ignominy of
Jesus' crucifixion (Dial. chaps. 89-96) and has the function of
reversing Trypho's charge that a curse lies on the crucified
Jesus, according to Dt. 21:23 (Dial. 96.1; cf. 32.1; 89.2; 90.1).
Justin argues that the Law holds no curse on the crucified
Messiah, but rather holds a curse on those who do not perfectly
adhere to it--a curse which is lifted by God through the sacrifice of Christ (Dial. 94.5-95.3).[64] The argument thus occurs
within a different context than previous discussions about the
Law and is intended as an answer to the problem of the crucifixion in view of Dt. 21:23 more than as an answer to the problem of the Law. However, it provides an additional point about
the unviability of the Mosaic Law as a criterion of life, a
point which is strikingly Pauline, and deserves consideration.

Justin writes:

Καὶ γὰρ πᾶν γένος ἀνθρώπων εὑρεθήσεται ὑπὸ κατάραν
ὃν κατὰ τὸν νόμον Μωϋσέως· Ἐπικατάρατος γὰρ εἴρηται
πᾶς ὃς οὐκ ἐμμένει ἐν τοῖς γεγραμμένοις ἐν τῷ βιβλίῳ
τοῦ νόμου τοῦ ποιῆσαι αὐτά. καὶ οὐδεὶς ἀκριβῶς πάντα
ἐποίησεν, οὐδ'ὑμεῖς τολμήσετε ἀντειπεῖν· ἀλλ'εἰσὶν οἱ
μᾶλλον καὶ ἧττον ἀλλήλων τὰ ἐντεταλμένα ἐφύλαξαν. εἰ δὲ
οἱ ὑπὸ τὸν νόμον τοῦτον ὑπὸ κατάραν φαίνονται εἶναι, διὰ
τὸ μὴ πάντα φυλάξαι, οὐχὶ πολὺ μᾶλλον πάντα τὰ ἔθνη φα-

----

[64]The point is made rather awkwardly in the immediate
context. Justin suggests that the Law indeed holds a curse
against all men who are crucified but not in the exceptional
case of Christ through whom God saves men who have committed
deeds truly deserving a curse, just as the command to make
the brazen serpent is not a violation of God's earlier command against the making of graven images since the brazen serpent is a special sign of the future crucifixion, the saving
mystery (Dial. 94.1ff.). Shotwell, p. 12, perhaps attributes
to Justin too much when he writes that the Apologist "states
the same argument that Paul uses in Gal. 3:10-14."

νήσονται ὑπὸ κατάραν ὄντα, καὶ εἰδωλολατροῦντα καὶ
παιδοφθοροῦντα καὶ τὰ ἄλλα κακὰ ἐργαζόμενα
(Dial. 95.1);

For every race of men will be found to be under
the curse according to the Law of Moses. For "cursed,"
it is said, "is every one who remaineth not in all the
things that are written in the book of the Law, to do
them." And no one ever did all exactly (not even you
will dare deny this), but some have kept the commands
more, and some less, than others. But if they who are
under this Law are plainly under a curse, because they
have not kept everything, how much more will all the
Gentiles plainly be under a curse, as serving idols,
and corrupting boys, with all other abominations.

In the above passage, Justin emphasizes that all of
mankind (πᾶν γένος ἀνθρώπων) is under the curse of the Law,
since no one has precisely observed all of the precepts of
the Law (οὐδεὶς ἀκριβῶς πάντα ἐποίησεν). The unfulfillability
of the Law is for Justin so self-evident that according to him
not even the Jews would, presumably as reasonable disputants,
dare to deny the point (οὐδ'ὑμεῖς τολμήσετε ἀντειπεῖν). We
have here essentially an argument a minore ad maius:[65] if the
Jews are, in terms of Dt. 27:26, under the curse of the Law,
then how much more are the gentiles who worship idols and commit all other outrageous deeds (εἰ δὲ οἱ ὑπὸ τὸν νόμον τοῦτον
ὑπὸ κατάραν φαίνονται εἶναι . . . οὐχὶ πολὺ μᾶλλον πάντα τὰ
ἔθνη). Justin goes on to suggest that this impasse of the
Law's curse confronting mankind is resolved through the
atoning death of Christ (Dial. 95.2-3; cf. 94.5).

Although the Rabbinic teachers knew of Dt. 28 and
discussed the problem of the fulfillability of the Torah,[66]
Justin's argument in Dial. 95.1 does not arise from the Rabbinic debates, even if he is aware of them. Rather, his argument is strikingly Pauline and both of the Deuteronomic citations which he quotes appear to be taken from Galatians 3 unless we have here the correction of a scribe.

Compare the readings:

---

[65]Sibinga, p. 95.

[66]Schoeps, pp. 175ff.

Dt. 27:26

LXX(Brook-McLean):	Gal. 3:10:	Dial. 95.1:
ἐπικατάρατος πᾶς ἄνθρωπος	ἐπικατάρατος πᾶς	ἐπικατάρατος πᾶς
ὃς οὐκ ἐμμενεῖ ἐν πᾶσιν	ὃς οὐκ ἐμμένει πᾶσιν	ὃς οὐκ ἐμμένει
τοῖς λόγοις	τοῖς γεγραμμένοις	τοῖς γεγραμμένοις
τοῦ νόμου τούτου	ἐν τῷ βιβλίῳ τοῦ νόμου	ἐν τῷ βιβλίῳ τοῦ νόμου
ποιῆσαι αὐτούς.	τοῦ ποιῆσαι αὐτά.	τοῦ ποιῆσαι αὐτά.

Dt. 21:23

LXX(Brook-McLean):	Gal. 3:13:	Dial. 96.1:
κεκαταραμένος ὑπὸ θεοῦ	ἐπικατάρατος	ἐπικατάρατος
πᾶς	πᾶς ὁ	πᾶς ὁ
κρεμάμενος	κρεμάμενος	κρεμάμενος
ἐπὶ ξύλου.	ἐπὶ ξύλου.	ἐπὶ ξύλου.

After a careful study of these readings, Sibinga de-
cides that Justin's text of these quotations is half way between Paul's and the Septuagint and that Justin probably did not
take the citations directly from Galatians.[67] Sibinga bases his
conclusion partly on emendations of the first citation which
bring Justin's reading of Dt. 27:26 closer to the Septuagint,
and partly on the fact that Justin changes Paul's interpretation
of the Deuteronomic quotes.[68] The evidence, however, does not
justify this conclusion. First of all, there can be no question
about the proximity of Justin's text of Dt. 21:23 and Gal. 3:13,
as we have them, which are identical and very different from
the Septuagint. As Sibinga himself observes,[69] Justin explicitly rejects the contention that God accurses the crucified One
(οὐχ ὡς τοῦ θεοῦ καταρωμένου τούτου τοῦ ἐσταυρωμένου, Dial.
96.1), as might be suggested by the Septuagint (κεκαταραμένος
ὑπὸ θεοῦ). This may very well be the reason why Justin chooses
the Pauline, rather than the Septuagintal, reading.

---

[67]Sibinga, pp. 98-99.

[68]Pp. 94-97. Paul applies Dt. 27:26 to the Jews, whereas Justin applies it to all men. Paul applies Dt. 21:23 to
Christ, but Justin does not. Justin accepts that Dt. 21:23 entails a curse on crucified men, but the case of God's Messiah is
for him an exception (Dial. 94.5). He also interprets Dt.
21:23 as a prophecy of what the Jews would do, cursing Christ
(Dial. 96.1).

[69]Ibid., p. 95.

Secondly, the change of the Pauline interpretation is not at all decisive as far as the question of whether or not Justin has used the Pauline quotations. Justin is not explicitly appealing to Paul, nor can he necessarily be expected faithfully to reproduce Paul's interpretation of the texts, even though he is borrowing from Paul as he seems to do. It is quite likely that he found Paul's application of Dt. 21:23 to Christ, as well as Paul's language γενόμενος ὑπὲρ ἡμῶν κατάρα, offensive. He thus had to modify the Pauline argument.

Furthermore, the textual emendations of Dt. 27:26 which are proposed by Sibinga are not so weighty or so securely supported to warrant Sibinga's conclusions. Manuscript evidence is lacking. Sibinga can only argue from the context of <u>Dial</u>. 95.1. But his arguments can be disputed. First, that Justin originally read πᾶς ἄνθρωπος with the <u>LXX</u>, instead of simply πᾶς with Gal. 3:10, because of his reference to πᾶν γένος ἀνθρώπων in <u>Dial</u>. 95.1, is weakly put forward by Sibinga in the form of a rhetorical question: would Justin have found occasion to bring πᾶν γένος ἀνθρώπων under a curse if the text of Dt. 27:26 read merely πᾶς instead of πᾶς ἄνθρωπος with the Septuagint?[70] Sibinga, however, fails to see that Justin does not simply say πάντες ἄνθρωποι but precisely πᾶν γένος ἀνθρώπων and that this expression for Justin is not an unusual expression triggered here allegedly by the Septuagint. Rather it is a common and very frequent designation of mankind in both of Justin's works (e.g., <u>Dial</u>. 23.1; 64.2; 88.4; 93.1; 124.1).[71] As far as the wider application of Dt. 27:26 to all nations is concerned, Sibinga himself notes that Justin likes to stress the universal character of Christianity and of Christian salvation.[72] There is, therefore, no need for Sibinga's above emendation.

The second emendation, reading πᾶσιν before τοῖς γεγραμμένοις because Justin emphasizes that οὐδεὶς ἀκριβῶς πάντα ἐποίησεν . . . διὰ τὸ μὴ πάντα φυλάξαι (<u>Dial</u>. 95.1), is common

---

[70]<u>Ibid</u>.

[71]See also <u>Ap</u>. 15.6; 25.1; 31.7; 39.3; 46.2; 50.12.

[72]Sibinga, p. 95.

among the editors.[73] But this reading appears also in Paul and
does not, therefore, necessarily bring Justin's text closer to
the Septuagint. Justin could well be dependent on Paul. The
third and final emendation proposed by Sibinga, reading τοῦ νόμου τούτου instead of simply τοῦ νόμου, because of Justin's
phrase οἱ ὑπὸ τὸν νόμον <u>τοῦτον</u> in <u>Dial</u>. 95.1, is indeed possible and one which would admittedly suggest affinities with the
Septuagint. However, the use of the pronoun οὗτος in the a-
forementioned phrase can be differently explained in the context of <u>Dial</u>. 95.1. If it is not merely an emphatic reference
to the antecedent κατὰ τὸν νόμον Μωϋσέως, it may well be a way
of avoiding the awkward linguistic combination ὑπὸ τὸν νόμον
ὑπὸ κατάραν which is conveniently broken by οὗτος (ὑπὸ τὸν νόμου τοῦτον ὑπὸ κατάραν). This last emendation, too, is not
sufficiently grounded to support Sibinga's conclusion.

On the other hand, the positive evidence linking Justin's use of these texts with Galatians is much stronger. The
reading of the text of Dt. 21:23 by Justin and Paul is identical. Justin's reading of τοῖς γεγραμμένοις ἐν τῷ βιβλίῳ τοῦ
νόμου and τοῦ ποιῆσαι αὐτὰ in connection with Dt. 27:26 is also
the same as Paul's. The phrase ὑπὸ κατάραν (εὑρεθήσεται ὑπὸ
κατάραν ὄν), repeated twice more by the Apologist in the context
of <u>Dial</u>. 95.1, is probably Pauline as well (cf. ὑπὸ κατάραν
εἰσίν, Gal. 3:10). Finally most decisive of all is Justin's association of the two Deuteronomic texts. This association can
hardly be coincidental. Nor is there a trace of any evidence of
a testimony tradition which either Justin alone, or both Justin
and Paul, as Sibinga likes to conjecture,[74] utilize. These
texts are rarely cited in early Christian sources[75] and never

---

[73]So Otto and Archambault, but not Goodspeed.

[74]<u>Ibid</u>., p. 97.

[75]Only Dt. 21:23 by way of Gal. 3:13, in contexts where
the reference to Paul or to Pauline writings is quite explicit.
See Irenaeus, <u>Adv. Haer</u>. 3.19.3 (ἐπικατάρατος πᾶς ὁ κρεμάμενος
ἐπὶ ξύλου) and Tertullian, <u>Adv. Marc</u>. 3.18.1 ("maledictus omnis
qui pependerit in ligno") and 5.3.10 ("maledictus omnis ligno
suspensus"). In the latter reference Tertullian states that
Marcion accepted Dt. 21:23 at face value and contended that
Christ was indeed cursed by the Creator God. Cf. the citation
of Gal. 3:13 and Dt. 21:21-22 in Ps. Tert., <u>Adv. Jud</u>. 10.1-3.

within the same context, except in Justin and Paul. One can
only conclude that, as far as the evidence is concerned, unless
we have here the unlikely intervention of a copyist,[76] the Deuteronomic texts are taken from the Letter to the Galatians.
Justin's argument concerning the unfulfillability of the Law and
the impasse of the Law's curse is dependent on Paul. Thus, Justin's third Scriptural argument regarding the invalidity of the
Law as a criterion of salvation is an adaptation of the Pauline
argument and establishes a clear link between Justin and Paul.

B. Arguments from Reality

Thus far we have examined arguments about the invalidity of the Law which Justin grounds in the immediate authority
of Scripture. But Justin supports his thesis of the invalidity
of the Law also with other arguments based on reality as he conceives of it. It is his contention that his arguments are drawn
both from Scripture and from reality. In Dial. 28.3, Justin
tells Trypho: ἀπό τε τῶν γραφῶν καὶ τῶν πραγμάτων τάς τε ἀποδείξεις ποιοῦμαι. ᾽Απὸ τῶν πραγμάτων signifies proofs from
facts, especially facts from the history of salvation, based on
the discernment of reason. The term πράγματα is particularly
associated by Justin with things which he regards as the historical fulfilment of Old Testament prophecies.[77] But more widely,
this same term denotes facts or aspects of the history of salvation, nature and the cosmos which are logically inferred.[78]

These arguments from reality are not extensively developed philosophical arguments, such as we find in the prologue
of the Dialogue. Nor is "reality" conceived of in the height-

---

[76]We have no evidence of such an intervention by a
copyist. Moreover, as we have noted above, Justin himself rejects that God accurses the crucified One, as may be inferred
from the Septuagintal reading of Dt. 21:23 (Dial. 96.1).

[77]See Dial. 91.3; 105.4; 114.2. In this sense, Justin's
whole Christological proof is a quasi-philosophical argument
which the Apologist calls μεγίστη καὶ ἀληθεστάτη ἀπόδειξις
(Ap. 30.1) and ἡ ἀπόδειξις Χριστοῦ (Dial. 120.5). This is the
touchstone of his argumentation in the Apology (chaps. 30ff.).
He also appeals to it frequently in the Dialogue (Dial. 7.1-2;
23.4; 28.2; 67.3; 91.3; 105.4; 114.2).

[78]See Dial. 23.4; 28.2; 67.3; 123.2.

ened philosophical sense. Rather, they are for the most part
simple arguments drawn from events, persons and instances of
the history of salvation, or from the practice of the Mosaic
Law, as well as from the realm of nature and the cosmos. Some
are attested in the Graeco-Roman pagan tradition critical of the
Jews and of Jewish practices. The others are derived from the
Christian tradition which Justin reworks and develops. All of
them have a common purpose, to demonstrate that the Mosaic Law
is temporal rather than eternal, incidental rather than essential, limited rather than universal, and thus to support Justin's thesis regarding the rightful cessation of the Law. As
such, they also provide justification and reinforcement of Justin's interpretation of the purpose of the Law as historical
legislation intended strictly for the Jews.

These arguments are not presented by Justin in any systematic way. Although some enjoy greater prominence than others, all of them occur in various parts of the Dialogue dealing
with the Law, sometimes combined with other concerns (e.g.,
Dial. 40.1-2; 46.1ff.), more often combined with one another
(e.g., Dial. 23.3-5; 27.5; 29.3). A good example of the latter
case is Dial. 29.3 at the end of the main unit on the Law, where
Justin tells Trypho:

> μὴ οὖν ἄχθεσθε, μηδὲ ὀνειδίζετε ἡμῖν τὴν τοῦ σώματος
> ἀκροβυστίαν, ἣν αὐτὸς ὁ θεὸς ἔπλασε, μηδέ, ὅτι θερμὸν
> πίνομεν ἐν τοῖς σάββασι, δεινὸν ἡγεῖσθε· ἐπειδὴ καὶ ὁ
> θεὸς τὴν αὐτὴν διοίκησιν τοῦ κόσμου ὁμοίως καὶ ἐν ταύτη
> τῇ ἡμέρᾳ πεποίηται καθάπερ καὶ ἐν ταῖς ἄλλαις ἁπάσαις,
> καὶ οἱ ἀρχιερεῖς τὰς προσφορὰς καθὰ καὶ ταῖς ἄλλαις
> ἡμέραις καὶ ἐν ταύτῃ κεκελευσμένοι ἦσαν ποιεῖσθαι, καὶ
> οἱ τοσοῦτοι δίκαιοι μηδὲν τούτων τῶν νομίμων πράξαντες
> μεμαρτύρηνται ὑπὸ τοῦ θεοῦ αὐτοῦ (Dial. 29.3).

> Be not therefore vexed, nor reproach us with the uncir-
> cumcision of our body, which God Himself formed, nor
> think it shocking that we drink hot water on the sab-
> baths; since even God has ordered the governance of the
> world on this and on all other days alike, and the high
> priests have been commanded to make the offerings as on
> the other days so also on this, and such numbers of
> righteous men, although they practised none of these
> ordinances, have received testimony from God Himself.

In one single paragraph Justin combines arguments from creation,
from the cosmos, from the Law and the history of salvation to
indicate the non-essential character of the Law. In what follows, these and similar arguments are examined separately.

(1) Most important for the Apologist is the argument
from the history of salvation, having two aspects. The first,
occurring as the last point in the above summarizing paragraph,
is simply the fact that many of the Old Testament righteous
lived and found full acceptance by God without the Law. Righteous men and women who lived during the earlier period of the
divine economy, prior to Moses and Abraham, says Justin, did not
have the Law, nor consequently did they observe it. However,
they pleased God. Therefore, reasons Justin, the Law was never
an essential criterion of righteousness, a necessary prerequisite to salvation.

In _Dial_. 19.3-5, the Apologist writes:

εἰ γὰρ ἀναγκαία [ἡ περιτομή], ὡς δοκεῖτε, οὐκ ἂν ἀκρόβυστον ὁ θεὸς ἔπλασε τὸν ᾿Αδάμ, οὐδὲ ἐπέβλεψεν ἐπὶ
τοῖς δώροις τοῦ ἐν ἀκροβυστίᾳ σαρκὸς προσενέγκαντος
θυσίας ῎Αβελ, οὐδ᾿ἂν εὐαρέστησεν ἐν ἀκροβυστίᾳ ᾿Ενώχ,
καὶ οὐκ εὑρίσκετο, διότι μετέθηκεν αὐτὸν ὁ θεός. Λὼτ
ἀπερίτμητος ἐκ Σοδόμων ἐσώθη, αὐτῶν ἐκείνων τῶν ἀγγέ-
λων αὐτὸν καὶ τοῦ κυρίου προπεμψάντων. Νῶε, ἀρχὴ γένους ἄλλου, ἅμα τοῖς τέκνοις ἀπερίτμητος εἰς τὴν κι-
βωτὸν εἰσῆλθεν. ἀπερίτμητος ἦν ὁ ἱερεὺς τοῦ ὑψίστου
Μελχισεδέκ, ᾧ καὶ δεκάτας προσφορὰς ἔδωκεν ᾿Αβραάμ,
ὁ πρῶτος τὴν κατὰ σάρκα περιτομὴν λαβών, καὶ εὐλόγη-
σεν αὐτόν . . . καὶ γὰρ μὴ σαββατίσαντες οἱ προωνο-
μασμένοι πάντες δίκαιοι τῷ θεῷ εὐαρέστησαν καὶ μετ᾿
αὐτοὺς ᾿Αβραὰμ καὶ οἱ τούτου υἱοὶ ἅπαντες μέχρι
Μωϋσέως.

For if it [_i.e._, circumcision] were necessary, as ye
think, God would not have formed Adam uncircumcised,
nor would He have looked with favour upon the gifts of
Abel who offered sacrifices in uncircumcision of the
flesh, nor would Enoch in uncircumcision have "pleased"
Him, and "he was not, for God translated him." Lot was
saved out of Sodom without circumcision, when those
very angels and the Lord led him forth. Noah, as the
head of another race, entered into the ark together
with his children, without circumcision. The priest
of God most High, Melchizedek, was without circumcision,
and he had tithes given him by Abraham as offerings,
and Abraham was the first to receive the circumcision
that is after the flesh, and was blessed by Melchizedek
. . . For, moreover, without keeping the sabbath all
the righteous men who have already been named pleased
God, and after them Abraham and all his sons until
Moses.

This is the first occurrence of the argument from the
history of salvation. It is found in a context where Justin
wants to demonstrate that the Law is necessary only for a special purpose (_Dial_. 18.2ff.) and for the Jews alone. Having
the Genesis narrative in mind, Justin states that circumcision

was not necessary for Abel, Enoch, Lot, Noah and Melchizedek
prior to Abraham, nor was the sabbath necessary either for these
Old Testament righteous or for Abraham and his posterity, until
the time of Moses. All of these righteous lived and pleased
God without observance of the Law. The above list begins with
Adam, a name which in other similar passages (Dial. 46.3; cf.
92.2) concerning the Old Testament righteous is omitted. The
point about the creation of man in an uncircumcised state seems
to be part of an independent argument and will be considered
later.

In Dial. 23.3, the same argument from the history of
salvation is more briefly stated and combined with other arguments from reality. If there were no need of circumcision and
other precepts of the Law prior to Moses and Abraham, says Justin, neither is there need of them now with the coming of
Christ: εἰ γὰρ πρὸ τοῦ ᾿Αβραὰμ οὐκ ἦν χρεία περιτομῆς οὐδὲ
πρὸ Μωϋσέως σαββατισμοῦ καὶ ἑορτῶν καὶ προσφορῶν, οὐδὲ νῦν, μετὰ τὸν . . . Χριστόν, ὁμοίως ἐστὶ χρεία (Dial. 23.3). The same
point is repeated in a more general way in Dial. 27.5[79] and also
in Dial. 29.3,[80] again combined with other similar arguments.
In Dial. 46.3, Justin expands the list of the Old Testament
righteous to include women and indicates that his list is not
exhaustive. The Apologist writes:

> Κἀγὼ ἔφην· ᾿Αβραὰμ καὶ ᾿Ισαὰκ καὶ ᾿Ιακὼβ καὶ Νῶε
> καὶ ᾿Ιώβ, καὶ εἴ τινες ἄλλοι γεγόνασι πρὸ τούτων ἢ με-
> τὰ τούτους ὁμοίως δίκαιοι, λέγω δὲ καὶ Σάρραν τὴν γυ-
> ναῖκα τοῦ ᾿Αβραάμ, καὶ ῾Ρεβέκκαν τὴν τοῦ ᾿Ισαάκ, καὶ
> ῾Ραχὴλ τὴν τοῦ ᾿Ιακώβ, καὶ Λείαν, καὶ τὰς λοιπὰς ἄλλας
> τὰς τοιαύτας μέχρι τῆς Μωϋσέως, τοῦ πιστοῦ θεράποντος,
> μητρός, μηδὲν τούτων φυλάξαντας, εἰ δοκοῦσιν ὑμῖν σω-
> θήσεσθαι (Dial. 46.3);

> And I said: Does it seem to you that Abraham and
> Isaac and Jacob and Noah and Job, and any other simi-
> larly righteous men before or after these, and, fur-
> ther, Sarah the wife of Abraham, and Rebecca the wife
> of Isaac, and Rachel the wife of Jacob, and Leah, and
> all the other women of that kind until the mother of
> of Moses, the faithful attendant, though they kept
> none of these things, will be saved?

---

[79] καὶ τοὺς πρὸ Μωϋσέως καὶ ᾿Αβραὰμ ὠνομασμένους δικαίους
καὶ εὐαρέστους αὐτῷ [τῷ θεῷ] γενομένους, μήτε τὴν ἀκροβυστίαν
περιτετμημένους μήτε τὰ σάββατα φυλάξαντας, διὰ τί οὐκ ἐδίδασκε
ταῦτα ποιεῖν;

[80] καὶ οἱ τοσοῦτοι δίκαιοι μηδὲν τούτων τῶν νομίμων
πράξαντες μεμαρτύρηνται ὑπὸ τοῦ θεοῦ αὐτοῦ.

112

Elsewhere in Dial. 67.7, he states that both the righteous and
the Patriarchs prior to Moses will enjoy God's inheritance without having observed any part of the Law.[81] In a final reference
the argument is reiterated in the form of an exegetical problem
(Dial. 92.2),[82] and shortly afterwards a parenthetical comment
is added, emphasizing the length of the pre-Mosaic period (πολλαὶ γὰρ γενεαὶ ἀνθρώπων πρὸ Μωϋσέως φαίνονται γεγενημέναι,
Dial. 92.5).

We have thus in Justin a periodization of salvation
history into (a) a pre-Law epoch prior to Moses and to Abraham,
(b) a Law epoch until Christ, which is related only to the
Jews, and (c) the universal epoch beginning with Christ.[83] To
be sure, Justin's three-fold periodization of salvation history
is not as explicit as von Campenhausen seems to suggest. The
three-fold classification of history is less defined than the
tripartite division of the Law. Justin nowhere speaks of a division of the history of salvation. There is nothing comparable
to the statement of Dial. 44.2 which classifies the Law and the
Old Testament into various parts. Nor is Justin interested in
the pre-Mosaic period for its own sake. Only on one occasion
and in passing does he state in positive terms[84] that Enoch and
others like him observed the true spiritual circumcision. Rather, his chief interest is to state that the Old Testament right-
ous neither had the Law nor consequently did they observe it,

---

[81]οἱ πρὸ Μωϋσέως γενόμενοι δίκαιοι καὶ πατριάρχαι,
μηδὲν φυλάξαντες τῶν ὅσα ἀποδείκνυσιν ὁ λόγος ἀρχὴν διαταγῆς
εἰληφέναι διὰ Μωϋσέως, σώζονται ἐν τῇ τῶν μακαρίων κληρονομίᾳ
ἢ οὔ (Dial. 67.7); Trypho answers positively. For the same
point see also Dial. 26.1.

[82]εἰ γάρ τις ἐξετάζειν βούλοιτο ὑμᾶς, ὅτι ᾽Ενὼχ καὶ Νῶε
ἅμα τοῖς τέκνοις, καὶ εἴ τινες ἄλλοι τοιοῦτοι γεγόνασι, μήτε ἐν
περιτομῇ γενόμενοι μήτε σαββατίσαντες εὑρέστησαν τῷ θεῷ, τίς ἡ
αἰτία τοῦ δι᾽ἄλλων προστατῶν καὶ νομοθεσίας μετὰ τοσαύτας γενεὰς
ἀξιοῦν τὸν θεὸν δικαιοῦσθαι τοὺς μὲν ἀπὸ ᾽Αβραὰμ μέχρι Μωϋσέως
διὰ περιτομῆς, τοὺς δὲ ἀπὸ Μωϋσέως καὶ διὰ περιτομῆς καὶ τῶν ἄλλων ἐντολῶν, τοῦτ᾽ἐστι σαββάτου καὶ θυσιῶν καὶ σποδῶν καὶ προσφορῶν.

[83]Von Campenhausen, Die Entstehung, pp. 116ff.

[84]οὐ ταύτην τὴν κατὰ σάρκα παρελάβομεν περιτομήν, ἀλλὰ
πνευματικήν, ἣν ᾽Ενὼχ καὶ οἱ ὅμοιοι ἐφύλαξαν (Dial. 43.2). Cf.
Dial. 45.4.

his purpose being to minimize the importance and the value of the Mosaic Law (μὴ σαββατίσαντες, Dial. 19.5; οἳ μήτε περιτομὴν τὴν κατὰ σάρκα ἔχοντες μήτε σάββατα ἐφύλαξαν, Dial. 23.1; τοὺς πρὸ Μωϋσέως καὶ ᾽Αβραὰμ ὠνομασμένους δικαίους . . . μήτε τὴν ἀκροβυστίαν περιτετμημένους μήτε τὰ σάββατα φυλάξαντας, Dial. 27.5; cf. 29.3; 46.3-4; 67.7).

What leads Justin to develop this argument? In the Dialogue this argument is addressed to Jews. But Justin's defense of the consistency of God in view of the variety of divine dispensations in history (Dial. 23.1; 30.1; 92.5) is not totally explained by Justin's debate with Judaism. Rather it suggests that his germinal periodization of history first arises out of his confrontation with Marcion. It was Marcion, not the Jews, who had interests to impugne the consistency and wisdom of the Creator. It was against Marcion and his followers that the purposefulness of the Mosaic Law as an historic dispensation had particularly to be defended. Thus Justin, once again, utilizes an argument against the Jews which he had previously developed against Marcion, quite probably in the Syntagma.

Confirmation of this fact may be found in Tertullian and Irenaeus. A similar defense of God's dispensations against the Marcionites occurs in the anti-heretical works of both of these writers who seem to continue Justin's argumentation: the same God, the God of the Old Testament, legislates according to circumstances different things at different times with beneficent purposes.[85] However, in the case of these writers, unlike in that of Justin, the argument is further elaborated and involves above all a concept of historical development of which there is no sign in the Dialogue.[86] Furthermore, both Irenaeus and Tertullian show a greater interest in the Old Testament Patriarchs and other righteous prior to Moses as bearers of the

---

[85]Irenaeus, Adv. Haer. 4.18-19 ("Una enim salus et unus Deus; quae autem formant hominem, praecepta multa, et non pauci gradus qui adducunt hominem ad Deum," 4.19.2); 4.34.7 ("Per multas dispositiones ostendens Deum"). Tertullian, Adv. Marc. 4.1 and 33; Adv. Jud. 2. See also Prigent, Justin et l'Ancien Testament, pp. 252-55, who finds definite links between Justin and, on the other hand, Tertullian and Irenaeus.

[86]See above, pp. 87-90.

unwritten natural law.[87] Finally, Tertullian using the same history of salvation argument against the Jews speaks specifically of different "periods" in the divine economy.[88] Cyprian, too, utilizes the argument that the Old Testament figures such as Abel, Enoch, Noah and Melchizedek were found righteous but were uncircumcised (Ad Quir. 1.8).

That the Old Testament righteous and Patriarchs did not have the Mosaic Law is not an original observation of any of the above writers. Already Paul suggests as much in Galatians 3, known to all of these writers, but even before him the relationship of the Old Testament Patriarchs to the Mosaic Law was a problem for the Jewish tradition. The Rabbinic teachers believed that certain laws for all mankind were given to Adam and again to Noah after the flood for all his descendants.[89] They also considered whether or not the Mosaic Law had been known to the Patriarchs, especially Abraham, who, they said, was thoroughly versed and kept both the written and the unwritten Law.[90] Philo's view of the Patriarchs as ἔμψυχοι καὶ λογικοὶ νόμοι is well known.[91]

Justin, however, shows no evidence of dependence on the Jewish tradition for his view of the Old Testament righteous

---

[87]Irenaeus identifies this law specifically with the Decalogue (Adv. Haer. 4.27.3). Tertullian, Adv. Jud. 2, has a more universal and more defined concept of natural law which according to him was also observed by the Patriarchs. Marcion, on the other hand, claimed that the Old Testament righteous such as Abel, Enoch, Noah and Abraham were not saved, since when Christ descended into Hades to preach they did not accept his message because they suspected that their God was tempting them once again as He had done during their life (Irenaeus, Adv. Haer. 1.25.2; cf. 4.15). The gnostics also charged the Old Testament Patriarchs with sins and crimes, against which both Irenaeus (Adv. Haer. 4.48) and Justin (Dial. 134.1; 141.4) defend. Celsus, who knew of the conflicts over the Old Testament between gnostics and Christians, repeats similar criticisms (c. Celsum 4.43).

[88]Adv. Jud. 2.9 ("et Iudaeis certis temporibus datam quando voluit et certis temporibus reformatam").

[89]Moore, I, 276.

[90]Ibid., pp. 277-78.

[91]Abr. 5. Abraham is also called ἄγραφος νόμος, Abr. 276. See further Wolfson, II, 180ff.

and of the pre-Mosaic period, even if he is acquainted with
this tradition. Rather he is dependent more immediately on
the Christian tradition. His list of the Old Testament righteous resembles the kind of Christian reflection on Old Testament figures as examples of faith and piety which is found in
Hebrews 11 and the Epistle of Clement.[92] This does not mean
that Justin is directly dependent on either Hebrews 11 or
I Clement. His mention of Rachel and Leah, names which are
quite rare in early Christian literature before him, and the
reference to the mother of Moses, which is unique, as well as
the fact that he leaves his list open (Dial. 46.3), all indicate that Justin is compiling his own list of the Old Testament
righteous and has the pentateuchal narratives also in mind.

Justin's interest in minimizing the value of the Law
and above all his use of the figures of Melchizedek and Abraham
suggest interesting similarities between Justin and, on the
other hand, Hebrews 7 and Paul. With respect to the figure of
Melchizedek whom Justin interprets as a type foreshadowing
Christ, the Apologist utilizes Gen. 14:18-20[93] and more extensively Ps. 109(LXX).[94] Although he does not quote Hebrews, nor
does he use the language of Hebrews,[95] the parallels are extremely interesting. Both Justin and the author of Hebrews
combine Gen. 14:18-20 and Ps. 109(LXX) in an exegesis comparing
Christ with Melchizedek. Both of them emphasize Melchizedek's

---

[92]Clement in different parts of his Epistle mentions
practically all of the Old Testament figures mentioned by Justin, with the notable exception of Melchizedek despite the fact
that he knows Hebrews and calls Christ "Highpriest" (I Clem.
36).

[93]He appeals to the Genesis narrative in Dial. 33.2
when he says ὁ Μελχισεδὲκ ἱερεὸς ὑψίστου ὑπὸ Μωϋσέως ἀναγέγραπται γεγενῆσθαι, but does not directly quote from it. His reference to ἱερεὸς ὑψίστου (Dial. 19.4; 33.2; 113.4), as well as
his point about the blessing of Abraham and Abraham's giving
tithes to Melchizedek (Dial. 19.4; 33.2) ultimately derive from
Gen. 14:18-20. Cf. Heb. 7:1-10.

[94]In Dial. 19.2, Justin alludes to this Psalm (οὗ κατὰ
τὴν τάξιν τὸν αἰώνιον ἱερέα ὁ θεὸς καταστήσειν διὰ τοῦ Δαυεὶδ
μεμήνυκεν). Later he quotes the whole Psalm and interprets it
on several occasions (Dial. 32.6; 33.1-2; 63.3; 83.1-3; 113.5).

[95]He calls Christ ἀρχιερέα only twice (Dial. 33.2; 116.
1) and ἱερέα, apparently taken from Ps. 109:4(LXX), far more
frequently.

116

blessing of Abraham and the latter's offering of tithes to
Melchizedek (Heb. 7:4-10; Dial. 19.4; 33.2). Both of them
stress the eternal priesthood of Christ and Christ's superiority over the Law.[96] These parallels are not sufficient to show
that Justin is dependent on Hebrews 7.[97] It is probable that
both Justin and the author of Hebrews use Old Testament texts
which are naturally associated with one another by their common
reference to Melchizedek.

     With respect to Justin and Paul the evidence is more
impressive. While Justin never refers to Paul, nor does he explicitly quote him, his interpretation of Abraham as an example
of justification through faith, not through circumcision, is
nevertheless strikingly Pauline and cannot be explained solely
on the basis of Genesis 15ff. The most important passages in
the Dialogue in this regard are the following:

'Αβραάμ, τοῦ ἐν ἀκροβυστίᾳ ἐπὶ τῇ πίστει μαρτυρηθέντος
ὑπὸ τοῦ θεοῦ καὶ εὐλογηθέντος καὶ πατρὸς πολλῶν ἐθνῶν
κληθέντος (Dial. 11.5).

Abraham, who when he was still uncircumcised received
witness from God for his faith, and was blessed, and
was called father of many nations.

καὶ γὰρ αὐτὸς ὁ 'Αβραὰμ ἐν ἀκροβυστίᾳ ὢν διὰ τὴν πίστιν,
ἣν ἐπίστευσε τῷ θεῷ, ἐδικαιώθη καὶ εὐλογήθη, ὡς ἡ γραφὴ σημαίνει· τὴν δὲ περιτομὴν εἰς σημεῖον, ἀλλ'οὐκ εἰς
δικαιοσύνην ἔλαβεν, ὡς καὶ αἱ γραφαὶ καὶ τὰ πράγματα
ἀναγκάζει ἡμᾶς ὁμολογεῖν. . . . εἰς σημεῖον ἡ περιτομὴ
αὕτη δέδοται, ἀλλ'οὐχ ὡς ἔργον δικαιοσύνης (Dial. 23.
4-5).

---

[96]However, the author of Hebrews contrasts the priesthood of Christ with the priesthood of the Mosaic cult which he
regards as the heart of the Law (Heb. 7:12). Justin refers to
Christ as the Eternal Priest throughout the Dialogue. But he
does not ever compare Christ with the priests of the Mosaic
cult. He is interested in pointing up that Melchizedek was uncircumcised, whereas Abraham at the time of his blessing and
tithing of Melchizedek was circumcised according to Justin
(Dial. 32.2; cf. 19.2). This is an error repeated by Tertullian in Adv. Marc. 5.9.9 and Adv. Jud. 3.1. For this, as well
as for his interpretation of Ps. 109(LXX) in Adv. Marc. 5.9 as
applying to Christ, not to Hezekiah as the Jews are said to
have insisted, Tertullian seems to be dependent on Justin.

[97]One might suggest that Justin, writing in Rome, knew
and had read Hebrews which was known to Clement some half century earlier. However, even if Hebrews was written in Italy,
it may not have been current there at the time of Justin.

For Abraham himself when in uncircumcision was justified and received blessing, on account of the faith
with which he believed God, as the (passage of) Scripture indicates. Now he received circumcision for a
sign, but not for righteousness, as both the Scriptures and the facts compel us to acknowledge. . . .
this circumcision has been given for a sign, and not
as a work of righteousness.

οἱ τῇ γνώμῃ ἐξομοιωθέντες τῇ πίστει τοῦ Ἀβραάμ (Dial.
44.2).

They who have become in their mind like to the faith
of Abraham.

οὐδὲ γὰρ Ἀβραάμ διὰ τὴν περιτομὴν δίκαιος εἶναι ὑπὸ
τοῦ θεοῦ ἐμαρτυρήθη, ἀλλὰ διὰ τὴν πίστιν· πρὸ τοῦ γὰρ
περιτμηθῆναι αὐτὸν εἴρηται περὶ αὐτοῦ οὕτως· Ἐπίστευσε δὲ Ἀβραάμ τῷ θεῷ, καὶ ἐλογίσθη αὐτῷ εἰς δικαιοσύνην (Dial. 92.3).

For not even to Abraham was witness borne by God that
he was righteous because of his circumcision, but because of his faith. For before he was circumcised it
was thus said of him: "And Abraham believed God, and
it was counted to him for righteousness."

Σὺν τῷ Ἀβραάμ . . . τὴν κληρονομίαν ληψόμενοι, τέκνα
τοῦ Ἀβραάμ διὰ τὴν ὁμοίαν πίστιν ὄντες (Dial. 119.5).

We shall inherit . . . together with Abraham . . . as
being children of Abraham because we have like faith
with him.

The above passages indicate that Justin appeals directly to the Old Testament (ὡς ἡ γραφὴ σημαίνει, Dial. 23.4)
which he quotes in Dial. 92.3 (Gen. 15:6). The citation of
Gen. 15:6 occurs of course also in Gal. 3:6 and Rm. 4:3 without significant variations. It is not impossible that, as in
the previous case of Dt. 27:26 and 21:23 which we have examined,
Justin is borrowing the citation from Paul. It is thoroughly
possible that at least the ultimate reference of Justin's use
of the Genesis text is Paul. The indications, however, which
definitely link Justin with the Apostle have to do with the
content of Justin's argument about Abraham. This argument
seems to presuppose in particular Romans 4 more than Genesis
15ff.

First of all, note Justin's interest in the "justification" of Abraham by God (ἐδικαιώθη, Dial. 23.4; ἐμαρτυρήθη,
Dial. 92.3; cf. 11.5). This is not so emphatic in the context
of Gen. 15, despite the statement καὶ ἐλογίσθη αὐτῷ εἰς δικαιοσύνην (Gen. 15:6) which attracts the attention both of the
Apostle and the Apologist. In similar fashion Justin's

118

terminology ἐδικαιώθη, ἔργον δικαιοσύνης (Dial. 23.5) and above all πίστις and πίστις 'Αβραάμ (Dial. 44.2), moves beyond the Genesis context into the Pauline world. Romans 4 begins with the question of whether or not Abraham ἐδικαιώθη (Rm. 4:2) and has much to say about the faith of Abraham (Rm. 4:5,9,12,16). Indeed the parallel which Justin draws between the faith of Abraham and the faith of Christians, giving the latter the status of children of Abraham (Dial. 44.2; 119.5), cannot be explained apart from Rm. 4:11-12 (cf. Gal. 3:7).[98] Most decisive of all is Justin's emphasis on the uncircumcision of Abraham at the time he received the promised blessing (Dial. 11.5; 23.4; 93.2) and, equally true, the accompanying insistence that Abraham received circumcision as a mere sign, not as an act of intrinsic righteousness (τὴν δὲ περιτομὴν εἰς σημεῖον, ἀλλ'οὐκ εἰς δικαιοσύνην, Dial. 23.4; cf. Rm. 4:11, καὶ σημεῖον ἔλαβεν περιτομῆς σφραγῖδα τῆς δικαιοσύνης τῆς πίστεως τῆς ἐν τῇ ἀκροβυστίᾳ).[99] These emphases are not at all necessary on the basis of the context of Gen. 15-17 alone. But they are perfectly explainable in terms of Rm. 4:9-11.

One can hardly argue that Justin is in this regard presenting his own interpretation of the Genesis narrative which simply parallels that of Paul. Also, no other Christian writer prior to Justin reproduces this Pauline argument as fully as Justin does.[100] One must conclude that the Apologist knew and utilized Paul without naming him. Facing the problem of the

---

[98]The same parallel occurs in Tertullian, Adv. Marc. 5.3.11-12, and Irenaeus, Adv. Haer. 4.35.1, both of whom, interestingly, refer to Paul. Tertullian reports that Marcion erased Abraham's name from Gal. 3 (Adv. Marc. 5.3.11). He believed that Abraham's God was only the Creator God, a God of a family clan (Adv. Marc. 1.10.3).

[99]The term σημεῖον occurs also in Gen. 17.11 where circumcision is said to be the sign of a covenant between God and Abraham. But the contrast with righteousness and faith is missing. For Justin's use of σημεῖον in connection with circumcision, see below, 135ff.

[100]We have two references in the Apostolic Fathers. In Barn. 30.7 there is a conflation of Gen. 15:6; 17:5 and Rm. 4: 11: τί οὖν λέγει τῷ 'Αβραάμ, ὅτε μόνος πιστεύσας ἐτέθη εἰς δικαιοσύνην; 'Ιδού, τέθεικά σε, 'Αβραάμ, πατέρα ἐθνῶν τῶν πιστευόντων δι'ἀκροβυστίας τῷ θεῷ. In I Clem. 10.6, Gen. 15:6 is quoted together with other passages from Genesis and Abraham is presented as an example of faith and hospitality (10.7). Cf. Jm. 2:23.

Law as sharply as Paul did, Justin adopts a similar view of the
history of salvation and attempts to minimize the significance
of the period of the Law as both temporary and secondary. The
Mosaic Law, being legislation only for the Jews and given on
account of their hardness of heart, argues Justin, adds nothing
essential to God's revelation. The Old Testament righteous
lived and pleased God without the Law. But Justin, unlike Paul,
does not concentrate on Abraham alone. Rather he looks from
Abraham backwards to all of the Old Testament righteous, and
extends the pre-Mosaic period indefinitely back to creation.
At the same time he draws an inference which is found only implicitly in Romans 4 and Galatians 3. If the Mosaic Law was
not necessary as a criterion of righteousness prior to Moses,
then, claims Justin, neither is it necessary as a prerequisite
to salvation now with the coming of Christ. Its complete cessation with the inauguration of the universal period of the New
Covenant and the New Law is thus justified. The only necessary
criterion of righteousness is now Christ and the Gospel.

This is the first aspect of the history of salvation argument having to do with the pre-Mosaic period. A second facet
is based on the destruction of Jerusalem in 70 A.D. as an event
of theological significance. Although far less prominent in the
Dialogue, occurring only in Dial. 40.1-5 and 46.2, this argument
is fairly important to Justin and adds a tone of finality to the
thesis of the cessation of the Law. According to Justin, the
destruction of Jerusalem and the Temple, implying of necessity
the cessation of the cult, demonstrates that the Mosaic Law was
only a temporary arrangement within the divine plan. He argues
the point with reference to the sacrifice of the Passover lamb
and the offering of the two goats on the Day of Atonement. He
writes:

καὶ ὅτι πρόσκαιρος ἦν καὶ αὕτη ἡ ἐντολή, οὕτως ἀπο-
δείκνυμι. οὐδαμοῦ θύεσθαι τὸ πρόβατον τοῦ πάσχα ὁ
θεὸς συγχωρεῖ, εἰ μὴ ἐπὶ τόπῳ ᾧ ἐπικέκληται τὸ ὄνομα
αὐτοῦ, εἰδὼς ὅτι ἐλεύσονται ἡμέραι μετὰ τὸ παθεῖν τὸν
Χριστόν, ὅτε καὶ ὁ τόπος τῆς Ἱερουσαλὴμ τοῖς ἐχθροῖς
ὑμῶν παραδοθήσεται καὶ παύσονται ἅπασαι ἁπλῶς προσφοραὶ γινόμεναι. . . . καὶ ὅτι καὶ ἡ τῶν δύο τράγων τῶν
νηστείᾳ κελευσθέντων προσφέρεσθαι προσφορὰ οὐδαμοῦ
ὁμοίως συγκεχώρηται γίνεσθαι εἰ μὴ ἐν Ἱεροσολύμοις
ἐπίστασθε (Dial. 40.1-2,5).

And that also this commandment was given only for a
season, I will now prove. God does not allow the sheep
of the Passover to be sacrificed at any other place
than that "on which His name has been called," knowing

that there would come a time after Christ had suffered, when even the place of Jerusalem would be handed over to your enemies, and all offerings should completely cease to be. . . . Now that there is no permission for the offering of the two goats which were commanded to be brought at the Fast to take place anywhere save in Jerusalem, you are fully aware.

Found in a context of the typological interpretation of the Passover lamb and of the goats of Atonement,[101] this argument is digressive. But it is not for that reason less important to Justin. Justin wants to emphasize that not only the precept of the Passover sacrifice (πρόσκαιρος ἦν καὶ αὕτη ἡ ἐντολή, Dial. 40.1), but all of the ritual precepts of the Law are temporary (παύσονται ἅπασαι ἁπλῶς προσφοραὶ γινόμεναι, Dial. 40.2; 46.2). He anchors this argument on Dt. 16:5-6 and the stipulation that the Passover sacrifice cannot be celebrated elsewhere than in Jerusalem. He alludes to this text in Dial. 40.2: οὐδαμοῦ θύεσθαι τὸ πρόβατον τοῦ πάσχα ὁ θεὸς συγχωρεῖ, εἰ μὴ ἐπὶ τόπῳ ᾧ ἐπικέκληται τὸ ὄνομα αὐτοῦ. God, according to Justin, foreknew that after the death of Christ Jerusalem would fall to the enemies of the Jews, suggesting that the temporal character and the cessation of the Mosaic cult was within the divine plan of history (Dial. 40.2).

In its specific form, this argument seems to be Justin's own and does not have as much currency in the early Christian centuries as one might think. In a more primitive form, it is found in Barn. 16.1-5 where, compiling various apocalyptic predictions of the destruction of the Temple, the author suggests that the Temple was destroyed according to the divine will because the Jews falsely placed their hope on the building rather than on God. Justin's point, however, is different. For the Apologist the destruction of the Temple indicates that the Law is temporary and was destined to cease according to the divine will. Tertullian in Adv. Jud. 5.3 refers to the prohibition that sacrifices may be offered only in the holy land ("nusquam alibi nisi in terra sanctam"), which he attributes to Leviticus,[102] but he does not mention the destruction of the Temple. Instead, he quotes Mal. 1:10-11 and argues that the prophecy of

---

[101] See above, p. 59f.

[102] Probably Lev. 17:3-6 and the injunction to present animals for slaughter at the local sanctuary.

the universal offering of sacrifices to God indicates that God
prefers spiritual rather than material sacrifices. Eusebius,
too, in Dem. Evan. 1.6.47, mentions the prohibition of sacrifices outside of Jerusalem, but in an entirely different context. Chrysostom much later in his Adversus Judaeos, especially
the third and fourth homilies, makes much of the temporal and
geographic limitation of the Jewish cult. He also refers both
to the Deuteronomic stipulation and to the destruction of Jerusalem which he attributes to the divine will.[103]

(2) A second argument from reality which Justin invokes
to demonstrate the contingency and lack of ultimate value in the
Law is the apparent contradiction between some of the Law's precepts. This argument is not developed to any extent by Justin.
It occurs twice in summarizing statements intending to show the
temporal and non-essential character of the Law (Dial. 27.5;
29.3). The relevant passages are the following:

ἐπεί, εἴπατέ μοι, τοὺς ἀρχιερεῖς ἀμαρτάνειν τοῖς σάβ-
βασι προσφέροντας τὰς προσφορὰς ἐβούλετο ὁ θεός, ἢ τοὺς
περιτεμνομένους καὶ περιτέμνοντας τῇ ἡμέρᾳ τῶν σαββάτων,
κελεύων τῇ ἡμέρᾳ τῇ ὀγδόῃ ἐκ παντὸς περιτέμνεσθαι τοὺς
γεννηθέντας ὁμοίως, κἂν ᾖ ἡμέρα τῶν σαββάτων; ἢ οὐκ ἠ-
δύνατο πρὸ μιᾶς ἡμέρας ἢ μετὰ μίαν ἡμέραν τοῦ σαββάτου
ἐνεργεῖν περιτέμνεσθαι τοὺς γεννωμένους, εἰ ἠπίστατο
κακὸν εἶναι ἐν τοῖς σάββασιν (Dial. 27.5);

Since, tell me, did God wish the high priests to sin,
when they offered the offerings on the sabbath, or them
that get circumcised, and also circumcise, on the sabbath-day, when He commanded that those that were born
should be circumcised without fail on the eighth day in
every case alike, even though it be the sabbath-day?
Or could He not cause them that are born to be circumcised one day before or one day after the sabbath, if
He knew it was wrong on the sabbaths?

καὶ οἱ ἀρχιερεῖς τὰς προσφορὰς καθὰ καὶ ταῖς ἄλλαις
ἡμέραις καὶ ἐν ταύτῃ κεκελευσμένοι ἦσαν ποιεῖσθαι
(Dial. 29.3).

And the high priests have been commanded to make the
offerings as on the other days so also on this.

---

[103]For the interpretation of the destruction of the
Temple, especially in the Jewish tradition, see H. J. Schoeps,
Die Tempelzerstörung des Jahres 70 in der jüdischen Religions-
geschichte. Coniectanea Neotestamentica, Vol. VI (Uppsala,
1942), reprinted in his Aus frühchristlicher Zeit (Tübingen,
1950), pp. 144-83. See also his book The Jewish-Christian
Argument (New York: Holt, Rinehart and Winston, 1963), pp.
32ff.

122

The first point concerns the "violation" of the sabbath by the priests who offer sacrifices on that day and yet are found guiltless before God and the Law. Justin has probably in mind the Matthean redaction οὐκ ἀνέγνωτε ἐν τῷ νόμῳ ὅτι τοῖς σάββασιν οἱ ἱερεῖς ἐν τῷ ἱερῷ τὸ σάββατον βεβηλοῦσιν καὶ ἀναίτιοί εἰσιν (Mtt. 12:5; cf. Nm. 28:9), although he uses ἀρχιερεῖς instead of ἱερεῖς. The Jewish tradition knew of this apparent discrepancy in the Law but found no contradiction in it. Rather, it was held simply that the Temple service "pushes out," i.e., overrides the rule of the sabbath.[104] Justin, however, implicitly draws another inference from this apparent inconsistency, namely, that the Law is not of absolute significance and therefore revocable.

The second point in the above passage plays on the inevitable paradox between the rule of circumcision on the eighth day and the rule of the inviolability of the sabbath. What is to happen when the eighth day falls on a sabbath? The Rabbinic tradition permitted exceptions for reasons of health and others, which Justin does not take into consideration, and also held once again that the rule of circumcision simply supersedes the rule of the sabbath.[105] But for Justin the apparent discrepancy demonstrates that the Law is not of ultimate significance.[106] The rule of the sabbath can be broken on the basis of injunctions of the Law itself without incurrence of evil or sin before God. Therefore, reasons Justin, the Law can also entirely cease to be valid, as it well did in Christ, without intrinsic loss or serious discrepancy in the history of salvation. Irenaeus refers to these points, but he mentions them for entirely different reasons.[107] Tertullian does not mention

---

[104] See Strack-Billerbeck, I, 620.

[105] Shab. 18.3; 19.1ff. See also Moore, II, 18-19.

[106] Franklin in his dissertation, p. 169, is not correct in this instance when he thinks that Justin poses these contradictions of the Law in order to find a deeper, presumably typological or allegorical, meaning.

[107] In order to show that the Law permitted certain acts on the sabbath day and thus to defend Jesus' healings on the sabbath against Marcion who insisted that by his deeds Jesus destroyed the Law (Adv. Haer. 4.16).

them either in his <u>Adversus Marcionem</u> or his <u>Adversus Ju-</u>
<u>daeos</u>.[108]

(3) Two final arguments, one from nature and another
from the cosmos, which Justin marshals to prove the incidental
and non-essential character of the Law, take us to a markedly
different horizon, pagan literature. It is well-known that edu-
cated pagans were informed, and according to some considerably
informed,[109] about the Jews and their religion. Some pagans
were strongly attracted to Jewish traditions, while others were
repelled by them. Roman writers such as Suetonius, Juvenal,
Tacitus and Seneca were especially critical of things Jewish as
inimical to the Empire. Tacitus in particular calls the Mosaic
Law sinister and despicable (<u>Hist</u>. 5.4-5). Pagan critique of
the Jews goes back as early as the third century B.C. to Manetho
the Egyptian priest, who wrote in Greek. The Church Fathers
knew of this pagan tradition critical of the Jews, and Christian
heretics made use of it, particularly in their derision of the
Law and of the Old Testament.[110] It is not surprising to find
that Justin, too, seems to be familiar with this tradition and
that he makes occasional use of it when writing on the Mosaic
Law.

The argument from nature or from creation is simply that
man is born in a state of uncircumcision. Circumcision would
then appear as an unnatural mutilation of the body, or at least
as something that God does not sufficiently value as to have had
man created in an original state of circumcision. The Talmud

---

[108]Instead, in order to demonstrate as Justin tries to
do that the sabbath is only of temporal rather than of ultimate
significance, he appeals to the Maccabbeans' and much earlier to
Joshua's waging war on the sabbath day (<u>Adv. Jud</u>. 4.6-11). With
regard to the latter, see above, p. 24, n. 36.

[109]R. Walzer, <u>Galen on Jews and Christians</u> (Oxford,
1949), p. 20; see also R. Bergmann, <u>Jüdische Apologetik</u>
(Berlin, 1908), and John Gager, <u>The Figure of Moses in Greek</u>
<u>and Roman Pagan Literature</u> (Harvard Dissertation, 1967, pub-
lished by Abingdon Press, 1972).

[110]Origen, for example, defends the Law against its derision by both pagans and heretics. See Hanson, pp. 300f. In
<u>c. Celsum</u> 2.4, he writes that Christians do not treat the things
written in the Law with disrespect. Cf. Irenaeus, <u>Adv. Haer</u>.
4.42.1.

contains examples of Jewish apologetic against such pagan criticisms. According to one example, Tineius Rufus, Roman gover-
nor of Judea at the time of Akiba, asks why the Jews circumcize
themselves, since God's work is more beautiful than man's, and
further, if God wants circumcision, why is a child not born
circumcized? Akiba answers that God wants man to lend a hand
to His work, perfecting it to some extent, and that the work of
man sometimes is more beautiful than that of God.[111] Later, at
the time of Origen, according to another haggadic tradition, a
philosopher asks R. Hoshaya, an Amoraitic teacher, why was Adam
not created circumcized if God values circumcision so much?
The answer again is that the creation of man, as all of the
other acts of creation during the six days, permits improve-
ment.[112]

Justin apparently was familiar with the above criticism
of circumcision and utilizes it to demonstrate that circumcision is not ultimately necessary. In Dial. 19.3 he writes: εἰ
γὰρ ἦν ἀναγκαία [ἡ περιτομή], . . . οὐκ ἂν ἀκρόβυστον ὁ θεὸς
ἔπλασε τὸν 'Αδάμ. And again in Dial. 29.3: μὴ οὖν ἄχθεσθε,
μηδὲ ὀνειδίζετε ἡμῖν τὴν τοῦ σώματος ἀκροβυστίαν, ἣν αὐτὸς ὁ
θεὸς ἔπλασε. (Cf. Dial. 23.3, μείνατε ὡς γεγένησθε). The argument is not further developed. It is interesting, however, that
in Dial. 23.5 we find an extended reflection on a closely related idea which may well be Justin's own. Speaking of the faith
of Abraham and of the fact that this Patriarch received circumcision as a matter of a sign, not as an act of righteousness
(εἰς σημεῖον, ἀλλ'οὐκ εἰς δικαιοσύνην, Dial. 23.4), Justin continues:

> καὶ τὸ μὴ δύνασθαι δὲ τὸ θῆλυ γένος τὴν σαρκικὴν περιτο-
> μὴν λαμβάνειν δείκνυσιν ὅτι εἰς σημεῖον ἡ περιτομὴ αὕτη
> δέδοται, ἀλλ'οὐχ ὡς ἔργον δικαιοσύνης· τὰ γὰρ δίκαια καὶ
> ἐνάρετα ἅπαντα ὁμοίως καὶ τὰς θηλείας δύνασθαι φυλάσσειν
> ὁ θεὸς ἐποίησεν. ἀλλὰ σχῆμα μὲν τὸ τῆς σαρκὸς ἕτερον καὶ
> ἕτερον ὁρῶμεν γεγενημένον ἄρρενος καὶ θηλείας, διὰ δὲ
> τοῦτο οὐδὲ δίκαιον οὐδὲ ἄδικον οὐδέτερον αὐτῶν ἐπιστά-
> μεθα, ἀλλὰ δι'εὐσέβειαν καὶ δικαιοσύνην (Dial. 23.5).

And the fact that the female sex cannot receive carnal
circumcision, shows that this circumcision has been
given for a sign, and not as a work of righteousness.

---

[111]Bergmann, p. 103, from the Tanchumah. I am indebted
to Bergmann for most of these references.

[112]Gen. r., 11.6.

> For God made even females able to keep all the acts of
> righteousness and virtue as well as men. But we see
> that one fashion of flesh for male and another for fe-
> male has been made, yet we know that neither one of
> them is either righteous or unrighteous for this rea-
> son but only for reasons of piety and righteousness.

According to the above passage, Justin thinks that the
female by nature lacks the capacity to receive circumcision.
Created differently from the male, it cannot be, reasons Justin,
that the female was naturally excluded from observing something
truly essential. Rather, circumcision is only an external sign
involving the shape of one's body which is ethically neutral
(οὔτε δίκαιον οὔτε ἄδικον). As such, circumcision has nothing
to do with true piety and righteousness, whereas the principles
of righteousness can be observed by both males and females. It
is a strange argument and one apparently without precedent among
pagan critics of Judaism. Tightly knit as it seems to be, it
has probably been developed by Justin himself as a further reflection on the uncircumcized status of Adam.[113] Tertullian
mentions that Adam was not circumcized,[114] but says nothing
about the case of the creation of the female. Among other
Christian writers whom we have considered only Cyprian mentions
both that Adam was uncircumcized and that the female by nature
is unable to receive circumcision (Ad Quir. 1.8).

(4) The final argument from the cosmos is quite allusive in Justin. In Dial. 23.3 Justin writes: τὰ στοιχεῖα οὐκ
ἀργεῖ οὐδὲ σαββατίζει. And in Dial. 29.3 he repeats more extensively: καὶ ὁ θεὸς τὴν αὐτὴν διοίκησιν τοῦ κόσμου ὁμοίως καὶ
ἐν ταύτῃ τῇ ἡμέρᾳ [τοῦ σαββάτου] πεποίηται καθάπερ καὶ ἐν ταῖς
ἄλλαις ἀπάσαις. This argument from the cosmos, namely, that the
elements of the universe do not according to God's arrangement
rest on the sabbath day is an attested pagan criticism of the

---

[113]There is a tradition in the Talmud which raises the
question of females and circumcision but does not answer it. On
Gen. 17:14 "And the uncircumcized male," Gen. r. 46.5 reads:
"Is there then an uncircumcized female? The meaning, however,
is that we must perform circumcision on the member which marks
the distinction between male and female." It is possible that
this question is debated among the Jews to some extent and that
Justin knew about it. Neither can the same possibility be excluded also with regard to the uncircumcision of Adam (See Gen.
r. 46.3).

[114]Adv. Jud. 2.11.

sabbath rule. The Stoics thought of work as something natural
and of inactivity as unnatural. Seneca, for example, severely
criticizes what he regarded as the idleness of the sabbath
among Jews.[115] Jewish apologetic also defends against such
criticism. According to a midrashic tradition, asked why God
does not rest on the sabbath but permits the winds to blow and
to increase also on this day, Rabbi Akiba answered that God is
the tenant of the whole world and freely can move in it even on
the sabbath just as anyone according to the Law can move in his
own courtyard.[116]

Justin apparently knew of this philosophical objection
to the sabbath and utilized it. But he does not at all develop
it. He merely mentions it along with other arguments. The intention is the same, to prove the non-essential character of
the Law, the lack of ultimate value in it, and thereby to support the larger thesis that the Law has rightfully ceased as a
life norm after Christ.

Thus Justin marshals several arguments on the basis of
observable reality to support his thesis about the cessation of
the Law. Aside from the three Scriptural arguments demonstrating the cessation of the Law, four additional arguments
taken from the history of salvation, the Law, creation and the
cosmos are introduced as supportive proofs of the invalidity of
the Law, based not on the authority of Scripture but on the
force of fact and the cogency of reason. Most prominent in the
Dialogue are the former arguments, especially the Scriptural arguments regarding the abrogation of the Old Covenant by the New
and that regarding what God truly desires of men, spiritual obedience, not performance of the ritual Law. But frequently invoked is also the argument from the history of salvation emphasizing that the Old Testament righteous of the pre-Mosaic period
were justified without the Law. All of the arguments share the
same purpose: the declaration that the Mosaic Law has no absolute significance in the divine plan and is not a necessary,
abiding criterion of salvation. Contrary to the claims of Trypho, and despite the character of the Law as God's revelation

[115]Bergmann, p. 99.

[116]Ibid., p. 101.

and its undeniable place in canonical Scripture, the Law is
temporal and non-essential, designed for a particular purpose.
The cessation of the validity of the Law, and the total replace-
ment of the Law by another absolute and universal Law, Christ,
is both legitimate and fully explicable, according to Justin,
on the basis of Scripture and reason. This is Justin's thesis
about the invalidity of the Law, supported by a host of arguments and expounded for his intended Jewish readers.

C. The Law as a Matter of Indifference

After all of the arguments compiled to demonstrate the
invalidity of the Law, it may be surprising that Justin seems
to hold no decisive theological objection to the observance of
the Law post Christum, but views the Law as something ultimately
indifferent. Justin does not develop this point at any length
anywhere in the Dialogue. Rather, his view of the Law as an indifferent matter breaks incidentally into his argumentation at
different places. Moreover, allowance of the observance of the
Law is made chiefly for Jewish Christians and after certain explicit qualifications.

In Dial. 18.3 Justin states that the precepts of the
Law, such as the sabbath and the festivals, are "things which
do not hurt at all" (τὰ μηδὲ βλάπτοντα). In the context of this
passage, he is speaking of the purpose of the Law and states
that Christians would also observe circumcision, as well as the
sabbath and all of the festivals, if they did not know why the
Law had been instituted, that is, for the Jews and on account of
their hardness of heart (Dial. 18.2b). He then rhetorically reinforces the point, suggesting that Christians who are able to
endure unspeakable tribulations for their faith would also have
the courage to observe circumcision, the sabbath and the festivals of the Law, things which do not hurt the Christians in any
way: τὰ μηδὲ βλάπτοντα ἡμᾶς (Dial. 18.3).

In Dial. 23.5, as has been noted, the Apologist states
that the shape of one's body has nothing to do with true righteousness. Male was created in one fashion and female was created in another. Both, however, were created in such a fashion
as to be able to practice true righteousness (τὰ δίκαια καὶ
ἐνάρετα). Circumcision or the lack of it is a neutral thing
having to do with one's physical features, Justin suggests.

128

Dial. chaps. 45-47 express most accurately Justin's
view of the Law as something ultimately indifferent. Here the
whole point of the discussion is whether or not observance of
the Law excludes one from salvation or is entirely incompatible
with faith in Christ. Questioned by Trypho, Justin first easily allows that those who observed the Law prior to Christ will
be saved because the Law contains within it the universal principles of righteousness as well as those ritual precepts ordained for the hardness of heart of the Jews (Dial. 45.4).
Those who lived prior to Christ, having observed the Law, have
simultaneously observed the eternal ethical principles within
the Law which are essential for salvation. Salvation prior to
Christ depends not on the ritual precepts of the Law but on the
universal and eternal truths contained in the Law (τὰ καθόλου
καὶ φύσει καὶ αἰώνια καλά, Dial. 45.4).

Pressing further, Trypho asks what if some wish to observe the Law now, i.e., after Christ, while also believing in
Christ. Can they be saved (Dial. 46.1)? Justin here reaffirms
what he has said about the character and purpose of the Law.
He reminds Trypho that not all of the Mosaic precepts can any
longer be observed, such as the Passover sacrifice and the other Temple offerings, because the Temple has been destroyed
(Dial. 46.2; cf. 40.2), indicating the temporal character of
the Law. He then rehearses the argument concerning the non-
essential character of the Law, that the precepts of the Law
which can now be observed, such as circumcision and ritual
washings, are not ultimately necessary since they were not observed by the righteous of the Old Testament prior to Moses and
Abraham (Dial. 46.3-4). Such ritual precepts were ordained on
account of the hardness of heart of the Jews and in order to
nurture remembrance of God among them (Dial. 46.5). As far as
Christians are concerned, states Justin, these ritual precepts
add nothing to righteousness and piety: οὐδὲν συμβάλλεσθαι
πρὸς δικαιοπραξίαν καὶ εὐσέβειαν (Dial. 46.7b).

But if, nevertheless, one wishes to practice the Law
while yet believing in Christ, insists Trypho, will he be saved
(Dial. 47.1)? The answer is yes, but Justin sets qualifications. The context of the discussion indicates that he is
talking about Jewish Christians. Such persons who may now wish
to practice the Law, states Justin, will be saved provided that
they do not attempt to proselytize gentile Christians to the

observance of the Law and do not insist on the Law as a necessary criterion of salvation, as Trypho himself had insisted
(Dial. 47.1; cf. 8.4). Furthermore, these persons must consent
to live within the fellowship of the Church, not as sectarians
rejecting such fellowship, as some Jewish Christians according
to Justin were doing (Dial. 47.2-3). Under these qualifications, observance of the Law is allowed for Jewish Christians,
but yet as a kind of concession. Reminiscent of the language
of Paul (Rm. 14:1-2), Justin states that Jewish Christians can
practice the Law if they are compelled to do so by a certain
immaturity of thought (διὰ τὸ ἀσθενὲς τῆς γνώμης, Dial. 47.2).
Justin explicitly designates this view as his own opinion, and
not as an accepted view of the majority of gentile Christians
with whom he pointedly disagrees (Dial. 47.2).

Most interesting of all is that Justin also entertains
the possibility of the observance of the Law even by gentile
Christians. Gentile Christians who may have been persuaded to
observe the Mosaic Law, while yet retaining their faith in
Christ, are not totally excluded from salvation. They, too,
according to Justin's opinion, may possibly be saved (καὶ σωθήσεσθαι ἴσως ὑπολαμβάνω, Dial. 47.4a). Their salvation, although they observe the Law, is in the realm of possibility.
On the other hand, Justin holds no hope for either gentile
Christians who deny Christ or for Jews who never believe in
him (Dial. 47.4b-c).

From the above it is clear that the Law, according to
Justin, is ultimately a matter of indifference. Salvation is
entirely dependent on acceptance of Christ and observance of
the eternal and universal ethical principles, not the ritual
Law. The ritual Law of Moses adds nothing to righteousness
(Dial. 46.7b). However, it is not something unequivocally in-
jurious either, even for gentile Christians. Where Justin
seems to be rhetorical, he more easily allows that gentile
Christians could theoretically observe the Law without harm
(Dial. 18.2-3). But where the actual life of the Church is at
stake, he is more cautious (Dial. 47.1ff., 4a). There he sets
down qualifications for the practice of the Law even by Jewish
Christians. Nevertheless he allows such practice in striking
contrast to the attitude of other Christians of his time. His
understanding of the character and purpose of the Law entails

no decisive theological objection against observance of the
Law.   His view of the Law as something non-essential and ultimately indifferent gives him the flexibility of allowing the
practice of the Law at least among Jewish Christians who live
within the Church.

CHAPTER FOUR

THE PURPOSE OF THE LAW

If the Mosaic Law, as Justin claims, is neither a necessary nor a universal criterion of salvation, then what is its
role? If the Law has now ceased to be valid, and has been sup-
planted by the New Law, Christ, why was the Law in the first
place legislated? If the Mosaic Law is God's Law, a part of
Sacred Scripture, then what is its purpose in the divine scheme
of things?

Justin is the first Christian writer who attempts in a
systematic way to answer these questions. Earlier writers, such
as Paul, the author of Hebrews and the author of Barnabas, all
of whom share the premise that the validity of the Law has
ceased with the coming of Christ, show very little concern about
the question of the original purpose of the Law as such. Paul
who raises the question (τί οὖν ὁ νόμος, Gal. 3:19), provides
only brief and allusive answers to this query (Gal. 3:19, 22-24;
cf. Rm. 5:20). He is more concerned with demonstrating the invalidity of the Law for the present situation,[1] than he is with
explaining the purpose for which the Law was originally instituted. The author of Hebrews expounds the superiority of the
New Covenant over the Old, sharply exposing the weakness of the
Law (Heb. 7:16ff.; 8:5, 13; 10.1ff.), but never troubles himself
with the question of why then was the legislation of the whole
system of the Law in the first place necessary.[2] The author of
Barnabas simply assumes that the purpose of the Law, which was
misunderstood by the Jews, was from the beginning a spiritual,
not a literal, one (Barn. 9.4ff.).

---

[1]Von Campenhausen, Die Entstehung, p. 44, n. 56.

[2]So R. Bultmann quoted by von Campenhausen, ibid., pp.
83-84.

Justin Martyr, however, repeatedly raises the question
of the purpose of the Law and attempts to construct an extensive
formulation of the answer. In most sections of the Dialogue
where he deals with the Law, explanations of why the Law was
first ordained are frequently at the forefront (Dial. 18.2ff.;
46.5f.; 67.10; 95.2ff.). His third division of the Law, and the
one which chiefly occupies his attention, involves what Justin
conceives of as the purpose of the Law: τίς δὲ ἐντολὴ καὶ πρᾶξις ὁμοίως εἴρητο . . . διὰ τὸ σκληροκάρδιον τοῦ λαοῦ ὑμῶν
(Dial. 44.2). Indeed, even a casual reading of the Dialogue
will not fail to show that, apart from the invalidity of the
Law, the second thesis of Justin's argumentation about the Law
has to do with the original purpose of the Law.

By purpose of the Law is meant here what Justin himself
explicitly claims to be the reason or reasons why the Law was
originally given (διὰ τί προσετάγη, Dial. 12.3; 18.2ff., et
al.). This means that Justin's partial allegorical and typological interpretations of the Law are here left aside. We will
not further be concerned with them.[3] Although such interpretations may from the viewpoint of early Christianity be construed
as explanations of the purpose or purposes of the Law, Justin
never appeals to them as such.

An additional point here needs attention. The two major
theses of Justin's argumentation on the Law, (1) the invalidity
of the Law and (2) the purpose of the Law, are closely related
to each other and are mutually supportive. The Law has according to Justin ceased to be valid precisely because its purpose
was specific and limited, not eternal and universal. On the
other hand, its purpose was specific and limited, indeed it
could not be anything else, because the Law had in fact ceased
to be valid with the coming of Christ. A certain logical pre-
cedence must be given to Justin's teaching about the invalidity
of the Law as a prior axiom in his argumentation about the Law.
This is why in the present study the chapter on the invalidity
of the Law precedes the chapter on the purpose of the Law. The
Apologist's argument about the purpose of the Law is a corollary
to, almost an additional argument for, the Law's invalidity: it

[3]See above, pp. 59-65.

both presupposes and at the same time reinforces the premise
that the validity of the Law has now absolutely ceased.[4]

A. The Purpose of Circumcision

While Justin attributes a general purpose to the Law as
historical legislation for the Jews, i.e., a discipline ordained
by God on account of and in order to deal with the recalcitrance
of the Jews (διὰ τὸ σκληροκάρδιον τοῦ λαοῦ ὑμῶν, Dial. 44.2), he
also attributes more specific purposes to the different precepts
and practices of the Law, such as circumcision, sacrifices and
dietary regulations (Dial. 19.5ff.). In the case of circumcision, the purpose which Justin perceives in this commandment
is so peculiar and so different from his general thesis about
the purpose of the Law that it deserves separate attention.[5]
Justin frequently isolates circumcision for special consideration (Dial. 16.2ff.; 19.2ff.; 23.3ff.; 43.1; 46.4; 95.2f.).

The relevant passages are the following:

> ἡ γὰρ ἀπὸ 'Αβραὰμ κατὰ σάρκα περιτομὴ εἰς σημεῖον ἐδό-
> θη, ἵνα ἦτε ἀπὸ τῶν ἄλλων ἐθνῶν καὶ ἡμῶν ἀφωρισμένοι,
> καὶ ἵνα μόνοι πάθητε ἃ νῦν ἐν δίκῃ πάσχετε, καὶ ἵνα
> γένωνται αἱ χῶραι ὑμῶν ἔρημοι καὶ αἱ πόλεις πυρίκαυ-
> στοι, καὶ τοὺς καρποὺς ἐνώπιον ὑμῶν κατεσθίωσιν ἀλλό-
> τριοι, καὶ μηδεὶς ἐξ ὑμῶν ἐπιβαίνῃ εἰς τὴν 'Ιερουσαλήμ.
> οὐ γὰρ ἐξ ἄλλου τινὸς γνωρίζεσθε παρὰ τοὺς ἄλλους ἀν-
> θρώπους, ἢ ἀπὸ τῆς ἐν σαρκὶ ὑμῶν περιτομῆς (Dial. 16.
> 2-3).

> For the circumcision according to the flesh, that was
> from Abraham, was given for a sign, that ye should be
> separated from the other nations and us, and that ye
> alone should suffer the things ye are rightly suffering
> now, and that your lands should be desolate and your
> cities burned with fire, and that foreigners should eat
> up the fruits before your face, and none of you go up
> unto Jerusalem. For by nothing else are ye to be known
> from other men, save by the circumcision that is in
> your flesh.

---

[4]Shotwell, p. 11, confuses the priority of these theses
for Justin when he thinks that Justin first settles the point
about the purpose of the Law and then proceeds to demonstrate
its invalidity. The case is the other way around. See Dial.
11.2ff., which is the beginning of Justin's argument on the
cessation of the Law.

[5]It may be noted that scholars who have written on Justin usually view what he has to say about circumcision as one
example of his central thesis about the Law's purpose.

134

οὐ γὰρ πᾶσιν ἀναγκαία αὕτη ἡ περιτομή, ἀλλ'ὑμῖν μόνοις, ἵνα, ὡς προέφην, ταῦτα πάθητε ἃ νῦν ἐν δίκῃ
πάσχετε (Dial. 19.2).

The reason is that this circumcision is not necessary for all, but for you alone, that, as I said
before, ye may suffer what you now are rightly suf-
fering.

ὑμῖν οὖν μόνοις ἀναγκαία ἦν ἡ περιτομὴ αὕτη, ἵνα ὁ
λαὸς οὐ λαὸς ᾖ καὶ τὸ ἔθνος οὐκ ἔθνος, ὡς καὶ 'Ωσηέ,
εἷς τῶν δώδεκα προφητῶν, φησί (Dial. 19.5).

To you therefore alone was this circumcision necessary, that the people may not be a people, and the
nation not a nation, as also Hosea, one of the
Twelve prophets, says.

καὶ γὰρ αὐτὸς ὁ 'Αβραὰμ ἐν ἀκροβυστίᾳ ὢν διὰ τὴν
πίστιν, ἣν ἐπίστευσε τῷ θεῷ, ἐδικαιώθη καὶ εὐλογήθη,
ὡς ἡ γραφὴ σημαίνει· τὴν δὲ περιτομὴν εἰς σημεῖον,
ἀλλ'οὐκ εἰς δικαιοσύνην ἔλαβεν, ὡς καὶ αἱ γραφαὶ καὶ
τὰ πράγματα ἀναγκάζει ἡμᾶς ὁμολογεῖν. ὥστε δικαίως
εἴρητο περὶ ἐκείνου τοῦ λαοῦ, ὅτι ἐξολοθρευθήσεται ἡ
ψυχὴ ἐκείνη ἐκ τοῦ γένους αὐτῆς, ἣ οὐ περιτμηθήσεται
τῇ ἡμέρᾳ τῇ ὀγδόῃ (Dial. 23.4).

For Abraham himself when in uncircumcision was justified and received blessing, on account of the faith
with which he believed God, as the (passage of) Scripture indicates. Now he received circumcision for a
sign, but not for righteousness, as both the Scriptures and the facts compel us to acknowledge. So that
the saying was rightly spoken about that people:
"That soul shall be destroyed out of its race, which
shall not be circumcised on the eighth day."

τίς ἡ αἰτία τοῦ δι'ἄλλων προστατῶν καὶ νομοθεσίας μετὰ τοσαύτας γενεὰς ἀξιοῦν τὸν θεὸν δικαιοῦσθαι τοὺς
μὲν ἀπὸ 'Αβραὰμ μέχρι Μωϋσέως διὰ περιτομῆς, τοὺς δὲ
ἀπὸ Μωϋσέως καὶ διὰ περιτομῆς καὶ τῶν ἄλλων ἐντολῶν,
τοῦτ'ἔστι σαββάτου καὶ θυσιῶν καὶ σποδῶν καὶ προσφορῶν, εἰ μή, ὡς προείρηται ὑπ'ἐμοῦ, ἀποδείξετε ὅτι διὰ
τὸ τὸν θεόν, προγνώστην ὄντα, ἐγνωκέναι ἄξιον γεννσό-
μενον τὸν λαὸν ὑμῶν ἐκβληθῆναι ἀπὸ τῆς 'Ιερουσαλὴμ καὶ
μηδένα ἐπιτρέπεσθαι εἰσελθεῖν ἐκεῖ· οὐδαμόθεν γὰρ ἀλλαχόθεν ἐστὲ γνωριζόμενοι, ὡς προέφην, εἰ μὴ ἀπὸ τῆς
περὶ τὴν σάρκα περιτομῆς (Dial. 92.2-3).

What was the reason that after so many generations God
thought it well that by other leaders and a fresh legislation, those who lived from Abraham till Moses
should be justified by circumcision, and those who were
after Moses both by circumcision and by the other commandments, namely, Sabbath, sacrifices and ashes and
offerings? What reasonable answer can you give, unless, as I have already said, you prove that it was
because God, as foreknowing everything, knew that your
people would deserve to be cast out from Jerusalem, and
none of them be allowed to enter here? For by no other
possible way are you recognized, as I have already said,
save by the circumcision in your flesh.

Justin quite clearly understands that various overseers were appointed over the Jews and different legislations were ordained for them during the course of their history. But of special interest to him is the difference in time between the legislation of circumcision and the legislation of the remainder of the Law. The main body of the Law was ordained through Moses, whereas circumcision was given much earlier through Abraham. Time and again Justin notes that circumcision begins with Abraham and distinguishes it from the remainder of the Law which was given through Moses (<u>Dial</u>. 16.2f.; 19.5; 23.4; 43.1; 92.2). This distinction provides the basis for his separate and peculiar interpretation of the purpose of circumcision.

The first passage quoted above, <u>Dial</u>. 16.2-3, is both the most explicit and also the fullest statement of the purpose of circumcision according to Justin. The passage forms the beginning of a long polemical digression in which Justin berates the Jews for having killed Christ as well as the Prophets before him (<u>Dial</u>. 16.4-17.4). It is stimulated by a previous Old Testament citation (Lev. 26:40-41/<u>Dial</u>. 16.1) having to do with a future judgment of the Jews. According to the first passage above, the purpose of circumcision is to function as a sign (σημεῖον), separating the Jews from other peoples.

The term σημεῖον is used by Justin in several ways in the <u>Dialogue</u>.[6] In connection with circumcision, it is derived either from Gen. 17:11 (ἐν σημείῳ διαθήκης) or perhaps more immediately from Gal. 4:11 (σημεῖον . . . περιτομῆς)[7] and simply means a physical mark of identity: οὐ γὰρ ἐξ'ἄλλου τινὸς γνωρίζεσθε παρὰ τοὺς ἄλλους ἀνθρώπους, ἢ ἀπὸ τῆς ἐν σαρκὶ ὑμῶν περιτομῆς (<u>Dial</u>. 16.3).[8]

---

[6]As the prophetic "sign" to Ahaz in connection with Is. 7:14 and the Virgin Birth (<u>Dial</u>. 43.5; 66.2; 84.1-2); as the typological "sign" of the Cross (<u>Dial</u>. 90.5; 91.4; 94.1-5; 112.1-2; 131.4) and as the "sign" of Jonah (<u>Dial</u>. 107.1; 108.1). See also Franklin's dissertation, pp. 49-50 and 76-78 for a study of this term.

[7]Justin does not directly quote either of the texts, but he works with Gen. 15-17 and Romans 4. See above, pp. 9-10 and 116ff.

[8]He repeats this in <u>Dial</u>. 92.3: οὐδαμόθεν γὰρ ἀλλαχόθεν ἐστὲ γνωριζόμενοι, ὡς προέφην, εἰ μὴ ἀπὸ τῆς περὶ τὴν σάρκα περιτομῆς.

For Justin, the purpose of circumcision is to identify the Jews in order to facilitate their just punishment by the Romans: ἵνα μόνοι πάθητε ἃ νῦν ἐν δίκῃ πάσχετε (Dial. 16.2). The references to the present sufferings of the Jews, especially that to the prohibition of the Jews from entering Jerusalem, are no doubt references to the Bar Cochba war and to Hadrian's law against the Jews. The Bar Cochba war is mentioned several times by Justin (e.g., Dial. 1.3; 9.3; Ap. 31;6; 47.1-6).[9] The sufferings of the Jews as a result of this war are, according to Justin, predicted by Scripture and take place by divine providence.[10] Circumcision in particular, thinks Justin, was ordained by God as a mark of identity of the Jews so that they would not escape God's retributive justice at the hands of the Romans for their responsibility in the death of Christ and also the death of the Prophets (Dial. 16.4).

The second and third of the above passages, Dial. 19.2 and 19.5, repeat somewhat less clearly the same theme. Both are found in the larger context of the argument that, since Adam was created in a state of uncircumcision and since the Old Testament righteous prior to Abraham neither had nor observed circumcision, circumcision is not necessary. Rather, states Justin, circumcision is necessary only for the Jews, so that in the course of time they may be rejected as the people of God, according to the prediction of Hosea (ἵνα ὁ λαὸς οὐ λαὸς ᾖ, Dial. 19.5).[11] The Apologist does not here reflect further on this point but quickly moves on to another argument.

According to the fourth passage, Dial. 23.4-5, circumcision is twice called σημεῖον but its purpose is not stated.

---

[9] According to Ap. 31.6, the Apology was written during the war. The setting of the Dialogue is also cast at the same time (Dial. 1.3; 9.3). However, the Dialogue was most likely composed much later. Not only does it presuppose the fall of Jerusalem (Dial. 108.3) and Hadrian's prohibition against the Jews (Dial. 16.2; 92.2), it also ante-dates the writing of the Apology (Dial. 120.6). On the date of the Dialogue see Goodenough, p. 88, and Barnard, Justin Martyr, p. 13.

[10] In Dial. 16.2, Justin alludes to Is. 1:7 as one such prophecy of judgment against the Jews which he quotes in Dial. 52.4. The text is also cited in Ap. 47.5 with the same intent.

[11] An isolated allusion to Hos. 1:9.

Instead, circumcision is contrasted to a work of righteousness, which for Justin is the essential thing, whereas circumcision is simply an external mark. The term σημεῖον apparently calls to Justin's mind the underlying purpose of circumcision as a mark of physical identity. He then finds the opportunity to insist that Scripture at the threat of death indeed demands circumcision of the Jews (presumably marking them for punishment): ὥστε δικαίως εἴρητο περὶ ἐκείνου τοῦ λαοῦ, ὅτι ἐξολο-θρευθήσεται ἡ ψυχὴ ἐκείνη ἐκ τοῦ γένους αὐτῆς, ἢ οὐ περιτμηθή-σεται τῇ ἡμέρᾳ τῇ ὀγδόῃ (Dial. 23.4/Gen. 17:14). Otherwise the citation of Gen. 17:14 in this context is not at all appropriate. Thus, with biting irony, Justin turns around the intent of this text which was cited earlier by Trypho as positive Scriptural evidence for the validity of circumcision (Dial. 10.3).[12]

The final passage which speaks of the purpose of circumcision is Dial. 92.2-3. Here Justin, citing other ritual precepts besides circumcision, asks why all such precepts were given as presumably necessary for salvation when so many generations prior to Moses and Abraham were approved by God without having observed circumcision and many other injunctions of the Law (Dial. 92.2). Here we are interested in Justin's answer only with regard to circumcision which he dissociates from the other precepts of the Law. The answer repeats nearly in full what Justin states in Dial. 16.2-3. God by foreknowledge knew that the Jews would come to deserve expulsion from Jerusalem and would be prevented from again entering the city (Dial. 92.2). Circumcision was ordained by Him as an unfailing mark of identity on the Jews insuring their just punishment in due time. Writes Justin: οὐδαμόθεν γὰρ ἀλλαχόθεν ἐστὲ γνωριζόμενοι . . . εἰ μὴ ἀπὸ τῆς περὶ τὴν σάρκα περιτομῆς (Dial. 92.3).

---

[12]Circumcision as an external "sign" contrasted to spiritual circumcision is also mentioned in Dial. 28.4 (see above, pp. 100ff.). Here the value of circumcision is played down by Justin on the grounds that circumcision was also practiced by other peoples to no avail. Justin does not, however, reflect on why then circumcision is a special "sign" only for the Jews. Since the idea of other peoples' also practicing circumcision comes to him from Jer. 9:25-26, quoted in Dial. 28.3, Justin probably considers the reference to the various peoples cited in this text, the Egyptians, Moabites and Edomites, a purely historical reference, as something from the distant past, not relevant to the situation at hand involving only the Jews.

138

This punitive interpretation of the purpose of circumcision is without precedent. Justin seems to be the first Christian writer to formulate it. How does he arrive at this peculiar interpretation? He does not state the reasons why he considers such an argument cogent, except for the idea that, according to him, circumcision is an unfailing mark of identification (Dial. 92.3). Since direct evidence is lacking, one can only venture some conjectures about Justin's reasoning here.

Circumcision and the sabbath, more than the other precepts of the Law, were widely known among gentiles as the most conspicuous customs of the Jews. With respect to circumcision, there existed the tradition among pagan authors from the time of Herodotus that this religious practice was borrowed from the Egyptians. The charge is repeated especially in Graeco-Roman times by such writers as Diodorus Siculus, Celsus and Julian.[13] Roman authors such as Horace, Martial and Juvenal heaped ridicule on the practice.[14] Tacitus specifically remarks that the Jews "adopted circumcision to distinguish themselves from other peoples by this difference."[15] Tacitus' statement, however, does not in its context imply anything more than the idea of the separation of the Jews. Trypho himself refers to the idea of separateness as a necessary requirement of the people of God when he charges that the Christians do not distinguish themselves from the gentiles at large, yet make claims of having a special standing before God (Dial. 10.3). Justin, however, seems to go beyond the idea of mere separation and emphatically insists that circumcision alone is the unfailing mark of Jewish identity, and this for a special purpose (Dial. 16.3; 92.3).

Justin could not easily relate the purpose of circumcision to the sinfulness of the Jews as he does in the case of the remainder of the ritual Law. The legislation of the Mosaic Law as a whole occurs, according to Justin, after Israel's worship of the golden calf and in order to check the Jews' pro-

---

[13]Bergmann, pp. 102 and 115.

[14]Ibid.

[15]"Circumcidere genitalia instituerunt ut diversitate noscantur," Hist. 5.5. The translation is C. H. Moore's Loeb Classical Library: Tacitus, II, 183. The reference is Bergmann's, p. 102.

clivity to sin (<u>Dial</u>. 19.5ff.).[16] However, no such statements
are made in connection with circumcision. On the contrary,
Justin thinks of the pre-Mosaic period as the period of the
righteous who were approved by God without observing the Mosaic
Law. Circumcision is given to Abraham not because of the problem of sin--indeed no such rationale could be derived from
Genesis 17--but as a sign (σημεῖον, Gen. 17:11; cf. Rm. 4:11).
But a sign of what? Justin distorts the meaning of this term
in Gen. 17:11 and declares that it is a sign of physical identity of the Jews, the secret purpose of which was not disclosed
until the Bar Cochba war!

That the tragedies which befell the Jews in Graeco-
Roman times were also interpreted by Christians as evidence of
divine displeasure against them, and that Old Testament judgmental texts would be cited as proof of the divine intent, is
not surprising (cf. Mk. 13:14ff.; Mt. 22:7; <u>Barn</u>. 16.5). Justin himself devotes considerable attention to such explanations
of the sufferings of the Jews, particularly those due to the
Bar Cochba war.[17] During the Apologist's times both Jews and
Christians suffered at the hands of the Romans. The difference
according to Justin is that the Jews suffer justly, in accordance with the divine will and as predicted by Scripture, whereas Christians suffer unjustly (<u>Dial</u>. 110.6; <u>Ap</u>. 47.1-6). The
tribulations of the Jews as a consequence of the Bar Cochba war
are expressions of divine punishment against them, not so much
for sins committed in the distant past, but for their responsibility in the death of Christ and other evils committed against
Christians (<u>Dial</u>. 16.2ff.).

But where does Justin base his supposition that specifically circumcision is an unfailing mark of identity of the
Jews and thus a foreordained sign facilitating divine judgment
through the hands of the Romans? Is it possible that the Romans
physically checked those who entered Jerusalem to assure a
strict application of Hadrian's prohibition or that they checked
individual cases of persons who had already entered Jerusalem
and were suspected as Jews? Justin himself reports that the
Romans not only guarded entry into Jerusalem very carefully,

---

[16]See below, pp. 146ff.

[17]<u>Dial</u>. 16.2ff.; 19.2; 110.6; <u>Ap</u>. 47.1-6.

140

but also had decreed the death penalty for any Jew who was caught within the confines of the city (Ap. 46.5).[18] One would certainly expect that some Jews, concealing their identity, would risk life in order to enter Jerusalem. Some probably succeded in entering Jerusalem surreptitiously. Perhaps Roman soldiers may in certain instances have physically checked their suspects in order to identify them by the mark of circumcision. If so, this would explain Justin's insistence that the Jews are unfailingly recognized by circumcision (Dial. 16.3; 92.3). This idea could then easily serve as a peg for Justin's theological interpretation of circumcision as a mark of identity facilitating God's retributive justice against the Jews. Whether or not the Romans conducted such searches is difficult to know, although it is not an improbable matter. However, Justin apparently was convinced that they did. It is from such supposition that he seems to have drawn his curious explanation of the purpose of circumcision.

The later exegetical tradition for the most part ignores Justin's interpretation. His argument reappears only in Tertullian and Irenaeus. Tertullian, quite probably indebted to Justin, writes in Adv. Jud. 3.4 that circumcision had to be given, but only as a sign of racial identity so that the Jews would in the end-time and in accordance with their deserts be prohibited from entering Jerusalem.[19] Tertullian then quotes Is. 1:7-8, a text which Justin also cites (Dial. 16.2; 52.4; Ap. 47.5). In Adv. Jud. 3.6, he repeats the same argument adding more explicitly that the purpose of circumcision was instituted by God's foreknowledge and that in Tertullian's days this purpose of facilitating the prohibition of Jews from entering Jerusalem had already been fulfilled.[20]

---

[18]Addressing the Roman officials, Justin writes in the Apology: ὅτι δὲ φυλάσσεται ὑφ'ὑμῶν ὅπως μηδεὶς 'Ιουδαῖος ἐν αὐτῇ γένηται, καὶ θάνατος κατὰ τοῦ καταλαμβανομένου 'Ιουδαίου εἰσιόντος ὥρισται, ἀκριβῶς ἐπίστασθε (Ap. 47.6).

[19]"Dari enim habebat circumcisio, sed in signum unde Israel in novissimo tempore dinosci haberet, quando secundum sua merita in sanctam civitatem ingredi prohiberetur," Adv. Jud. 3.4.

[20]"Haec igitur dei providentia fuit . . . quod et quia futurum erat nuntiabatur, et quia factum videmus recognoscimus," Adv. Jud. 3.6.

This argument reoccurs in Irenaeus but in less complete form. According to Irenaeus, circumcision was given as a sign so that the Jews might continue "to be identified" ("in signo . . . ut cognoscibile perseveret genus Abrahae," Adv. Haer. 4.27.1). He does not state, however, why this function of circumcision was necessary, nor does he mention either the Bar Cochba war or Hadrian's prohibition against the Jews. Rather, he goes on to interpret circumcision as a typological sign of spiritual significance.[21] Perhaps he presupposes Justin's interpretation without mentioning it. This would explain his reference to circumcision as a sign of identification of the Jews.

After Irenaeus, and among the later Church Fathers, Justin's interpretation of the purpose of circumcision seems to be totally ignored, a forgotten vestige of early Christian polemics against the Jews.

B. The Purpose of the Ritual Law

The first reference to the purpose of the Law occurs indirectly in Dial. 12.3 where Justin criticizes the Jews for thinking that they act according to true piety by observing the sabbath, yet without knowing why the sabbath was ordained: μὴ νοοῦντες διὰ τί προσετάγη. This purpose is explicitly stated in Dial. 18.2 where Justin mentions inclusively circumcision, the sabbath and the festivals. Christians, too, says Justin, would observe the ritual precepts if they did not know why they were first ordained, namely, on account of the hardness of heart and also the lawlessness of the Jews: τὴν περιτομὴν τὴν κατὰ σάρκα καὶ τὰ σάββατα καὶ τὰς ἑορτὰς πάσας ἁπλῶς ἐφυλάσσομεν, εἰ μὴ ἔγνωμεν δι᾽ ἥν αἰτίαν καὶ ὑμῖν προσετάγη, τοῦτ᾽ ἔστι διὰ τὰς ἀνομίας ὑμῶν καὶ τὴν σκληροκαρδίαν (Dial. 18.2). In almost all of the sections of the Dialogue where Justin deals with the Law (e.g., chaps. 10-30; 43-47; 67.2-10; 92.2-5), time and again he reiterates the same point: the Law was given on account of the sins and the hardness of heart of the Jews.

The following passages are instructive:

---

[21]"In signo ergo data sunt haec: non autem sine symbolo erant signa . . . sed secundum carnem circumcisio praesignificabet spiritalem," Adv. Haer. 4.27.1.

142

διὰ τὰς ἀδικίας ὑμῶν καὶ τῶν πατέρων ὑμῶν εἰς σημεῖον,
ὡς προέφην, καὶ τὸ σάββατον ἐντέταλται ὁ θεὸς φυλάσσειν ὑμᾶς καὶ τὰ ἄλλα προστάγματα προσετετάχει (Dial.
21.1).

Now because of your sins and those of your fathers God
charged you to keep the sabbath as a sign, as I said
already, and has also given you His other ordinances.

διὰ τὰς ἁμαρτίας τοῦ λαοῦ ὑμῶν καὶ διὰ τὰς εἰδωλολα-
τρείας, ἀλλ'οὐ διὰ τὸ ἐνδεῆς εἶναι τῶν τοιούτων προσφορῶν, ἐνετείλατο ὁμοίως ταῦτα γίνεσθαι (Dial. 22.1).

In the same way He commanded offerings because of the
sins of your people, and because of their idolatries,
and not because He was in need of such.

ἀπὸ 'Αβραὰμ ἤρξατο περιτομὴ καὶ ἀπὸ Μωϋσέως σάββατον
καὶ θυσίαι καὶ προσφοραὶ καὶ ἑορταί, καὶ ἀπεδείχθη
διὰ τὸ σκληροκάρδιον τοῦ λαοῦ ὑμῶν ταῦτα διατετάχθαι
(Dial. 43.1).

Circumcision began with Abraham, and with Moses sabbath and sacrifices and offerings and feasts, and it
has been proved that these were appointed because of
the hardness of the heart of your people.

τίς δὲ ἐντολὴ καὶ πρᾶξις ὁμοίως εἴρητο . . . διὰ τὸ
σκληροκάρδιον τοῦ λαοῦ ὑμῶν (Dial. 44.2).

And another command and action was in the same way
spoken . . . on account of the hardness of your people's heart.

διὰ τὸ σκληροκάρδιον τοῦ λαοῦ ὑμῶν πάντα τὰ τοιαῦτα
ἐντάλματα νοεῖτε τὸν θεὸν διὰ Μωϋσέως ἐντειλάμενον
ὑμῖν (Dial. 46.5).

Ye perceive that on account of the hardness of the
heart of your people God enjoined on you by Moses all
such precepts.

τὰς προσφορὰς καὶ τὰς θυσίας δι'ἔνδειαν ὁ θεὸς ἐνετείλατο ποιεῖν τοὺς πατέρας ὑμῶν, ἢ διὰ τὸ σκληροκάρδιον αὐτῶν καὶ τὸ εὐχερὲς πρὸς εἰδωλολατρείαν (Dial.
67.8);

Did God charge your fathers to offer offerings and
sacrifices because He needed them, or because of the
hardness of their hearts, and their inclinations to
idolatry?

τὸ δὲ σαββατίζειν καὶ τὰς προσφορὰς φέρειν κελευσθῆ-
ναι ὑμᾶς, καὶ τόπον εἰς ὄνομα τοῦ θεοῦ ἐπικληθῆναι ἀ-
νασχέσθαι τὸν κύριον, ἵνα, ὡς προείρηται, μὴ εἰδωλο-
λατροῦντες καὶ ἀμνημονοῦντες τοῦ θεοῦ ἀσεβεῖς καὶ ἄθεοι γένησθε, ὡς ἀεὶ φαίνεσθε γεγενημένοι (Dial. 92.4).

But your being commanded to keep the sabbath and to
make offerings, and being granted by the Lord a place
in which the name of God was to be invoked, was for
fear lest, as has been said, you should worship idols
and forget God, and so become irreligious and godless,
as you appear always to have been.

Three observations may be made on the basis of the above passages. First, while the terms σκληροκαρδία and σκληροκάρδιον are Justin's key terms descriptive of the sinfulness of the Jews, other terms without consistency or particular differentiation are also used, such as ἀνομίαι (Dial. 18.2), ἀδικίαι (Dial. 21.1), ἁμαρτίαι (Dial. 22.1), εἰδωλολατρεῖαι (Dial. 22.1; 67.8) or simply κακίαι (Dial. 27.4), all of which refer to what Justin generally regards as the reason of the legislation of the Mosaic Law.

The charge of σκληροκαρδία is a noted case in the Christian tradition because of the logion of Jesus on divorce (Mtt. 19:8/Mk. 10:5). Justin probably knew this logion, although he does not quote it.[22] Ptolemy quotes it, but he uses it to show that the Mosaic Law contains stipulations enacted by men as well as by God, rather than to castigate the sinfulness of the Jews.[23] In the early Christian tradition, the charge of blindness is more prominent as a criticism against unbelieving Jews.[24] The term σκληροκαρδία is surprisingly rare (Acts 7:51; Barn. 9.5) as part of Christian anti-Jewish polemic. We do not find a particularly heavy focus on the sinfulness of the Jews or their perverse character as a people in the Christian tradition prior to Justin.

Justin, however, never loses the opportunity of pointing up the sinfulness and the evil inclination of the Jews. The Jews are incorrigibly blind, hopelessly lacking in understanding, and forever lawless.[25] Their wickedness and hardness of heart persist to the present day as evidenced by their killing of Jesus, their instigations against Christians, their syna-

---

[22] He quotes the final logion of this pericope (Mtt. 19: 11-12) in Ap. 15.4. Marcion had made much of Jesus' difference with Moses on this point and Tertullian quotes the reference to σκληροκαρδία as a proper explanation of this difference (Adv. Marc. 4.34).

[23] Pan. 33.4.-10.

[24] Mtt. 13:14-15 and parallels; Mtt. 15:14; 23:16-20; Jn 12:40; Acts 28:26-27; Rm. 11:8-10.

[25] Dial. 12.2; 20.4; 27.4; 55.3 et al.

144

gogual cursing of Christians, and their stubborn unrepentance.[26]
Except for the eschatological remnant which is to be saved,[27]
Justin holds no hope for the Jews. It is against this background that the Apologist constantly rehearses the purpose of
the legislation of the Law as enacted because of the hardness
of heart of the Jews.

Secondly, Justin tries to demonstrate his case about the
purpose of the Law from the authority of Scripture. Both the
content of his argument and his terminology are drawn from numerous Old Testament texts, especially prophetic texts, which
offer lengthy litanies of Jewish transgressions.[28] Justin exploits particularly the prophetic critique of the cult and draws
an inference from it regarding his understanding of the purpose
of the Law which is not part of the original meaning of these
prophetic texts. As far as Justin is concerned, Scripture tes-
tifies to the fact that both through Moses and the Prophets God
equally attempted to deal with the Jewish proclivity to sin.[29]
Trypho, despite his objections, has no choice but to accept the
cogency of Justin's Scriptural proof about the purpose of the
Law: αἱ γραφαὶ ἀναγκάζουσί με ὁμολογεῖν (Dial. 67.8,11).

Thirdly, it may be noted that according to Dial. 43.1
(καὶ ἀπεδείχθη διὰ τὸ σκληροκάρδιον τοῦ λαοῦ ὑμῶν ταῦτα διατετάχθαι), the purpose of the Law has already been demonstrated
by Justin prior to this point in the Dialogue. Subsequent references to why the Law was ordained are, as Justin occasionally
notes, repetitions either of matters to which Trypho has already
consented or for the benefit of Trypho's new companions who
joined the discussion on the second day.[30]

---

[26]Dial. 16.4f.; 17.1ff.; 39.1; 44.1; 46.6; 53.2; 68.1;
92.4; 93.4-5; 95.4; 108.1-3; 133.1; 133.6.

[27]See above, pp. 39ff.

[28]See below, pp. 152-53.

[29]Dial. 27.2,4; 28.2; 46.5-6; 67.3,10.

[30]Dial. 67.4,8,11; 92.5.

Justin's proof of the purpose of the Law is given in
the first and main unit on the Law (Dial. chaps. 10-30), particularly in Dial. chaps. 18-30. (Dial. chaps. 11ff. deal with
the first thesis of the Apologist regarding the invalidity of
the Law). Although these chapters by no means form a smooth
development of a single theme,[31] they nevertheless attain a certain concentration of argument on the purpose of the Law based
on a string of biblical quotations (Dial. 18.2b-3; 19.5b-23.2;
27.1-4; 30.1). In particular, Dial. 19.5b-23.2 is the heart of
Justin's argument, the most sustained effort on his part to show
why the Mosaic Law was instituted. This is Justin's Scriptural
proof of the purpose of the Law, a proof which ends with a conclusion (Dial. 23.1-2) repeated twice within the larger unit
(Dial. 27.1-4; 30.1). We turn to a closer examination of this
argument.

In Dial. 18.2 Justin returns to the subject of the Law
following the lengthy polemical digression of Dial. 16.4-18.1.
From this point up to Dial. 23.1-2, where Justin draws final inferences about the Law and leaves his interlocutors at a loss
for an answer (Dial. 23.3), a fairly cohesive unit may be dis-
cerned. Justin begins with the thesis of the purpose of the Law
in Dial. 18.2b, enumerates several arguments against the validity of circumcision (Dial. 19.2ff.), and then develops his main
argument regarding the purpose of sacrifices (Dial. 19.6a; 22.
1-11), the sabbath (Dial. 19.6c; 21.1-4), and fasting (Dial. 20.
1-4). It is clear that we have here a discernable pattern:
circumcision, sacrifices, the sabbath and fasting. The transi-
tion from arguments regarding the invalidity of the Law to arguments regarding the purpose of the Law is marked by Dial. 19.5
which refers to the polemical purpose of circumcision (ἵνα ὁ
λαὸς οὐ λαὸς ᾖ καὶ τὸ ἔθνος οὐκ ἔθνος), as we have noted. Circumcision, declares Justin, is necessary only for the Jews and
as a sign of their rejection as God's people in accordance with
Hosea's prophecy. Justin then goes on to explain also the purpose of sacrifices, the sabbath and fasting (καὶ θυσίας . . .
καὶ σαββατίζειν . . . καὶ . . . βρωμάτων, Dial. 19.6; 20.1).

---

[31]They include arguments about the invalidity of the
Law (Dial. 19.2ff.; 23.3-24.2; 27.5-28.6; 29.3) and also argu-
ments concerning the third theme of the Dialogue, the true
Israel (Dial. 24.3-26.4; 29.1-2; 30.2ff.).

It is Justin's contention that, prior to Moses, the Law
was not necessary with the exception of circumcision which was
given for a special reason. The Law became necessary only at
the time of Moses. Why? Because of the sins of the people in
the desert, especially the idolatrous worship of the golden
calf: μέχρι Μωσέως, ἐφ οὗ ἄδικος καὶ ἀχάριστος εἰς τὸν θεὸν ὁ
λαὸς ὑμῶν ἐφάνη ἐν τῇ ἐρήμῳ μοσχοποιήσας (Dial. 19.5). It was
for this reason that God ordained the Law over the people:
ὅθεν ὁ θεὸς ἁρμοσάμενος πρὸς τὸν λαὸν ἐκεῖνον καὶ θυσίας φέρειν
. . . καὶ σαββατίζειν . . . καὶ γὰρ βρωμάτων τινῶν ἀπέχεσθαι
προσέταξεν (Dial. 19.6-20.1). Thus the Law as a whole was legislated through Moses on account of the sins of the Jews, particularly the worship of the golden calf. This is the substance
of Justin's interpretation of the purpose of the ritual Law.

The Apologist is the first Christian writer who associates the legislation of the Mosaic Law with the worship of the
calf. Traditional Christian critique of the Jews included the
charge of idolatry centered on the worship of the calf (I Cor.
10:7; Acts 7:40ff.; Barn. 4.7-8; 14.1-3). The author of Barnabas in particular claims that the Jews lost their right to the
Covenant because of the worship of the calf. Basing himself on
the narrative of Exodus 32, from which he extensively quotes, he
interprets Moses' breaking of the tablets as a permanent forfei-
ture of the Covenant (Barn. 4.8; 14.3). The Jews were not wor-
thy to receive the Covenant, which Moses received, on account of
their sins: οὐκ ἐγένοντο ἄξιοι λαβεῖν διὰ τὰς ἁμαρτίας αὐτῶν
(Barn. 14.1).[32]

Justin, however, connects the legislation of the Law itself with the worship of the calf. The Law according to the
Apologist was not necessary until the time of Moses and the com-
mitment of this idolatrous act (Dial. 19.5-6). The Law, and especially the whole sacrificial system, was instituted because of
the worship of the calf and for the purpose of restraining the

---

[32]Cf. 14.4: Μωϋσῆς μὲν ἔλαβεν, αὐτοὶ δὲ οὐκ ἐγένοντο
ἄξιοι. Verweijs, p. 229, thinks that Justin shares with the
author of Barnabas (Barn. 4.7-8) the idea that the sin of the
golden calf was the occasion of the legislation of the Law.
However, the author of Barnabas contends that the Jews lost the
Covenant because of the worship of the calf, and says nothing
about the calf as the occasion of the giving of the Law, which
is Justin's contention.

idolatrous proclivities of the Jews. This is the central point of Justin's argument concerning the purpose of the Mosaic Law.

In later Christian writings, only the <u>Didascalia</u> makes much of the same kind of argument. According to this third-century work, the ritual Law of Moses was imposed as punishment on the Jews because of the sin of the worship of the golden calf. But the ritual Law is called "second legislation" (δευτέρωσις)[33] and is contrasted to the Decalogue which for the writer of the <u>Didascalia</u> comprises the true Law. According to the same writer, the "second legislation" or ritual Law is abolished by Christ, whereas the true Law which was issued first, the Decalogue, is reaffirmed by him. Echoes of the same teaching may also be found in the <u>Pseudo-Clementines</u> and the <u>Apostolic Constitutions</u>.[34] There is no evidence, however, that these documents are directly dependent on Justin though they may well presuppose his interpretation.

Although the Law as a whole was, according to Justin, legislated on account of the sinfulness of the Jews, particular precepts were also ordained for particular reasons. These reasons are not sharply differentiated. In <u>Dial.</u> 19.6-20.1, Justin indicates that (a) sacrifices were instituted in order to restrain the Jews from idolatry (καὶ θυσίας φέρειν ὡς πρὸς τὸ ὄνομα αὐτοῦ ἐνετείλατο, ἵνα μὴ εἰδωλολατρῆτε), (b) the sabbath was commanded so that the Jews would nurture remembrance of God (καὶ

---

[33]R. H. Connolly, <u>Didascalia Apostolorum</u> (Oxford, 1929), pp. lvii-lxix, offers an extensive discussion of the matter, but makes no mention of Justin. See also Strecker's appendix in Bauer's <u>Orthodoxy and Heresy</u>, p. 256, and n. 44, and also Marcel Simon, "The Ancient Church and Rabbinical Tradition," <u>Holy Book and Holy Tradition</u>, ed. F. F. Bruce and E. G. Rupp (Grand Rapids: Eerdmans, 1968), pp. 102-09. This use of the term δευτέρωσις is to be distinguished from an older one in the Christian tradition referring to the teachings of the Rabbis. Justin does not use the term δευτέρωσις at all, but uses παράδοσις for the oral Rabbinic traditions.

[34]Rec. 1.26 and <u>Ap. Const.</u> 6.20.1. H. J. Schoeps, <u>Theologie und Geschichte des Judenchristentums</u> (Tübingen, 1949), p. 180, thinks that the theory of the "second legislation" is dependent on the Jewish Christian concept of the false pericopes in the Old Testament. Strecker, in the appendix to Bauer's <u>Orthodoxy and Heresy</u>, p. 256, n. 44, however, disputes this because the concept of the false pericopes shows no dependence on Exodus 32, the basis of the theory of the "second legislation." See also Strecker's <u>Judenchristentum</u>, pp. 162ff.

148

σαββατίζειν οὖν ὑμῖν προστέταχεν, ἵνα μνήμην λαμβάνητε τοῦ θεοῦ), and (c) abstaining from certain foods was required so that the Jews would similarly maintain remembrance of God (καὶ γὰρ βρωμάτων τινῶν ἀπέχεσθαι προσέταξεν ὑμῖν, ἵνα καὶ ἐν τῷ ἐσθίειν καὶ πίνειν πρὸ ὀφθαλμῶν ἔχητε τὸν θεόν).

The charge of idolatry is the most frequent and most conspicuous one in the Dialogue. Again and again Justin accuses the Jews of idolatry. On one occasion he directly calls them idolaters (εἰδωλολάτραι, Dial. 93.4). According to Justin, not only sacrifices, but also all of the Temple ritual and the Temple itself were instituted by God so that the Jews might worship the true God and refrain from idolatry (Dial. 19.6; 22. 1,11; 67.8).

The charge of idolatry centers above all around the worship of the golden calf to which Justin refers numerous times (Dial. 19.5; 20.4; 73.6; 102.6; 132.1). It is in this connection particularly that the Jews are called ungrateful (ἀχάριστοι) lapsing into worship of the calf after having witnessed God's great acts of deliverance.[35] But this is seen by Justin as only the main instance of the people's constant proclivity to idolatry. The Apologist also mentions other instances, such as Amos' condemnation of the worship of Moloch and the Star of Raephan (Dial. 22.1,3/Amos 5:26), Elijah's struggles against the worship of Baal (Dial. 39.1/III Kgdm 19: 10,18; cf. Dial. 46.6; 136.3) and Jeremiah's reference to worship of the Host of Heaven (Dial. 136.3/Jer. 7:18). Frequent is also the charge that the Jews offered sacrifices and in particular that they sacrificed their children to demons.[36]

---

[35]Dial. 19.5; 20.4; 73.6; 102.6; 131.3-132.1.

[36]τὰ τέκνα ὑμῶν ἐθύετε τοῖς δαιμονίοις. See Dial. 19:6; 27.2; 46.6; 73.6; 133.1. In Dial. 46.6, Justin mentions Isaiah as the source of this charge, probably Is. 57:5, without however quoting it anywhere. Justin's formulation of the charge is linguistically closer to the reading of Ps. 105:37 (LXX) which Justin does not quote: καὶ ἔθυσαν τοὺς υἱοὺς αὐτῶν καὶ τὰς θυγατέρας αὐτῶν τοῖς δαιμονίοις. Is. 57:5 reads quite differently: οἱ παρακαλοῦντες ἐπὶ τὰ εἴδωλα ὑπὸ δένδρα δασέα, σφάζοντες τὰ τέκνα αὐτῶν ἐν ταῖς φάραγξιν ἀνὰ μέσον τῶν πετρῶν. Throughout the Dialogue, the charge of idolatry against the Jews is often contrasted to the rejection of idols by the gentile Christians who have forsaken their previous idolatrous ways (Dial. 11.4; 46.6-7; 91.3; 113.6; 119.2,5; 130.4).

Next to sacrifices, the second ritual precept to which
Justin assigns a particular purpose is the sabbath. The sabbath
was according to him ordained in order that the Jews might maintain remembrance of God (Dial. 19.6). Justin derives this interpretation of the sabbath from Ez. 20:19-26 which he quotes in
Dial. 21.2-4. In Dial. 19.6 he cites the central point of this
passage: τοῦ γινώσκειν ὅτι ἐγώ εἰμι ὁ θεός (cf. Ez. 20:20).[37]
In Dial. 21.2ff., he quotes the entire pericope. Here his introductory comment combines several elements. Just prior to
this quotation Justin writes:

> καὶ ὅτι διὰ τὰς ἀδικίας ὑμῶν καὶ τῶν πατέρων ὑμῶν εἰς
> σημεῖον, ὡς προέφην, καὶ τὸ σάββατον ἐντέταλται ὁ θεὸς
> φυλάσσειν ὑμᾶς καὶ τὰ ἄλλα προστάγματα προσετετάχει,
> καὶ σημαίνει ὅτι διὰ τὰ ἔθνη, ἵνα μὴ βεβηλωθῇ τὸ ὄνομα
> αὐτοῦ παρ'αὐτοῖς, διὰ τοῦτο εἴασέ τινας ἐξ ὑμων ὅλως
> ζῶντας (Dial. 21.1).

> Now because of your sins and those of your fathers God
> charged you to keep the sabbath as a sign, as I said
> already, and has also given you His other ordinances.
> He also signifies that because of the Gentiles--lest
> His name should be profaned among them--He allowed some
> of you at least to remain alive.

According to the passage, the sabbath was legislated on
account of the transgressions of the Jews, as well as the transgressions of their fathers, an idea contained in the citation
from Ezekiel (καὶ παρεπικράνετέ με, καὶ τὰ τέκνα ὑμῶν ἐν τοῖς
προστάγμασί μου οὐκ ἐπορεύθησαν, Dial. 21.2/Ez. 20:21). It was
ordained as a sign (σημεῖον) in connection with these transgressions. Justin suggests here that he is repeating an earlier point (ὡς προέφην). But he has not used the term σημεῖον
in connection with the sabbath. Apparently he is confusing it
with his reference to circumcision (Dial. 16.2). The term σημεῖον is found in the Old Testament quote, which probably explains Justin's use of it in connection with the sabbath, but
its meaning there is an entirely different and positive one
(εἰς σημεῖον ἀνὰ μέσον ἐμοῦ καὶ ὑμῶν τοῦ γινώσκειν ὅτι ἐγὼ κύριος ὁ θεὸς ὑμῶν, Dial. 21.2/Ez. 20:20). In the text observance of God's sabbath is a sign of obedience to Him and a

---

[37]This text is not quoted by writers earlier than Justin. As far as later writers are concerned, Prigent, Justin,
pp. 241ff. and 256, finds affinities between Justin on the one
hand and, on the other, Tertullian and Irenaeus, in the use of
this text through dependence by the latter writers on Justin's
Syntagma.

150

sign of acknowledgment of His lordship. Justin, however, draws
a completely different inference. The sabbath, for him, just as
the other precepts of the Law which he here inclusively associates (καὶ τὰ ἄλλα προστάγματα, Dial. 21.1), constitute a sign of
the transgressions and sins of the Jews. Ezekiel's complaints
against the breaking of the rule of the sabbath, God's Law, are
now cited as the reason for the giving of the sabbath in the
first place! Justin finishes his comment with a judgmental note
which he derives from the same text (Dial. 21.3/Ez. 20:22).

Justin does not elsewhere isolate the sabbath for special interpretation. In Dial. 43.1, he includes the sabbath
along with circumcision, sacrifices, offerings and festivals,
all of which according to him were commanded because of the
hard-heartedness of the Jews. In Dial. 46.2d, the sabbath is
mentioned together with circumcision, fasting and ritual washings all of which, repeats Justin, were ordained because of the
Jewish stubborness. In Dial. 92.4, the sabbath is combined with
offerings as well as the Temple itself all of which, states Justin, serve as restraints against idolatry and as means of remembrance of God.

The third ritual institution, fasting, which Justin distinguishes in Dial. 20.1ff., has for him the same purpose as the
sabbath: καὶ γὰρ βρωμάτων τινῶν ἀπέχεσθαι προσέταξεν ὑμῖν, ἵνα
καὶ ἐν τῷ ἐσθίειν καὶ πίνειν πρὸ ὀφθαλμῶν ἔχητε τὸν θεόν (Dial.
20.1). Justin cites Ex. 32:6 and Dt. 32:15 for support in this
case. Both of these texts have to do with the worship of the
calf occurring in the context of festive eating and drinking.
Justin does not interpret the texts. He allows it to be understood that just as eating and drinking led to the worship of the
calf so, on the contrary, refraining from such acts and fasting
lead to remembrance of God.

Justin's use of the above texts indicates that he works
independently with the Septuagint. He cites Ex. 32:6 rather
freely in order to form a parallel with Dt. 32:15 and thus to
emphasize the act of "eating" (ἔφαγε/ἔφαγεν, Dial. 20.1). The
other text, Dt. 32:15, is closely cited after the Septuagint,
but a peculiar version of the Septuagint which renders the full
Hebrew text.[38] This combination of texts does not occur prior

---

[38]See Sibinga, pp. 138 and 144.

to Justin. Ex. 32:6 is cited by Paul (I Cor. 10:7) and Dt.
32:15 is partly cited by Clement (I Clem. 3.1). In both cases
the readings are quite different than Justin's.[39] The same combination occurs later in Tertullian (De ieiunio 6.2). Prigent
surmises here a dependence on Justin.[40]

Justin completes his argument about fasting noting that
such restrictions were not placed on Noah except with regard to
the eating of flesh with blood (Dial. 20.1e). This is another
variation of his argument from the history of salvation demonstrating the non-essential character of the Law.[41] After a
brief exchange about distinctions between the eating of meats
and the eating of herbs (Dial. 20.2-3),[42] Justin repeats that
fasting regulations were ordained by God through Moses because
the Jews worshipped the golden calf and that the purpose of such
regulations is to restrain the Jews from idolatry as well as to
encourage remembrance of God among them (Dial. 20.4).

Justin does not elsewhere distinguish different ritual
precepts, assigning to them specific purposes. He generally refers to the various ordinances in different combinations and assigns to them the same inclusive purpose: all of the precepts
of the Law were for him ordained because of the hard-heartedness
and the sinfulness of the Jews. What is most important is that
he uses the prophetic texts to paint the sinfulness of the Jews

---

[39]It is interesting that Clement's reading of Dt. 32:15
seems to have been influenced by Ex. 32.6, as Sibinga, p. 138,
observes. We may thus have a pre-Justinian association of these
texts, or at least a sign of how they could be associated on the
basis of their content. But the evidence is too weak to posit
a testimonia source for Justin's combination of the texts. His
different readings of both texts makes it more likely that Justin himself is responsible for the combination, or at least that
he cites them independently from his own Septuagintal source
even if the combination of texts possibly was suggested to him
by a testimonia tradition.

[40]Justin, pp. 257ff.

[41]See above, pp. 110ff.

[42]Justin here states that distinctions in the eating of
herbs are different than Jewish fasting restrictions, since they
depend on the nutritional qualities of the herbs rather than
whether or not the herbs are clean or unclean ritually speaking.

152

in the darkest colors and to derive from the prophetic critique
of the Mosaic cult an inference very different from the one intended by the Prophets. The rejection of the cult by Amos,
Isaiah and Jeremiah on account of the (ethical) sins of the Jews
becomes in Justin's hands evidence of God's ultimate rejection of the Law and, further, the sinfulness of the Jews becomes the reason for the very institution of the Law. The Law,
according to Justin, was in the first place legislated because
of the sins of the Jews and for the purpose of dealing with the
sinful inclination of the Jewish people.

How the Apologist works may well be illustrated by a
series of four texts which form the last part of Justin's overall argument about the purpose of the Law in Dial. chap. 22.
Starting with the refrain that God ordained offerings not because He was in need of them but because of the sins and idolatrous acts of the Jews, Justin tries to demonstrate his thesis
by quoting consecutively Amos 5:18-6:7 (Dial. 22.2-5), Jer. 7:
21-22 (Dial. 22.6), Ps. 49:1-23(LXX) (Dial. 22.7-10) and, after
a very brief interpretive comment, Is. 66:1 (Dial. 22.11). The
lengthy citation from Amos provides a passionate rejection of
festivals and sacrifices because of Jewish idolatries. The
citation from Jeremiah declares that God did not request sacrifices at the time of Israel's deliverance from the Egyptian
bondage. The lengthy Psalm states that God will judge Israel
not on the basis of ritual practices, but on the basis of ethical deeds and spiritual dispositions. Finally the brief quote
from Isaiah suggests that the Temple is entirely inadequate for
the true worship of God and that it was ordained for quite another reason, to restrain the Jews from idolatry.[43]

Justin does not interpret the above texts. His interpretive comment of Dial. 22.11, just as his introductory remark
of Dial. 22.1, simply repeats that sacrifices were ordained not
because God was in need of them but because of the sins of the

---

[43]In his comment of Dial. 22.11, where Justin notes
that the Temple is called God's οἶκος ἡ αὐλή, we may have an
allusion to Is. 1:11-13 (πατεῖν τὴν αὐλήν μου) known in the
Christian tradition as a proof-text for the rejection of sacrifices of the Law (Barn. 2.5ff.; Irenaeus, Adv. Haer. 4.29.1;
Tertullian, Adv. Jud. 5.6). Justin, however, does not quote
this text, but quotes Is. 66:1 which speaks more directly about
the Temple itself. This is a traditional proof-text for the
rejection of the Temple (Acts 7:49-50; Barn. 16.2). Otherwise,
Prigent, Justin, p. 262.

Jews (διὰ τὰς ἁμαρτίας ὑμῶν, Dial. 22.11). Quoted one after another, the texts have an obvious impact. The rejection of the
Mosaic cult, as well as the litany of sins found especially in
Amos 5:18-6:7 and Psalm 49(LXX), suggest to Justin the reason
why the Law was in the first place legislated, i.e., on account
of the sinfulness of the Jews. The prophetic critique of the
cult becomes Justin's authoritative basis for his interpretation
of the original purpose of the Law as legislation for the Jews.

In the above instances Justin seems again to be working
directly with the Septuagint, although the above texts frequently occur in the Christian interpretation of the Mosaic Law.
Parts of the lengthy passage from Amos are cited in Acts 7:42-
43, Irenaeus, Adv. Haer. 4.26.1, and Tertullian, Adv. Marc.
5.4.6. Psalm 49(LXX) is extensively quoted by Clement, I Clem.
35.7-12,[44] and very briefly by Irenaeus, Adv. Haer. 4.29.1, and
also Tertullian, Adv. Jud. 5.5. The far lengthier quotations by
Justin suggest that the Apologist has before him the full texts
of the Septuagint.[45] Of the remaining texts, Jer. 7:21-22 is
cited by the author of Barnabas, Barn. 2.7, and by Irenaeus,
Adv. Haer. 4.29.3. The latter cites a fuller text (Jer. 7:21-
25). Is. 66:1 is cited in Acts 7:49 and Barn. 16.2. Justin
quotes these texts in a free fashion. The readings of the texts
in Acts, Barnabas and the work of Irenaeus are substantially
different. There is no evidence of a firm testimonia tradition
behind them. Although knowledge of all of the above texts
probably comes to Justin from the Christian tradition, he seems
to work independently with the Septuagint and combines the texts
in his own way for his interpretation of the purpose of the Law.

C. Justin's Historical Interpretation of the Law

We have seen that Justin interprets the Mosaic Law as
historical dispensation for the Jews. He insists on the exclusive association of the Law with the Jewish people. But this
association is not of special concern to previous Christian

---

[44]Clement, however, cites the passage for another purpose, that is, as a general warning to the Christian sinner.

[45]For a study of these texts, see also Prigent, Justin,
pp. 260-63. In the case of Amos 5:18-6:7, Prigent finds that
the first part of the citation is from a version of the Septuagint which renders in part the Hebrew text and theorizes that
Justin expands the citation from his own Septuagintal source.

154

writers. It is regarded as something self-evident. For Paul, the Law is the custodian of the Jews during the period between Moses and Christ (Gal. 3:17ff.). The Apostle's chief concern is to affirm that the Law has come to an end with Christ through whom God's salvation, apart from the Law, is equally available both to Jews and gentiles (Gal. 3:6ff.; Rm. 1:16-17; 3:21ff.; 4:1ff.). He argues that the Law is a limited historical dispensation (Gal. 3:17), but does not insist on the assumed link between the Law and the Jews. Some of his explanations of the role of the Law in the history of salvation concern the human situation in general (Rm. 5:12ff.; 7:7ff.).

The author of Hebrews is less specifically concerned about the association of the Law with the Jews. For him the Law centers on the Mosaic cult which is totally ineffective and abolished by the sacrifice of Christ (Heb. 7:12,18; 8:13; 10:4ff.). He views the Law less in connection with the Jews and more in connection with its role as a typological prefigurement and quasi-platonic shadow of the true reality of salvation through Christ's sacrifice (Heb. 10:1ff.).[46]

The author of Barnabas completely ignores the Law as historical dispensation. For him the true intent of the Law is only a spiritual one. The literal observance of the Law was a perverse misunderstanding by the Jews influenced by a demon (Barn. 9.4).

Even Ptolemy, who writes around the time of Justin, or probably a little later, does not draw special attention to the Law as a legislation for the Jews. In his treatise on the Law, he mentions that Moses on his own initiative legislated the rule of divorce on account of the σκληροκαρδία of the Jews, as Jesus presumably had explained.[47] He also states that a part of God's Law, the law of retaliation, was legislated because of the (moral) weakness of those who were to receive it (διὰ τὴν ἀσθένειαν τῶν νομοθετηθέντων).[48] Otherwise Ptolemy is not concerned with

---

[46] See T. Stylianopoulos, "Shadow and Reality: Reflections on Heb. 10:1-18," GOTR 17 (1972), 215-30.

[47] Pan. 33.4.4.

[48] Ibid., 33.5.5.

interpreting the Law as having any historical function or being
a dispensation specifically for the Jews. He is more interested
in the ethical part of the Law, the Decalogue, which for him en-
dures and which Jesus fulfils. The whole ritual Law is interpreted by Ptolemy allegorically as a body of images which teach
spiritual truths.[49]

Justin, however, insists that the ritual Law was legislated only for the Jews. He contrasts the universality of the
New Law with the particularity of the Old: ὁ γὰρ ἐν Χωρῆβ παλαιὸς ἤδη νόμος καὶ ὑμῶν μόνον, ὁ δὲ [καινὸς νόμος] πάντων ἁπλῶς
(Dial. 11.2). The sabbath was ordained for the Jews: ὑμῖν
προσετάγη (Dial. 12.3). Circumcision was ordained for the Jews
alone: δι' ἣν αἰτίαν καὶ ὑμῖν προσετάγη (Dial. 18.3; ὑμῖν μόνοις, Dial. 19.2,5). All of the Law was legislated on account
of the hardness of heart of the Jewish people: διὰ τὸ σκληρο-
κάρδιον/σκληροκαρδίαν τοῦ λαοῦ ὑμῶν (Dial. 18.2; 43.1 et al.).[50]

Why does Justin mark such a difference from the Christian tradition in this regard? Why does he insist on a historical function of the Law when his Christian predecessors, such
as the author of Barnabas, were far more interested in the allegorical or typological meaning of the Law? Justin's interpretation of the purpose of the Law as historical dispensation for
the Jews has in view the marcionite criticism of the Law.[51]

Three important passages in particular connect Justin's
view of the purpose of the Law with the heretical teachers whom
Justin mentions in the Dialogue, as we have noted.[52] These passages are the following:

---

[49] Ibid., 33.5.8ff.

[50] See also Dial. 27.2; 44.2; 46.5; 47.2; 67.4.

[51] I owe this insight to von Campenhausen, Die Entstehung,
pp. 112-13. But Justin's argument is now addressed to Jews.
Prior to von Campenhausen's incisive evaluation, scholars assumed that Justin followed the traditional allegorization of the
Law. Hanson, p. 292, for example, writes: "Most of the en-
actments of Torah, for Justin, were intended to be reinter-
preted in a non-literal or allegorical sense; the Jews have misunderstood the interpretation of the Law, for it should be taken
not literally, but Christologically."

[52] See above, pp. 20ff.

'Εὰν δὲ ταῦτα οὕτως μὴ ὁμολογήσωμεν, συμβήσεται ἡμῖν
εἰς ἄτοπα ἐμπίπτειν νοήματα, ὡς τοῦ αὐτοῦ θεοῦ μὴ ὄντος
κατὰ τὸν 'Ενὼχ καὶ τοὺς ἄλλους πάντας, οἳ μήτε περιτομὴν τὴν κατὰ σάρκα ἔχοντες μήτε σάββατα ἐφύλαξαν μήτε
δὲ τὰ ἄλλα Μωϋσέως ἐντειλαμένου ταῦτα ποεῖν, ἢ τὰ αὐτὰ
αὐτὸν δίκαια μὴ ἀεὶ πᾶν γένος ἀνθρώπων βεβουλῆσθαι
πράσσειν· ἄπερ γελοῖα καὶ ἀνόητα ὁμολογεῖν φαίνεται.
δι'αἰτίαν δὲ τὴν τῶν ἁμαρτωλῶν ἀνθρώπων τὸν αὐτὸν ὄντα
ἀεὶ ταῦτα καὶ τὰ τοιαῦτα ἐντετάλθαι ὁμολογεῖν, καὶ φι-
λάνθρωπον καὶ προγνώστην καὶ ἀνενδεῆ καὶ δίκαιον καὶ
ἀγαθὸν ἀποφαίνειν ἐστιν (Dial. 23.1-2).

Now if we do not acknowledge the soundness of these arguments, we shall find ourselves falling into absurd
ideas, either that it is not the same God who was in the
time of Enoch, and of all the other (saints) who neither
had circumcision after the flesh nor kept either the sabbaths or the other commands, for it was Moses who ordered these things to be done; or else that He has not
desired that all mankind should always practise the same
acts of righteousness. And to acknowledge this seems ri-
diculous and silly. But we must acknowledge that it is
because of the fault of sinful men that He who is ever
the same has given these and such-like commandments, and
must declare that He loves men, and knows all beforehand,
and is in want of nothing, and is righteous and good.

'Αλλὰ τῇ αὐτῶν κακίᾳ ἐγκαλεῖτε, ὅτι καὶ συκοφαντεῖσθαι
δυνατός ἐστιν ὁ θεὸς ὑπὸ τῶν νοῦν μὴ ἐχόντων, ὡς τὰ αὐτὰ
δίκαια μὴ πάντας ἀεὶ διδάξας. πολλοῖς γὰρ ἀνθρώποις ἄ-
λογα καὶ οὐκ ἄξια θεοῦ τὰ τοιαῦτα διδάγματα ἔδοξεν εἶναι,
μὴ λαβοῦσι χάριν τοῦ γνῶναι ὅτι τὸν λαὸν ὑμῶν πονηρευόμενον καὶ ἐν νόσῳ ψυχικῇ ὑπάρχοντα εἰς ἐπιστροφὴν καὶ
μετάνοιαν τοῦ πνεύματος κέκληκε (Dial. 30.1).

But charge it to your own wickedness, that God can even
be falsely accused by them that have no sense, for not
having always taught all men the same acts of righteousness. For to many men such subjects of God's teaching
seemed to be irrational and unworthy of Him, for they
had not received grace to know that He has called your
people, when acting evilly, and being ill with disease
of soul, unto conversion and repentance of spirit.

ἐπεί, εἰ μὴ τοῦτό ἐστι, συκοφαντηθήσεται ὁ θεός, ὡς μήτε
πρόγνωσιν ἔχων μήτε τὰ αὐτὰ δίκαια πάντας διδάσκων καὶ
εἰδέναι καὶ πράττειν (πολλαὶ γὰρ γενεαὶ ἀνθρώπων πρὸ Μωϋσέως φαίνονται γεγενημέναι), καὶ οὐκ ἔστι λόγος ὁ λέγων
ὡς ἀληθὴς ὁ θεὸς καὶ δίκαιος καὶ πᾶσαι αἱ ὁδοὶ αὐτοῦ
κρίσεις, καὶ οὐκ ἔστιν ἀδικία ἐν αὐτῷ (Dial. 92.5).

For except this be the reason (to avoid idolatry) the
accusation will be brought against God that He neither
has foreknowledge, nor teaches all men to know and
practise the same righteous ordinances, for plainly
there were many generations of men before Moses. Hence
that will be no valid saying which says that "God is
true and righteous and all His ways are judgments, and
there is no iniquity in Him."

The first passage, <u>Dial</u>. 23.1-2, forms the conclusion of Justin's central argument on the Law (<u>Dial</u>. chaps. 11-23). This is evident not only from the content of <u>Dial</u>. 23.1-2, which is a double inference drawn on the basis of Justin's previous argumentation, but also from the Apologist's request in this context for a full response from Trypho.[53] Contends Justin: if his interpretation of the Law as temporal legislation for the Jews is not accepted, then unthinkable inferences about God would follow, that is, either that one is not dealing with the same God in the pre-Law period before Moses and Abraham, when the righteous neither had nor observed the Law, or that God inconsistently does not require observance of the same righteous principles always and by all men (<u>Dial</u>. 23.1).

This is not a purely hypothetical formulation. The inconsistency of God was a favorite marcionite criticism of the Demiurge. The dilemma which Justin poses to Trypho is an issue in the marcionite critique of the Old Testament although Justin, as in the case of the inconsistency of the command to fashion the brazen serpent,[54] does not here explicitly refer to Marcion. His answer concerning the historical function of the Law, now directed to Jews, is an answer to a marcionite problem about God and the Law. This answer is repeated in <u>Dial</u>. 23.2 where Justin affirms that the Mosaic Law was ordained by God on account of sinful men, the Jews, and that God Himself is defined by unassailable attributes (ὁ αὐτὸς ὢν ἀεί . . . καὶ φιλάνθρωπος καὶ προγνώστης καὶ ἀνενδεῆς καὶ δίκαιος καὶ ἀγαθός). The grouping of these adjectives has also an anti-marcionite ring.[55]

The second passage, <u>Dial</u>. 30.1, recapitulates the same conclusion at the end of the main unit on the Law (<u>Dial</u>. chaps. 10-30). That God can be "slandered" (συκοφαντεῖσθαι) as inconsistent by unthinking men should, according to Justin, be charged to the wickedness of the Jews which necessitated the

---

[53]Says Justin to Trypho and his companions: ἐπεὶ εἰ μὴ ταῦτα οὕτως ἔχει ἀποκρίνασθέ μοι, ὦ ἄνδρες, περὶ τῶν ζητουμένων τούτων ὅ τι φρονεῖτε, <u>Dial</u>. 23.2b. But they, seemingly overwhelmed, have nothing to say, and Justin breaks into a kerygmatic appeal (<u>Dial</u>. 23.3).

[54]See above, p. 30.

[55]See above, pp. 27-28.

158

legislation of the Law. To many men the precepts of the Mosaic
Law seem irrational and unworthy of God. But the truth of the
matter is, declares Justin, that such men have not received the
grace to know the purpose of the Law which is to call to repentance an evil and spiritually ill people, the Jews: τὸν λαὸν
ὑμῶν πονηρευόμενον καὶ ἐν νόσῳ ψυχικῇ ὑπάρχοντα εἰς ἐπιστροφὴν
καὶ μετάνοιαν τοῦ πνεύματος κέκληκε [ὁ θεός] (Dial. 30.1).
Once again, these criticisms of the Law are not criticisms simply of general pagan readers of the Old Testament, and certainly not of the Jews, but of Justin's Christian heretical opponents. They who "slander" God as inconsistent and impugn the
Law as "irrational" and "unworthy of Him" are the ones who
"blaspheme" against Him, the Christian heresiarchs and their
followers whom Justin mentions (Dial. 35.4ff.; 80.3; 82.3).
Justin's interpretation of the purpose of the Law is part of
his anti-heritical polemic, although his argument in the Dialogue is now addressed to Jews.

The final passage, Dial. 92.5-6, occurs much later in
Justin's exposition but reflects the same interests. Unless
Trypho and his companions agree, observes Justin, that the variety of dispensations was ordained by God in order to deal
with the sinful proclivity of the Jews (Dial. 95.2-4), God
could be "slandered" as neither having foreknowledge nor teaching all men the same righteous principles: συκοφαντηθήσεται ὁ
θεός, ὡς μήτε πρόγνωσιν ἔχων μήτε τὰ αὐτὰ δίκαια πάντας διδάσκων
καὶ εἰδέναι καὶ πράττειν (Dial. 95.5). Then the Scriptural word
that God is true and just, and that His ways are right judgments
and that no iniquity lies in Him[56] would not stand. But this
word is true, says Justin, and God's dispensations have in view
also the salvation of the Jews (Dial. 95.6). Such things as the
sabbath and offerings were appointed so that the Jews would not
commit idolatry but would be mindful of God, as Justin has previously shown: καὶ ὅτι διὰ ταῦτα ἐνετέταλτο ὁ θεὸς τὰς περὶ
σαββάτου καὶ προσφορῶν ἐντολάς, προαποδέδεικταί μοι (Dial. 95.
5a). In this case as well, hints of Justin's anti-heretical polemic appear to be the basis of his explanation of why the Law
was originally legislated.

[56]Justin is here quoting Dt. 32:4 and Ps. 91:16 (LXX).

In all of these instances, Justin's interpretation of the purpose of the Law as historical legislation for the Jews is linked to his anti-gnostic and anti-marcionite polemic. His explanation of why the Law was originally given is presented as the alternative answer to gnostic and marcionite criticisms of God, the Mosaic Law and the Old Testament. In particular, Justin seems to concede to Marcion that the Law was indeed intended for the Jews, i.e., that it must be interpreted in its historical and literal meaning, but he draws entirely different inferences about God and the Law than does Marcion. While he accepts and in fact emphasizes the function of the Law as historical dispensation, Justin at the same time defends the perfection of God and the meaningfulness of the Law within the divine dispensation.

Defense both of the perfection of God and the meaningfulness of the Law lies behind Justin's efforts to present the Law as a remedial and beneficent, rather than as a punitive discipline. It is true that, according to Justin, the Law would not have been necessary apart from the nature of the Jews as a hard-hearted people. But the precepts of the Law are neither irrational nor unworthy of God. The Law was given as a kind of divine "accommodation" suitable to the evil propensity of the Jews (ὅθεν ὁ θεὸς ἁρμοσάμενος πρὸς τὸν λαὸν ἐκεῖνον [τὸν νόμον], Dial. 19.6; 67.10). The Law is a restraint against idolatry (Dial. 19.6 et al.). It provides remembrance of God (Dial. 19.6ff.; 27.4; 46.5). It calls for conversion and repentance (Dial. 30.1). It does not matter that the Jews remained obdurate and unrepentant to the end.[57] The Law itself is a benevolent response by God Who is always good, just, prescient, consistent and loving. Thus the Law, according to Justin, was historically legislated for the Jews not as a puni-

---

[57] A point frequently repeated in the Dialogue, e.g., 19.6; 39.1; 46.6; 92.4; 93.4-5; 130.3 et al. Justin does not raise the question of the implications of the ultimate ineffectiveness of the Law in its stated purpose. As is known, some gnostics described the Demiurge as a "fumbling deity" who could not effectively deal with the Jews. Justin, however, is satisfied to emphasize the evil character of the Jews, which he assumes is the reason for the ineffectiveness of the Law.

tive or merely preventive discipline, as Marcel Simon suggests,[58] nor as a reproach, as Goodenough thinks,[59] but as a
remedial measure suited to a spiritually ill people. Otherwise, the goodness and perfection of God would remain open to
attack by the Marcionites.[60]

The connection of Justin's historical interpretation
of the Law with his anti-heretical polemic is corroborated when
one compares him with Tertullian and Irenaeus whose writings
against the second-century heresiarchs are extant. In his
Adversus Marcionem, Tertullian devotes the entire second book
to the defense of the true God and of the Mosaic legislation.
He defends the severity of God as compatible with reason and
justice and intended to be remedial, not arbitrary (Adv. Marc.
2.15). The Law, even its minute prescriptions for private and
public life, has the purpose of dealing with the hardness of
heart of the Jews, restraining their evil inclinations and en-
couraging continence (2.18-19). The Law simply bound man to
God; no one ought to find fault with it for its purpose was a
beneficent, not onerous, one (2.19.1-2). The apparent contradictions in the Old Testament regarding the Law have adequate
explanation (2.21-22). For example, the prophetic critique of
the cult, which rejects sacrifices and the sabbaths although
these were instituted in the Law, implies that God does not
really need such things, but accepts them as a token of respect-
ful homage (2.22). The dispensation of the Creator was reformed by Christ, rather than destroyed; restored, rather than
abolished.

Thus Tertullian in a more comprehensive and developed
form reflects all the concerns that one finds in Justin: the
defense of the goodness of God, the purpose of the Law as legislation for the Jews, the remedial character of the Law, and the

---

[58] Verus Israel, p. 199. Verweijs, p. 278, also thinks
that the Law was given to the Jews as punishment, according to
Justin.

[59] P. 117.

[60] Tertullian more explicitly defends the beneficent
purpose of the Law and the goodness of God against Marcion:
"ut nemo eam (i.e., the Law) reprobare debeat . . . Ad hoc be-
neficium, non onus, legis adiuuadum etiam prophetas eadem bo-
nitas dei ordinauit, docentes deo digna," Adv. Marc. 2.19.2.

effort to harmonize the differences in divine dispensations
while maintaining the unity and perfection of God. With respect to the latter, the effort to explain the consistency of
the one and the same God and, on the other hand, the diversity
of dispensations, leads Tertullian to a more defined theory of
development in the divine dispensations (Adv. Marc., book 4).
For him, the Law is preparatory to the Gospel forming the faith
of men by gradual stages in anticipation of the perfect light
of the Christian discipline (Adv. Marc. 4.17.2).[61] Justin,
however, retains the older view of the radical abolition of the
Law by Christ,[62] while recognizing the difference in divine
dispensations and offering his interpretation of the purpose of
the Law as adequate explanation of this state of affairs in the
history of salvation.

Irenaeus, who battles a wider circle of gnostics, tes-
tifies to similar interests about the Mosaic Law. Irenaeus
treats the legislation of the Law and its implications in book
4 of his Adversus Haereses. In this book he states that there
are many covenants and many precepts in the divine dispensations, but there is one and the same God (Adv. Haer. 4.9.1-3).
God sketches the plan of salvation like an architect, promul-
gating the Mosaic Law as instruction and discipline for the
Jews (4.14.2; 15.1). The legislation of the Law was given after the worship of the golden calf (4.15.1). Irenaeus thinks
of the Law's purpose as both remedial and punitive (4.16.5).
He calls the Law "bondage" (4.13.2; 15.1; 16.5). However, he,
too, insists against the gnostics that the Law has a pedagogical purpose suitable to the condition of the Jews and that God
does not need the savors of sacrifices or any such thing (4.14.
1-3; 15.1-2; 17.1-5). On the whole the Law plays a positive
role in the history of salvation for Irenaeus even though the
obdurate character of the Jews has made the purpose of the Law

---

[61]"Hanc etenim dicimus operam legis fuisse procurantis
euangelio: quorundam tunc fidem paulatim ad perfectum disci-
plinae Christianae nitorem primis quibusque praeceptis balbu-
tientis adhuc benignitatis informabat." His theory of development is fully set out in his Adversus Judaeos, book 2.

[62]See above, pp. 87ff.

ineffective.[63] In Irenaeus we also find a more defined sense of historical development as compared to Justin. According to Irenaeus, God who formed all things reveals Himself through many dispensations, forming, instructing and preparing men for the purpose of their being totally subject to God in Christ (Adv. Haer. 4.20.6-8).[64]

Justin's historical interpretation of the purpose of the Law was thus shaped by previous confrontation with the gnostic heresiarchs and especially with Marcion over the Old Testament. In the Dialogue, this argument is turned against the Jews as a corollary to the thesis of the invalidity of the Law, but the heretical teachers and their followers are unmistakably in the background.

The Mosaic Law, according to Justin, is intrinsically non-essential and unnecessary. Its only purpose in the history of salvation is to function as a temporary legislation for the Jews alone.[65] He agrees with the marcionite position that the historical function of the Law must be accepted, but draws quite different inferences. He does not in the main take recourse to allegorization of the Law but accepts its literal meaning. But to safeguard the perfection of God and at the same time the purposefulness of the Law as divine dispensation,

---

[63]Irenaeus takes note of the gnostic charge that the giver of the Law was of limited power because Israel was in the end disobedient and was ruined. His answer is free will: many are called but few are chosen, as Christ said (Adv. Haer. 4.15.2).

[64]Further on Irenaeus' view of historical development, see Karl Prümm, "Göttliche Planung und menschliche Entwicklung nach Irenäus Adversus Haereses," Schol. 13 (1938), 206-24, 342-66; Jean Daniélou, "Saint Irénée et les origines de la théologie de l'histoire," RechSR 34 (1947), 227-31; and R. A. Marcus, "Pleroma and Fulfilment: The Significance of History in St. Irenaeus' Opposition to Gnosticism," VigChr. 8 (1954), 193-224.

[65]This does not mean that the purpose of the Law is still valid for the Jews after Christ, as Verweijs, pp. 228-29, thinks. The Law has ended as temporary dispensation in the history of salvation (Dial. 11.2; 24.1; 43.1). The Jews who have not believed in Christ, failing to respond to the supreme moment of God's salvation, can now find themselves only in a curious twilight in which Justin assumes they are forever lost except for the eschatological remnant of the Jews who will by God's grace repent.

he paints the character of the Jews as a people with the darkest colors on the basis of the prophetic condemnation of the Jews.[66] Although he misinterprets the intent of the prophetic texts regarding the Mosaic cult and also retains a view of Scripture as a Sacred Book of absolute perfection, the achievement[67] of Justin lies in this: he recognized the historical function of the Law and the diversity of divine dispensations in history. He was the first Christian writer to work out an explanation of these matters over against the second-century heresiarchs without losing hold either of the authority of Scripture or the unity of God.

---

[66]The Christian tradition, and certainly the gnostics and Marcionites (see Tertullian, Adv. Marc. 2.22 and Irenaeus, Adv. Haer. 4.17), utilized prophetic texts critical of the Mosaic cult as evidence of the invalidity and worthlessness of the Law. But Justin goes beyond this and finds in the prophetic critique the very reason for the legislation of the Law, that is, the sinfulness of the Jews.

[67]Von Campenhausen, p. 106.

CONCLUSIONS

Justin Martyr played a significant role in the controversy over the Law and the Old Testament in the second century.
His lost <u>Syntagma</u>, an extensive work against the great second-
century heresiarchs, especially Marcion, probably centered on
the question of the interpretation of the Old Testament.[1]   His
<u>Dialogue with Trypho</u>, dealing with the Mosaic Law, Christology
and the true Israel, is an extant record of his controversy
over the Old Testament with Judaism.   In the latter document,
Justin has composed a comprehensive evaluation of the Mosaic
Law in <u>Dial</u>. chaps. 10-30 and in other parts of this writing
(<u>Dial</u>. chaps. 40-47, 67, 92-93 and 95).   From the present study
of Justin's treatment of the Law, the following conclusions may
be drawn:

(1)   While Justin's life and work involved him in debates with pagans and Jews as well as heretical Christians, his
interpretation of the Law in the <u>Dialogue</u> is cast primarily in
the context of the Jewish-Christian debate.   Trypho is portrayed
as a Jew.   The three major themes of the <u>Dialogue</u> are the central issues of the Jewish-Christian debate.   The authority of
the Old Testament is the exclusive court of appeals.   Neither
the authority of Jesus, nor that of an apostle, for example
Paul, as in the case of Ptolemy's treatise on the Law, is cited.
Above all, Justin's conviction that an eschatological remnant
of Jews is still being saved by conversion to Christianity in
the Apologist's very days (<u>Dial</u>. 32.2c; 55.3; 64.2-3) indicates
that the <u>Dialogue</u> is a writing for Jews.   Although one may assume that the <u>Dialogue</u> was also written for Christians, we must
reject the hypothesis that this document was in any way similar

---

[1]Prigent, <u>Justin et l'Ancien Testament</u>, pp. 10ff.   The
disputes of these thinkers involved for the most part the interpretation of the Old Testament.

166

to the Apology written for a pagan or pagans as Goodenough[2] and
Hyldahl[3] have advocated. The specific focus of the Dialogue may
well have been a concrete missionary front, possibly limited
geographically, where Christians and Jews, and particularly gentile Christians and Jewish Christians, crossed lines. The proselytistic encounter between Justin and Trypho (Dial. 8.2-4; cf.
47.1-4), Justin's view that some Jews were still open to conversion, the presence of Jewish Christians within the catholic
Church (Dial. 47.2) as well as hints of missionary activity
going on between Christians and Jews and between Jewish Christians and gentile Christians (Dial. 47.1,3-4) make the latter
view likely.

(2) On the other hand, Justin's treatment of the problem of the Law shows distinct awareness of the second-century
heresiarchs and their followers whom he mentions (Dial. 35.2-6;
80.2-4; 82.1-3; cf. Ap. 26.5-8; 58.1-2). The problem of the
Law, a major issue in the ongoing Jewish-Christian debate, was
raised sharply and anew around the middle of the second century
by the gnostics and especially Marcion. Ptolemy's Letter to
Flora indicates the intensity and scope of this debate.[4] Justin
was a major figure in the struggle and responded to the gnostic
teachers, and especially Marcion, with the Syntagma (Ap. 26.8).
In this work he quite probably dealt with the problem of the
Law. In the Dialogue, as Prigent[5] and von Campenhausen[6] have
shown, there is evidence that the heretical front is of considerable concern to Justin and that certain lines of argument on
the Law have been shaped by previous confrontation of the Apologist with the heretical teachers (Dial. 23.1-2; 30.1; 92.4-5).
Arguments originally directed against Marcion are now directed
against the Jews. In some instances, even marcionite criticisms
of the Law and the Old Testament known to Justin are now turned
against the Jews, as one clear case demonstrates (Dial. 94.

[2]The Theology of Justin Martyr, pp. 99-100.

[3]Christentum und Philosophie, pp. 20ff. and 292ff.

[4]See especially Pan. 33.3.1-3.

[5]Justin et l'Ancien Testament.

[6]Die Entstehung, pp. 112-13.

1-2).[7] In other cases, Justin modifies arguments of his heretical opponents to suit his purposes. For example, the argument
that the Law is intrinsically valueless because the Patriarchs
and other righteous of the Old Testament prior to Moses were not
required to observe it[8] is quite probably an adaptation of a
gnostic or marcionite argument that the legislation of the Law
is an inconsistency of the fumbling Demiurge who gave different
laws at different times.

Most importantly, Justin's historical interpretation of
the Law, and his tripartite division of the Law, were a result
of his debates with the great second-century heresiarchs. It
was the challenge of gnostic and marcionite hermeneutic that
led Justin, the first Christian author explicitly to do so, to
recognize the variety of divine dispensations, while maintaining and defending against the heretical teachers the unity of
God and the authority of Scripture.

(3) The Law for Justin is chiefly the ritual Law of the
Jews, contrary to Verweijs' opinion.[9] The problem of the Law
for the Apologist is primarily the problem of the meaning of the
cultic precepts of the Law such as circumcision, the sabbath,
fasting regulations, festivals, offerings, sacrifices and the
like. This is the issue at the forefront of Justin's treatment
of the Law. This also confirms that the Dialogue is a book of
controversy with Judaism. The problem of the Law in Ptolemy's
Letter to Flora, where the Law is discussed as a problem among
Christians, is by comparison quite different and centers on the
ethical part of the Law, the Decalogue.

(4) Justin's argumentation on the Law, having in view
the Jewish-Christian debate, emphasizes first of all the cessa-

---

[7]The contradiction between God's command to fashion a
brazen serpent and the earlier commandment which prohibited
graven images, reported by Tertullian, Adv. Marc. 2.21-22, as
a marcionite criticism of the Old Testament. See above, p. 30.

[8]Justin effectively utilizes this argument against the
Jews a number of times. See above, pp. 110ff.

[9]Evangelium und neues Gesetz, pp. 228-29. Verweijs
thinks that Justin does not restrict the teaching of the end of
the Law to the ceremonial Law.

tion of the Law and its invalidity with the coming of Christ, the New Law (Dial. chaps. 11ff.). In the second place, Justin underscores the purpose of the Law as temporal legislation for the Jews. Although he regards the Law as a remedial measure, he nowhere conceives of the Law as having pedagogical value nor does he speak of the fulfilment of the Law by Christ. Unlike Tertullian and Irenaeus who construct a theory of development in order to defend the unity of the two dispensations against the gnostics and Marcion, Justin remains within the older Christian tradition and insists on the radical abolishment of the Law by Christ. However, he seems to regard the Law as something ultimately indifferent for he allows Jewish Christians who live within the Church to practice it (Dial. 47.2).

(5) As a Christian teacher, Justin collects many Scriptural and non-Scriptural arguments to demonstrate his theses. For the most part he utilizes the Septuagint from which he quotes both frequently and extensively. Many texts are known to him from the Christian tradition, but in his use of these texts the Apologist depends directly on the Septuagint rather than on other Christian sources. In one interesting case, however, Justin is clearly dependent on Paul and Galatians 3.[10] There is no doubt that Justin knew of Paul. Unlike Ptolemy, however, he does not quote him nor does he mention him because the Dialogue is written for Jews and the authority of the discussion with Trypho is the Old Testament.

From the present study of Justin it is evident that the Apologist engaged in extensive controversies with both heretical Christianity and Judaism over the interpretation of the Law and the Old Testament around the middle of the second century. In his Dialogue with Trypho we have a comprehensive evaluation of the Law most likely written prior to Ptolemy's Letter to Flora. The record of the Apologist's work shows that among Christians thinkers of the second century Justin is a figure of no mean stature.

---

[10]The use of Dt. 21:23 and 27:26 which is quoted from Gal. 3:10-13, as well as the use of the Pauline argument concerning the impasse of the curse of the Law because no man is able to observe it in its entirety. See above, pp. 104ff. Justin seems to be dependent as well on Romans 4 for his argument about the faith of Abraham and circumcision. Again see above, pp. 116ff.

APPENDIX

ARE PAGANS THE ADDRESSEES OF THE DIALOGUE?

In modern times, several authors have claimed that the
Dialogue has been written for pagan readers. First Harnack[1]
suggested that pagans, along with Jews and Christians, are also
addressed in the Dialogue. Then Goodenough,[2] independently and
for different reasons, argued at length that the Dialogue is a
writing addressed not to a Jew, but either to a Christian or a
pagan, preferrably a pagan. Recently Niels Hyldahl,[3] taking into consideration both Harnack's suggestion and Goodenough's
view, attempts to settle the case for the Dialogue as a writing
for pagans. Finally Reiner Voss,[4] who knows of Hyldahl's position, accepts the hypothesis of the Dialogue as a work addressed
to pagans and adds to it a literary argument.

These scholars have cited the following evidence in support of their hypothesis:

(1)   the name of the stated addressee, Marcus Pompeius,
which is strongly Roman and therefore indicates a pagan, rather
than either a Christian or Jewish addressee.[5]

(2)   specific references to gentiles who are presumably

---

[1]In a lengthy footnote, Judentum und Judenchristentum,
pp. 51-52, n. 2.

[2]The Theology of Justin Martyr, pp. 96-100.

[3]Philosophie und Christentum, pp. 16-22.

[4]Der Dialog in der frühchristlichen Literatur, p. 38.
However, he states that the Dialogue actually found mostly
Christian readers.

[5]Goodenough, especially pp. 98 and 100.

addressed on many occasions throughout the _Dialogue_, e.g., _Dial_.
23.3; 24.3; 29.1; 32.5 and others.[6]

(3) the philosophical prologue of the _Dialogue_ (chaps.
1-6), as well as Justin's concept of the Christian faith as a
philosophy (_Dial_. 8.1-2), which presumably imply a pagan or pagan readers.[7]

(4) the literary form of the _Dialogue_ which favors
cultured pagan readers.[8]

In this Appendix, my purpose is to assess all of this
evidence point by point. At the end of this investigation, additional arguments will be presented that bear on the question
of whether or not pagans are the addressees of the _Dialogue_.

(1) The first of the above arguments centers on the
name of the stated addressee of the _Dialogue_. As Goodenough
suggests,[9] it is true that the name Marcus Pompeius, which is
in part Roman, may imply a pagan or Christian, rather than a
Jewish reader.[10] However, Marcus Pompeius is mentioned only
twice in the _Dialogue_, once simply by ὦ φίλτατε (_Dial_. 8.3) and
again by his full name ὦ φίλτατε Μᾶρκε Πομπήϊε at the end of the
work (_Dial_. 141.5). These references yield of themselves little
or nothing concerning the addressees of the _Dialogue_. They are
isolated references almost completely lost in this endless work
having as focus the encounter between a Christian and a Jew.
That the _Dialogue_ originally featured a dedication which included the name of the addressee and also "possibly a key to the
purpose of the book,"[11] has no support by either textual or

---

[6]Hyldahl, pp. 18ff.; Harnack, _Judentum und Judenchris-
tentum_, pp. 51-52, n. 2.

[7]Goodenough, pp. 99-100; Hyldahl, pp. 20ff. and 292ff.

[8]Voss, p. 38.

[9]Goodenough does not offer the name of the stated addressee, but rather the philosophical prologue of the book, as
decisive for his view concerning the recipients of the _Dialogue_.

[10]But adoption of Greek and Roman names by Jews in Hellenistic times was not unusual as in the case of Josephus Fla-
vius. The name Marcus is a good Jewish name.

[11]Goodenough, p. 97. See also Harnack, p. 47, n. 3.

internal evidence. On the contrary, if it is likely that the
Dialogue is an imitation of the Platonic style, the work may begin as it does for maximum dramatic effect. This would mean
that the question of the identity of Marcus Pompeius, like the
instance of Luke's Theophilus (Lk. 1:3; Acts 1:1), recedes to
the background with minimal significance concerning the question
of the addressee or addressees of this work. Both the dedication, if it ever existed, and the two references to the stated
addressee may simply be a literary gesture, as Hirzel had already suggested.[12] Neither suffices as evidence of the true addressee or addressees of the Dialogue.

Moreover, there is one instance of evidence in the
Dialogue which compels one to move beyond Marcus Pompeius, a
single addressee, as the intended reader of this work and seems
to confirm the formality of Justin's address to him. Dial.
80.3b is the only occasion where Justin takes note of his own
intention to write this document. Talking with Trypho and his
companions, Justin in Dial. 80.3b hints that the contents of the
Dialogue are also intended for a wider audience than Trypho and
the Jews (οὐκ ἐφ'ὑμῶν μόνον). The passage reads:

> ὅτι δ'οὐκ ἐφ'ὑμῶν μόνον τοῦτο λέγειν με ἐπίστασθε, τῶν
> γεγενημένων ὑμῖν λόγων ἁπάντων, ὡς δύναμίς μου, σύντα-
> ξιν ποιήσομαι, ἐν οἷς καὶ τοῦτο ὁμολογοῦντά με, ὃ καὶ
> πρὸς ὑμᾶς ὁμολογῶ, ἐγγράψω.

> But that you may know that I do not say this before you
> alone, I will make, so far as in me lies, a collection
> of all the speeches made by us, in which I will write
> that I acknowledge whatever I am acknowledging to you.

In the wider context, the discussion in Dial. chap. 79
is about fallen angels. In Dial. chap. 80 (εἶπε δέ μοι), it
changes to the issue of the Christian eschatological hopes, the
millenium, the rebuilding of Jerusalem and the resurrection.
Trypho questions Justin as to whether or not Christians truly
acknowledge the millenial hope and the hope of gathering together in Jerusalem with Christ, along with the Old Testament Patriarchs, Prophets and other righteous Jews and Jewish proselytes who lived prior to Christ. Or has Justin previously made

---

[12]Rudolf Hirzel, Der Dialog: ein literarhistorischer
Versuch (Leipzig, 1895), II, 368ff.

such Christian claims[13] in order to overwhelm Trypho in the discussion, presumably by taking everything away from the Jews? Justin retorts that he means exactly what he says and that, in order to show his perfect willingness to affirm the same claim not only before Trypho and his companions, but also before others, he will commit the whole conversation to writing (Dial. 80.3b).

The above passage does not disclose either the full purpose nor the actual addressees of the Dialogue. It deals only with an incidental point in the lengthy discussion. The reference to readers of the Dialogue other than Trypho and his friends is oblique and unclear. But the passage does provide a clue that the work is also intended for a wider audience than Trypho and his friends, an audience which is in this instance the test of Justin's willingness to assert the particular point under discussion.

Harnack suggests that pagans are here in view.[14] However, the context indicates no evidence that pagans constitute in this instance Justin's audience. On the contrary, besides the Christians, some of whom according to Justin accept the millenial hope while others do not (Dial. 80.2), the context casts in sharp light the gnostics who, Justin reports, reject both the hope of the millenium as well as the hope of the resurrection (Dial. 80.3-5). The forceful, though of course negative, way in which the "godless and impious heretics" (ἄθεοι καὶ ἀσεβεῖς αἱρεσιῶται) appear on the horizon at this point suggests that they, Justin's gnostic opponents, are in this instance particularly in view, for polemical purposes,[15] not pagans. To what

---

[13]But where? No such previous discussion may be found in the Dialogue in its present form. Perhaps the omission is due to the lacuna of Dial. 74.3. It is doubtful that Justin is here referring to the earlier more general remarks of Dial. 24.3 and 26.1.

[14]He cites this passage in Judentum und Judenchristentum, pp. 51-52, n. 2, along with several other passages.

[15]They are anticipated already by the καὶ in Dial. 80. 2c (πολλοὺς δ'αὖ καὶ τῶν τῆς καθαρᾶς) and are still in view in 80.5 (καὶ σαρκὸς ἀνάστασιν γενήσεσθαι). See also the reference to gnostics in 82.3, where they seem to be mentioned in another connection, that of true and false prophets and teachers (Dial. 81.4ff.). But the larger context is the same. In Dial. 81.4 Justin is still talking about the millenium, calling upon the

extent the gnostics are encountered in the Dialogue is another question.[16] Suffice it here to say that Dial. 80.3b allusively reflects multiple addressees, or at least multiple fronts, Jews, Christians and gnostics, other than pagans. It is also an indication that the references to Marcus Pompeius are not sufficient evidence for the view that the Dialogue is a writing addressed to pagans.

(2) A second argument supporting the same hypothesis is that certain passages of the Dialogue seem to ring out as appeals to gentiles. Harnack suggested that Dial. 29.1; 64:2e; 80.3b and 119.4 imply pagan readers.[17] Earlier Th. Zahn had suggested that Dial. 23.3 and 24.3 are addressed to the companions of Trypho, who are presumably gentile converts to Judaism, although not yet full proselytes.[18] Zahn suggested that also Dial. 32.5 is a reference to pagans.[19] It is on such references, and especially on Zahn's evidence, that Hyldahl partly rests his own case regarding the addressees of the Dialogue.[20] He supposes that such references involve gentiles who are pagans and that they also indicate the pagan readers of this work. But is this the case?

---

witness of the author of Revelation who, according to Justin, "prophesied" the millenium. This then triggers his subsequent statements about false prophets and teachers, the gnostics.

[16]See above, pp. 20ff.

[17]Judentum und Judenchristentum, pp. 51-52, n. 2.

[18]"Studien zu Justin III," ZKG 8 (1885-1886), 56-61. But Zahn does not claim that the whole Dialogue is addressed to pagans. Zahn, supposing a high degree of historical reality in the Dialogue, sets out to answer the question of who are Trypho's friends and concludes that they are his gentile students who have been won over to Judaism by him but not yet circumcized. Justin, however, never refers to Trypho as a teacher and clearly distinguishes him from the Rabbinic teachers (Dial. 38. 1; 48.2; 62.2; 137.2). One of Justin's last remarks to Trypho is that he should choose Christ rather than his own teachers (Dial. 142.2).

[19]Ibid.

[20]P. 19. He thinks that the gentile converts of Trypho are token representatives of the pagan readers of the Dialogue. He seems to follow Zahn already in "Tryphon und Tarphon," especially pp. 86ff.

174

Each of the above passages must be separately examined.[21]

(a) <u>Dial</u>. 23.3:

Καὶ μηδὲν μηδενὸς ἀποκρινομένου· Διὰ ταῦτά σοι, ὦ Τρύφων, καὶ τοῖς βουλουμένοις προσηλύτοις γενέσθαι, κηρύξω ἐγὼ θεῖον λόγον, ὃν παρ'ἐκείνου ἤκουσα τοῦ ἀνδρός.[22]
ὁρᾶτε ὅτι τὰ στοιχεῖα οὐκ ἀργεῖ οὐδὲ σαββατίζει. μείνατε ὡς γεγένησθε. εἰ γὰρ πρὸ τοῦ Ἀβραὰμ οὐκ ἦν χρεία
περιτομῆς . . . οὐδὲ νῦν.

And when no one answered I added: Therefore to you,
Trypho, and to those who wish to become proselytes (to
the true faith), I proclaim the Divine message which
I heard from that (old) man (whom I mentioned before).
You see that Nature does not idle nor keep the sabbath.
Abide as ye have been born. For if before Abraham
there was no need of circumcision . . . neither in
like manner is there any need now.

In this passage, Justin makes one of his many appeals
for the conversion of Trypho and his companions to the Christian faith.   Zahn thinks that the above use of the term προσήλυτοι is in the technical sense, designating exclusively gentile converts to Judaism, not converts whether Jews or pagans
to Christianity.   It is on this idea that Zahn essentially
rests his theory about the companions of Trypho.   For Zahn the
προσήλυτοι of <u>Dial</u>. 23.3 are none other than Trypho's friends,
gentile converts to Judaism, who, however, are not yet full
proselytes but only φοβούμενοι τὸν θεόν (<u>Dial</u>. 10.4).   According to Zahn, they have not yet been circumcised as Justin himself supposedly intimates, saying to them alone and not to Trypho: μείνατε ὡς γεγένησθε, <u>i.e.</u>, uncircumcised (<u>Dial</u>. 23.3).

Zahn is admittedly ingenious, yet not convincing.
First, neither the term προσήλυτος nor the phrase φοβούμενοι
τὸν θεὸν are used by Justin in the technical sense which Zahn's
interpretation requires.   The terms προσήλυτος and προσήλυσις
are clearly used for converts to the Christian faith (<u>Dial</u>.

---

[21]Except for <u>Dial</u>. 80.3b which was discussed above, pp.
171-73.

[22]The old man by the sea who converted Justin to the
Christian faith (<u>Dial</u>. 3.1ff.).   This is the only reference
to him apart from the prologue and it is an intriguing one.
It probably reflects Justin's dependence on the Christian
tradition for what he writes in the <u>Dialogue</u>.

28.2; 122.5).[23] Furthermore, there is no evidence in the context of Dial. 10.4 to show that φοβούμενοι τὸν θεόν is not used
here in a general, rather than technical, way. The general usage of this phrase is in fact indicated by its other occurrences
in Dial. 24.3; 98.5 and especially Dial. 106.1-2 where it designates all men, believers and potential believers: πάντας τοὺς
φοβουμένους τὸν θεόν.[24] Finally, throughout the Dialogue, Justin distinguishes between Trypho and the Rabbinic teachers,[25]
not between Trypho and his companions,[26] so that in the context
of Dial. 23.3 as well, μείνατε ὡς γεγένησθε equally includes
Trypho. The larger argument (εἰ γὰρ πρὸ τοῦ Ἀβραὰμ οὐκ ἦν
χρεία περιτομῆς, and so on, Dial. 23.3ff.) involves appeals to
the history of salvation and to creation, periods when, according to Justin, circumcision neither existed nor was it necessary.[27] Justin's remarks are addressed both to Trypho and
Trypho's companions. In the context, Trypho is also the direct
addressee (σοί, ὦ Τρύφων, καὶ τοῖς βουλομένοις προσηλύτοις)!

---

[23]Thus also Otto, p. 81, n. 4, and all other commenta-
tors take as well Dial. 23.3 as an appeal to Jews to become
Christian proselytes. But Zahn brushes the use of the terms
in Dial. 28.2 and 122.4 aside as a convenient imitation of the
proper Jewish usage.

[24]The usage here is apparently derived from Ps. 21:23-
24(LXX) which is quoted in Dial. 106.2.

[25]Dial. 9.1; 36.2; 38.1-2; 62.2; 68.7; 71.1; 110.1;
112.4-5; 117.4; 120.5; 134.1; 137.2; 140.2 and 142.2.

[26]According to the setting of the Dialogue, there were
at least four companions with Trypho on the first day of the
discussion (Dial. 56.13,16), two having departed early (τῶν δὲ
σὺν αὐτῷ δύο, χλευάσαντες καὶ τὴν σπουδὴν ὑμῶν ἐπισκώψαντες,
ἀπηλλάγησαν, Dial. 9.3). On the second day, two others join
the discussion and one of them is called Mnaseas (Dial. 85.6;
94.4; cf. 78.6; 85.4; 92.5 and 118.4). Justin takes no time to
introduce them in any special way and nowhere does he distinguish them as being in any way different from Trypho. It may
be noted here that Zahn himself recognizes that Justin does not
draw the alleged distinction clearly, i.e., Justin does not according to Zahn reproduce history accurately on this matter because he lacks talent as a writer, pp. 59-60.

[27]This is often repeated in the Dialogue, e.g., Dial.
19.3-4; 27.5; 29.3; 43.2 et al. See above, pp. 109ff.

Thus μείνατε and γεγένησθε[28] equally apply to Trypho, just as ὁρᾶτε in the same passage also applies to him.

The passage which reflects all these elements together and shatters Zahn's theory is <u>Dial</u>. 28.1-2:

> Καὶ ὁ Τρύφων· Καὶ πρότερον ἀκηκόαμέν σου τοῦτο προ-
> βάλλοντος καὶ ἐπεστήσαμεν. . . . Κἀγώ· Ἐπειδὴ ἀπό
> τε τῶν γραφῶν καὶ τῶν πραγμάτων τάς τε ἀποδείξεις
> καὶ τὰς ὁμιλίας ποιοῦμαι, ἔλεγον, μὴ ὑπερτίθεσθε μη-
> δὲ διστάζετε πιστεῦσαι τῷ ἀπεριτμήτῳ ἐμοί. βραχὺς
> οὗτος ὑμῖν περιλείπεται προσηλύσεως χρόνος· ἐὰν φθά-
> σῃ ὁ Χριστὸς ἐλθεῖν, μάτην μετανοήσετε, μάτην κλαύ-
> σετε· οὐ γὰρ εἰσακούσεται ὑμῶν.

> Trypho said: We have already heard you put this for-
> ward, and we paid attention to what you said. . . .
> And I said: Since I draw my proofs and exhortations
> both from the Scriptures and from the facts themselves,
> do not put the matter off, or hesitate to believe me,
> who am uncircumcised. It is but a short time that is
> left you for coming over to us, if Christ come sudden-
> ly, you will repent in vain, you will lament in vain;
> for He will not hear you.

Justin here not only uses the noun προσήλυσις in connection with his inviting Trypho and his companions to become
<u>Christian</u> proselytes, but also groups Trypho and his companions
together without distinction, as the plural in both Trypho's and
Justin's lips indicates. Most telling of all is the implicit
contrast which Justin draws on the one hand between himself, an
uncircumcized gentile (ἀπερίτμητος) and, on the other hand,
those whom he is here addressing, Trypho and his companions, who
are circumcized Jews.

Thus the addressees of <u>Dial</u>. 23.3 are not gentile converts to Judaism as Zahn thought, but Trypho and his companions
who are Jews. Consequently they are not representatives of the
pagan readers of the <u>Dialogue</u> as Hyldahl supposes.

(b) <u>Dial</u>. 24.3 and (c) <u>Dial</u>. 29.1 are parallel cases
and may be examined together. The first passage reads:

> δεῦτε σὺν ἐμοὶ πάντες οἱ φοβούμενοι τὸν θεόν, οἱ θέ-
> λοντες τὰ ἀγαθὰ Ἰερουσαλὴμ ἰδεῖν. δεῦτε πορευθῶμεν
> τῷ φωτὶ κυρίου· ἀνῆκε γὰρ τὸν λαὸν αὐτοῦ, τὸν οἶκον
> Ἰακώβ. δεῦτε πάντα τὰ ἔθνη, συναχθῶμεν εἰς Ἰερου-
> σαλήμ.

---

[28] Otto Translates "nati estis" ("you were born") not
"facti estis" ("you were made"), p. 82, n. 7. But this does not
essentially affect our point. The translations of Archambault
and Williams seem to follow Otto here.

Come with me all who fear God, who wish to see the
good things of Jerusalem. Come, let us go in the
light of the Lord, for He has set His people free,
even the House of Israel. Come, all ye nations, let
us be gathered together at Jerusalem.

And the second passage:

Δοξάσωμεν τὸν θεόν, ἅμα τὰ ἔθνη συνελθόντα, ὅτι καὶ
ἡμᾶς ἐπεσκέψατο· δοξάσωμεν αὐτὸν διὰ τοῦ βασιλέως
τῆς δόξης, διὰ τοῦ κυρίου τῶν δυνάμεων. εὐδόκησε
γὰρ καὶ εἰς τὰ ἔθνη, καὶ τὰς θυσίας ἥδιον παρ'ἡμῶν
ἢ παρ'ὑμῶν λαμβάνει.

Let all of us Gentiles come together and glorify
God, because He has looked down upon us; let us glo-
rify Him by the King of glory, by the Lord of hosts.
For He hath taken pleasure even in the nations, and
He receives the sacrifices more gladly from us than
from you.

The matter is quite different with respect to the above
passages, for here we have unambiguously to do with gentiles:
τὰ ἔθνη.[29] Significantly these gentiles are addressed in the
hortatory subjunctive as the direct audience of Justin. But do
these references signify non-Christian pagans? The evidence indicates that in these instances, not pagans in general but rather Christians, i.e., gentiles who are already converts to the
Christian faith, constitute Justin's audience.

The literary character of these passages constructed out
of Old Testament texts[30] and defined by a liturgical flavor offers the first clue to Justin's audience in these instances.
David Gill not long ago neatly argued in a brief note[31] that
Dial. 29.1 is a liturgical fragment which Justin works into his
text at this point. He observed that as an appeal to Trypho and
his companions, Dial. 29.1 is completely out of place here and

---

[29]From the first passage Zahn wanted the reference to
the φοβούμενοι τὸν θεόν. He apparently did not notice that the
second passage is in style strikingly similar and also contains
the same appeal to the ἔθνη. Otherwise, he might have argued
his case differently. The second passage is Harnack's main reference for the suggestion that receptive pagans are also addressed in the Dialogue.

[30]In the case of Dial. 24.3 Justin builds on the Septuagintal texts of Ps. 127:1,4-5; Jer. 3:17 and Is. 2:5-6 from
where he apparently derives the δεῦτε, and in the case of Dial.
29.1 on Ps. 23:10(LXX).

[31]"A Liturgical Fragment in Justin, Dialogue 29,1,"
HTR 59 (1966), 98-100.

that its original context must have been quite different, the
Christian liturgy. His main point is that this text is a liturgical fragment which Gill tries to reconstruct. He does not see
that its parallel, Dial. 24.3, is also of the same texture (another liturgical fragment?), nor does he observe the strong
kerygmatic tone of the whole Dialogue,[32] which show how Justin
can occasionally break forth into a kind of lyricism, a tri-
umphal note of celebration, clothed certainly in liturgical language, if not also in expressions representing actual fragments
of early Christian hymns and prayers. If Gill is of course entirely right, it is all the more plain that the addressees here
are not pagans, but gentiles who are Christians, the worshipping Church.

That these are Christian gentiles is demonstrated both
by the context of the passages as well as by the wider use of
the term ἔθνη in the Dialogue. Dial. 24.3 presupposes the contrast between the true and false Israel, between the Jews on the
one hand and, on the other, the gentiles who are already Christian believers (πεπιστεύκαμεν, Dial. 24.1b). The ἔθνος δίκαιον
and λαὸς φυλάσσων πίστιν (Dial. 24.2) are the gentiles (ἔθνη)
who, unlike Israel, have already responded to God's call (Dial.
24.2; cf. 119.4). The same are designated in Dial. 25.1, where
Justin identifies and includes himself with them (σὺν ἡμῖν),[33]
and also quite plainly in Dial. 26.1 (τά . . . ἔθνη τὰ πιστεύσαντα εἰς αὐτόν). The other passage, Dial. 29.1, both by context and content, also has to do with gentiles who have already
believed in Christ and are already baptized Christians contrasted to the Jews (e.g., τὰς θυσίας ἥδιον παρ'ἡμῶν ἢ παρ'ὑμῶν

---

[32]E.g., κηρύξω ἐγὼ θεῖον λόγον, Dial. 23.3; βοῶ, Dial.
24.1. The prophetic texts which Justin quotes have the same
character. Justin, as in the case of Dial. 24.3, where form-
critically he seems to imitate Is. 2:5-6, often is drawn to
this style, weaving the prophetic texts into his own discourse.
Cf. Dial. 12.2; 15.1; 28.2-3 et al.

[33]Otto here notes, but does not adopt, the reading σὺν
ὑμῖν of manuscript A which does not harmonize with the previous
discourse in the first person plural. Zahn, however, p. 58, a-
dopts this reading because it seems perfectly to suit his hypothesis that Trypho's companions are here addressed. But the
contrasting οὗτοι which follows would then, on Zahn's own
terms, be a very awkward reference to Trypho as a single person.

λαμβάνει, Dial. 29.1c; τίς οὖν ἔτι μοι περιτομῆς λόγος . . . ἐκείνου τοῦ βαπτίσματος χρεία ἁγίῳ πνεύματι βεβαπτισμένῳ, Dial. 29.1d; ἐν τοῖς ὑμετέροις ἀπόκεινται γράμμασι, μᾶλλον δὲ οὐχ ὑμετέροις ἀλλ᾿ ἡμετέροις, Dial. 29.2d).

The theme of the true Israel is a major theme in the Dialogue, treated with concentration in Dial. 119-25 (see also Dial. 116ff.) and 130-41.[34] It is a theme which is in the air throughout the Dialogue, breaking forth at many points of the discussion.[35] The same theme is the subject also of Dial. chaps. 24-26 and 28-30, the larger context of our passages. Here the Jews and Christians are contrasted as the false and true people of God. The context clearly corroborates that the references to the ἔθνη in Dial. 24.3 and 29.1 are to Christian gentiles.

Justin's use of the term ἔθνη in the Dialogue confirms this conclusion. Justin in a concentrated fashion uses the term ἔθνη primarily as a designation for the Christians. The term ἔθνη is Septuagintal language derived from especially prophetic texts which Justin quotes as predictions of the true Israel, the Church, now fulfilled.[36] To be sure, he can use the same term to designate also unbelieving pagans in general,[37] but in each case there is hardly room for doubt as to whom Justin is referring. Unbelieving pagans are τὰ ἄλλα ἔθνη (Dial. 17.1), gentiles who serve idols, commit all kinds of abominations (Dial. 95.1), and stand off against the Christians as their persecutors (τὰ ἄλλα ἔθνη . . . [τὰ] ἀναιροῦντα τοὺς μόνον ὁμολογοῦντας

---

[34]See above, p. 7 and n. 3.

[35]Dial. 11.4-5; 32.5; 39.1-5; 43.2 et al. It is present whenever the "we"/"you" contrast comes to the fore.

[36]See Dial. 11.3-5; 24.4; 26.2-4; 28.5 and 30.2-3 where Ps. 18(LXX) is presupposed, perhaps omitted by a scribe. In Dial. chaps. 118-41, of course, where Justin properly deals with this theme, he adduces numerous proof-texts as prophecies fulfilled in Christianity.

[37]See Ap. 27.1; 42.4; Dial. 10.3; 17.1; 21.1 et al. Justin often refers to pagans or mankind in general with the expression πᾶν γένος ἀνθρώπων (Ap. 15.6; 25.1; 31.7; 39.3; 46.2; 50.12; Dial. 23.1; 88.4; 93.1; 95.1-2; 124.1.

180

ἑαυτοὺς εἶναι Χριστιανούς, <u>Dial</u>. 96.2).[38] The Christian gentiles, however, are those of whom Isaiah and other Prophets
spoke (εἰς φῶς ἐθνῶν, <u>Dial</u>. 11.3-4; cf. 26.2-3; 28.5-6 et <u>al</u>.),
the believing gentiles (τά . . . ἔθνη τὰ πιστεύσαντα, <u>Dial</u>.
26.1; οἱ . . . ἀπὸ τῶν ἐθνῶν ἁπάντων διὰ τῆς πίστεως τῆς τοῦ
Χριστοῦ θεοσεβεῖς καὶ δίκαιοι γενόμενοι, <u>Dial</u>. 52.4; cf. 91.3),
who have already been illumined (τὰ ἔθνη τὰ πεφωτισμένα, <u>Dial</u>.
122.3). These gentiles constitute another people (λαὸς ἕτερος,
<u>Dial</u>. 119.3), another Israel (ἄλλος 'Ισραήλ, <u>Dial</u>. 123.5), the
people promised to Abraham (<u>Dial</u>. 11.5; 119.4), with whom Justin
fully identifies (ἡμεῖς λαὸς ἕτερος . . . ἡμᾶς ἐξελέξατο . . .
ἡμᾶς δὲ ἅπαντας, <u>Dial</u>. 119.3-5;[39] ἡμᾶς τὰ ἔθνη, οὓς ἐφώτισεν,
<u>Dial</u>. 122.5), and the true children of God (θεοῦ τέκνα ἀληθινὰ
καλούμεθα καὶ ἐσμέν, <u>Dial</u>. 123.9). But these gentiles are to be
distinguished not only from Jews, which is quite evident for
Justin, but also from pagans in general:

Καὶ ἡμᾶς δὲ ἅπαντας δι'ἐκείνης τῆς φωνῆς ἐκάλεσε, καὶ
ἐξήλθομεν ἤδη ἀπὸ τῆς πολιτείας, ἐν ᾗ ἐζῶμεν κατὰ τὰ
κοινὰ τῶν ἄλλων τῆς γῆς οἰκητόρων κακῶς ζῶντες· καὶ
σὺν τῷ 'Αβραὰμ τὴν ἁγίαν κληρονομήσωμεν γῆν, εἰς τὸν
ἀπέραντον αἰῶνα τὴν κληρονομίαν ληψόμενοι, τέκνα τοῦ
'Αβραὰμ διὰ τὴν ὁμοίαν πίστιν ὄντες (<u>Dial</u>. 119.5).

And all of us also did He call by that voice, and we
went forth from the state of life in which we were
living, yea, and living evilly according to the common
ways of all other inhabitants of the earth. And we
shall inherit the Holy Land together with Abraham, re-
ceiving our inheritance for a boundless eternity, as
being children of Abraham because we have like faith
with him.

These, the Christian gentiles, are the ἔθνη who are addressed in

---

[38]The note of anti-Christian persecution is often
sounded in the <u>Dialogue</u>. See <u>Dial</u>. 9.1; 11.4; 18.3; 30.2; 35.8;
39.5-6; 96.2; 110.4; 119.6; 121.2. In <u>Dial</u>. 110.4 Justin lists
a number of tortures and means of death, saying that Christians
courageously face up to them, so that the tortures have the opposite result of their aim, attracting others (also Justin prior
to his conversion, <u>App</u>. 12.1) and increasing the number of
Christians, rather than diminishing them. In several places,
as part of his own anti-Jewish polemic, Justin taunts that perhaps the reason why Jews do not become Christians is that they
fear similar persecution (<u>Dial</u>. 39.6; 44.1; 46.6), although he
knows that Jews as well suffered much persecution in his days
because of the Bar Cochba war (<u>Dial</u>. 16.2ff.; 19.2; 110.6).

[39]A passage which according to Harnack implies Greek and
not Jewish readers. True, but one must specify Greek readers
who are already Christians, not pagans in general.

<u>Dial</u>. 24.3 and 29.1. They are the new house of Jacob (<u>Dial</u>.
24.3; cf. 123.9), those who in the end-time will gather together
in Jerusalem (<u>Dial</u>. 24.3; cf. 80.1,2,5; 81.1ff.) and can in the
present glorify God through Christ as baptized and worshipping
believers, <u>i.e</u>., as the Church (<u>Dial</u>. 29.1; cf. 63.5).

(d) <u>Dial</u>. 32.5:

καὶ ταῦτα δὲ πάντα ἃ ἔλεγον ἐν παρεκβάσεσι λέγω πρὸς
ὑμᾶς, ἵνα ἤδη ποτὲ πεισθέντες τῷ εἰρημένῳ καθ᾽ ὑμῶν ὑπὸ
τοῦ θεοῦ, ὅτι Υἱοὶ ἀσύνετοι ἐστέ . . . παύσησθε καὶ ἑ-
αυτοὺς καὶ τοὺς ὑμῶν ἀκούοντας πλανῶντες, καὶ παρ᾽ἡμῶν
μανθάνοντες τῶν σοφισθέντων ἀπὸ τῆς τοῦ Χριστοῦ χάριτος.

And all these things which I said by way of digression
do I say unto you, in order that by obeying at last
God's word against you, namely, "Ye are children without
understanding" . . . you may cease leading both yourselves and them that hear you astray, and be learning
from us who have been made wise by the grace of Christ.

This passage is also suggested by Zahn as a reference to non-
Christian gentiles. It is an allusive passage but it indeed
contains an intriguing reference to non-Christian gentiles. The
crucial question is: who are those who listen to the Jews and
are, according to Justin, led astray by them (παύσησθε . . .
τοὺς ὑμῶν ἀκούοντας πλανῶντες).

At this point of the <u>Dialogue</u>, Justin is in the Christological discussion (<u>Dial</u>. chaps. 31ff.). He is responding to
Trypho's initial objection about the humble appearance of
Christ, first by way of a digression (παρέκβασις). With the
plural παρεκβάσεσι Justin takes note of his frequent asides
throughout the <u>Dialogue</u> in which he declares or attempts to demonstrate that only Christians possess the correct interpretation of Scripture. In these digressions he often combines repeated criticisms of the Jews with appeals for their conversion.[40] The passage as it stands contains at the beginning an
obscurity which can be clarified by an emendation of the text
to read καὶ ταῦτα δὲ πάντα, ἔλεγον, ἐν παρεκβάσεσι λέγω and so
on,[41] but this is not crucial to the matter at hand. The

[40]<u>Dial</u>. 28.2-3; 32.2-5; 39.1ff.; 44.1ff. <u>et al</u>.

[41]Omit the "α" as an error by dittography (πανταἀελεγον)
and punctuate as indicated above, not following Otto and Goodspeed. This resolves the difficulty of the text which reads as
if Justin had already spoken to Trypho and his companions on a
previous occasion other than the present one. The difficulty is

essential question is who are those who, according to Justin, listen to the Jews and are led astray by them?

Zahn states that they are gentiles who, like Trypho's friends, are students of Jewish teachers.[42] He does not discuss the passage further. Are there any other clues in the *Dialogue* concerning their identity? Or does this represent simply a passing remark by Justin? The only other place where gentiles are said to be open to persuasion by Jews is *Dial.* chap. 47, but here we have to do with Christian gentiles persuaded by Jewish Christians to observe the Mosaic Law. Justin states that he knows of Christian gentiles who have adopted Jewish practices and have subsequently either continued to maintain their confession of Christ or have denied it altogether (*Dial.* 47.4). Naturally he repudiates both this kind of proselytism as well as those gentile Christians who succumb to it, expressing little or no hope at all especially for those who altogether turn their back to the Christian faith.[43]

Is there any relationship between the problem of *Dial.* chap. 47 and those who are "misled" by the Jews according to *Dial.* 32.5? The evidence makes it quite unlikely. First, there is no explicit connection made between the two. Secondly, the Jews who proselytize gentile Christians according to chap. 47 are Jewish Christians (*Dial.* 47.1ff.), whereas the plural "you" implied in *Dial.* 32.5 definitely refers to Trypho and to non-Christian Jews. Justin's reminder in *Dial.* 47.1 of Trypho's attempt to proselytize him (*Dial.* 8.4) is evidently only an incidental point of comparison and sheds no light on the passage of *Dial.* 32.5.

---

apparent in Williams' translation: "And all these things which I said by way of digression do I say unto you," p. 64. With the emendation, "ἔλεγον" would be the normal and ongoing reference to the stated addressee or Justin's readers, e.g., *Dial.* 41.1 (ὧ ἄνδρες, ἔλεγον, and so on) and the text would be completely clear. Otto, p. 108, n. 14, sees the difficulty, but proposes a more complicated emendation.

[42]P. 59. Harnack, too, curiously refers to "Rabbi Trypho und einigen von dessen Schülern," *Judentum und Judenchristentum*, p. 53. But as we have noted Trypho is differentiated from the Jewish teachers in the *Dialogue* and cannot be one of them.

[43]See above, pp. 128-29.

Thirdly and most decisively, <u>Dial</u>. 32.5 indicates that
those who are "misled" by the Jews are not at all Christians,
but pagans as Zahn stated. Justin's statement that καὶ παρ'
ἡμῶν μανθάνοντες τῶν σοφισθέντων ἀπὸ τῆς τοῦ Χριστοῦ χάριτος
(<u>Dial</u>. 32.5) sets off the Christians not only from the Jews
(καὶ ἑαυτούς), but also from those who are "led astray" by the
Jews (καὶ τοὺς ὑμῶν ἀκούοντας πλανῶντες). The latter, therefore, can be only unbelieving gentiles.

What we seem therefore to have in <u>Dial</u>. 32.5 is an indirect, isolated reference to non-Christian gentiles inclined
toward Judaism. The indirect reference is, as far as it is
possible to ascertain, and certainly within the total scope of
the <u>Dialogue</u>, made quite in passing. It is similar to Justin's
fleeting but intriguing comment about τοὺς ἐκτρεπομένους τῆς
ὀρθῆς ὁδοῦ (<u>Dial</u>. 8.2) which is also vague in its own context.[44]
It is of course tempting to link these statements of Justin and
to associate them with Marcus Pompeius, the stated addressee
and perhaps, in Harnack's words, "receptive pagan" whom Justin
wishes to win over to Christianity. But this supposition would,
according to all evidence, stand as a conjecture of the highest
improbability. Not only is that isolated reference lost in the
<u>Dialogue</u>, but also Justin's sense of straight-forwardness, even
boldness,[45] does not seem to permit the above supposition. A
writer of Justin's passion and candor is not likely to leave
matters of important concern to him in the background of undeveloped statements. <u>Dial</u>. 32.5 contains an indirect and allusive reference to pagans who are receptive to Judaism but who
cannot be considered the addressees of the <u>Dialogue</u>. Nowhere

---

[44]In <u>Dial</u>. 8.2 Justin is addressing Trypho. The remark
would specifically suit in the most relevant manner those who
already have found the true way, but are going astray, i.e.,
Christians attracted either by Gnosticism (e.g. <u>Dial</u>. 30.1;
35.4ff.; 82.3; cf. <u>Ap</u>. 58.2) or Judaism (<u>Dial</u>. 47.3). There
is no evidence of this, however, in <u>Dial</u>. 8.2.

[45]A fearless possession of truth, or fearlessness precisely because of the conviction that truth is possessed marks
Justin's self-understanding (<u>Ap</u>. 2.1,4; 12.6ff.; 23.1; 25.1;
30.1 et al.; <u>Dial</u>. 7.1; 8.1; 39.5; 96.2; 110.4,6; 121.4 et al.).
Justin thinks that he brings forward not merely human teachings
or arguments, but those which come from God and Scripture, and
one cannot say anything better than Scripture (<u>Dial</u>. 55.3; 68.1;
80.3; 85.5).

184

in this work does Justin show any interest in such pagans.[46]

(e) <u>Dial</u>. 64.2e:

καὶ τὸ αὐτὸ καὶ πρὸς πάντας ἁπλῶς τοὺς ἐκ παντὸς γένους ἀνθρώπων, συζητεῖν ἢ πυνθάνεσθαί μου περὶ τούτων
βουλομένους πράττω.

And so will I do with, in fact, all of every race of
men, who desire to make enquiries, or to ask questions
of one about these matters.

This is a passage of universalistic concern and one that Harnack
suggested as implying pagan readers for the <u>Dialogue</u>. In the
context, Justin is replying to Trypho's aloof remark that Jesus
can indeed remain the Lord and Messiah but of Christians alone.
The Jews as worshippers of God, says Trypho, have no need of
confessing Christ (<u>Dial</u>. 64.1). Justin answers that if he were
equally contentious he would break off the discussion and would
leave Trypho and the Jews to their fate. But because he fears
the judgment of God, he will not pass verdict on any of the
Jews, who may be part of the eschatological remnant yet to be
redeemed.[47] Rather, he will patiently continue answering their
questions no matter what objections they may raise (<u>Dial</u>. 64.2).
Then Justin makes the statement above, saying that he does in
fact do the same for <u>all</u> <u>men</u> who are willing to discuss issues
of the Christian faith with him and possibly be persuaded.

Although Justin here has pagans in view, a fundamental
qualification is necessary. It is one thing to say that Justin
has also pagans in view within his total outlook, and quite
another to claim that pagans in a concrete way are also the addressees of the <u>Dialogue</u>.

That pagans are partly in view within the <u>Dialogue</u> cannot be doubted above all because of the powerful universalism
that informs Justin's faith. Justin has found the truth.[48] If
he continues to be a philosopher and to wear the <u>pallium</u>, it is
because he knows the truth which makes one perfect and happy,

---

[46]The only place where he speaks of gentile proselytes
to Judaism, <u>Dial</u>. chaps. 122-23, Justin is anxious to identify
them solidly with the Jews for his particular argument (<u>Dial</u>.
123.1-2) and is even less hopeful of attracting them than the
Jews themselves (<u>Dial</u>. 122.1-2).

[47]See above, pp. 42-44.

[48]<u>Dial</u>. 8.1; cf. 3.7; 7.1; <u>Ap</u>. 2.1-2; 23.1; 30.1).

and which he must declare to all men (Dial. 1.2; 8.2). Christians pray for the conversion not only of the Jews, but of all
peoples (Dial. 35.8). Justin would wish that all men could
bountifully share the grace given to him to understand Scripture (Dial. 58.1c). Elsewhere he movingly notes that Christians, even though cursed by Jews and persecuted by pagans, say
to all: you are our brothers, come to know the truth (ἀδελφοί
ἡμῶν ἐστε, ἐπίγνωτε μᾶλλον τὴν ἀλήθειαν τοῦ θεοῦ, Dial. 96.
2c).[49]

Thus Justin is imbued with a catholic vision. The above
statement of Dial. 64.2e is a similar expression of Justin's
universalistic outlook. It indicates his eagerness to engage
any man in conversation concerning the Christian faith with the
hope of persuading him. But it does not disclose the addressees
of the Dialogue, which is another question.

(f)   Dial. 119.4:

> οὐκοῦν οὐ εὐκαταφρόνητος δῆμός ἐσμεν, οὐδὲ βάρβαρον
> φῦλον οὐδὲ ὁποῖα Καρῶν ἢ Φρυγῶν ἔθνη, ἀλλὰ καὶ ἡμᾶς
> ἐξελέξατο ὁ θεὸς καὶ ἐμφανὴς ἐγενήθη τοῖς μὴ ἐπερωτῶ-
> σιν αὐτόν. 'Ιδοὺ θεός εἰμι, φησί, τῷ ἔθνει, οἳ οὐκ
> ἐπεκαλέσαντο τὸ ὄνομά μου. τοῦτο γάρ ἐστιν ἐκεῖνο τὸ
> ἔθνος, ὃ πάλαι τῷ 'Αβραὰμ ὁ θεὸς ὑπέσχετο, καὶ πατέρα
> πολλῶν ἐθνῶν θήσειν ἐπηγγείλατο.

> Wherefore we are not a people to be despised, nor a
> clan of barbarians, nor like the nations of the Carians
> or the Phrygians, but God has even chosen us, and has
> been made manifest to them that enquired not after Him.
> "Behold, I am God," He says, "to the nation, who called
> not upon My name." For this is that nation which God
> long since undertook to give Abraham, and promised to
> make him father of many nations.

This last passage was also cited by Harnack as support
for his suggestion that pagans as well are addressees of the

---

[49]Justin in fact knows that some pagans daily turn to
Christ: ἔτι καθ'ἡμέραν τινὰς μαθητευομένους εἰς τὸ ὄνομα τοῦ
Χριστοῦ . . . καὶ ἀπολείποντας τὴν ὁδὸν τῆς πλάνης (Dial. 39.2).
Those who "leave the way of error" are pagans as indicated by
Dial. 39.4; 41.4; 47.1; 109.1; 113.6-7. Nevertheless, these
references, except of course Dial. 39.2, have to do with those
who are already Christians, i.e., as former pagans who have al-
ready been saved from πλάνη. In an interesting article, "Bap-
tismal Theology and Practice in Rome as Reflected in Justin
Martyr," in Russia and Orthodoxy, III, ed. Andrew Blane and
Thomas Bird (The Hague: Mouton Press, 1974), pp. 9-34, George
Williams finds that Justin gives testimony to three degrees of
baptism: for Jews, for Christian progeny, and for gentile converts.

186

Dialogue. In the context, Justin is dealing with the third
theme of the Dialogue, the true and false Israel, treated with
concentration in Dial. chaps. 119-25. Harnack apparently surmised that Justin's references to gentiles imply pagan readers.
In particular, he pointed to the contrast between the barbarians
on the one hand and, on the other, presumably cultured pagans
with whom Justin identifies (οὐδὲ βάρβαρον φῦλον . . . ἀλλὰ καὶ
ἡμᾶς ἐξελέξατο ὁ θεός), as indicating that the Dialogue is also
intended for Greek readers. However, Justin is here talking a-
bout Christians. He does not here or anywhere else in the Dialogue identify himself with Greek pagans in general, but only
with gentiles who are already Christians. He distinguishes between believing and non-believing gentiles.[50]

Furthermore, the people who are contrasted to ἡμᾶς (the
Christians) are in the wider context not the "barbarians" but
the Jews. The contrast in the specific passage with the "barbarians," although it has a certain apologetic ring not noted by
Harnack, arises from Justin's preceding claim about the high
status of the Christians as a people. This claim runs as follows:

> ἡμεῖς λαὸς ἕτερος ἀνεθήλαμεν . . . ἡμεῖς δὲ οὐ μόνον
> λαὸς ἀλλὰ καὶ λαὸς ἅγιός ἐσμεν, ὡς ἐδείξαμεν ἤδη. Καὶ
> καλέσουσιν αὐτὸν λαὸν ἅγιον, λελυτρωμένον ὑπὸ κυρίου.
> οὐκοῦν οὐκ εὐκαταφρόνητος δῆμός ἐσμεν, οὐδὲ βάρβαρον
> φῦλον (Dial. 119.3-4).

> We sprouted up afresh as another people . . . we are
> not only a people, but also a holy people, as we have
> already proved: "And they shall call it a holy people,
> redeemed by the Lord." Wherefore we are not a people
> to be despised, not a clan of barbarians.

The emphasis on the privileged status of Christians before God
triggers the fleeting depreciatory reference to the "barbarians"
which plays no role at all in the Dialogue.

But the presupposed contrast with the Jews is decisive.
In the passage under discussion, Justin quotes from Dt. 14:2,
Is. 65:1 and Gen. 17:5, texts which he considers predictions of
the rise of the gentile Church. The Apologist's intent both
here and in the wider context, where he quotes numerous other
Old Testament texts, is to demonstrate his thesis about the true
Israel as compared to the false one. The one is promised by

---

[50]As has been noted above, pp. 179ff.

Scripture. The other is censured by Scripture. Justin concludes his present argument with an explicit contrast between
Christians and Jews: ἡμεῖς . . . ὁμοιόπιστον οὖν τὸ ἔθνος καὶ
θεοσεβὲς καὶ δίκαιον, εὐφραῖνον τὸν πατέρα, ὑπισχνεῖται αὐτῷ
[τῷ ᾽Αβραάμ], ἀλλ᾽οὐχ ὑμᾶς, οἷς οὐκ ἔστι πίστις ἐν αὐτοῖς (Dial.
119.6). This is the ongoing contrast of the third major theme
of the Dialogue which is assumed throughout the work. Thus
Dial. 119.4 has to do with gentiles who are Christians, not unbelieving pagans.

We have examined all of the passages cited by various
authors in support of the hypothesis that pagans are partly or
primarily the addressees of the Dialogue. Our findings may be
here summarized. Dial. 23.3 is directed to Trypho and his
Jewish companions, not to gentiles who are converts to Judaism.
Dial. 24.3 and 29.1 are addressed to Christian gentiles. Dial.
32.5 indeed contains an allusive reference to non-Christian gentiles leaning toward Judaism, but in no way suggests that these
are the intended readers of this writing. Dial. 64.2e is a general reference to all men, including pagans, but these are not
the addressees of the Dialogue. Dial. 80.3b favors either
Christians or Justin's gnostic opponents, but not pagans. Finally, Dial. 119.4 involves again gentiles who are already
Christians, not pagans at large. None of the above passages
supports the hypothesis of a pagan readership of the Dialogue.

(3) A third argument of the hypothesis that pagans are
the addressees of the Dialogue is derived from the philosophical
prologue of Justin's work (Dial. chaps. 1-6), as well as from
Justin's concept of the Christian faith as a "philosophy" (Dial.
8.1). Both Goodenough, who interprets the prologue as the key
to the purpose of the Dialogue, and Hyldahl, who writes his book
as a study of the prologue, have on these grounds claimed that
the intended reader or readers of the Dialogue are preferrably
or even exclusively pagans.

Goodenough finds as a main problem the discontinuity between the prologue, which deals with philosophical questions,
and the main body of the work, which discusses issues arising
presumably out of the Jewish-Christian debate.[51] His solution

[51]Goodenough, pp. 96ff.

is that "once the Dialogue is recognized as addressed to a man
interested in philosophy and not as a record of a controversy,
or a text book for controversy, against Judaism, the continuity
of the introduction with the body of the Dialogue becomes
clear."[52] For Goodenough the Dialogue is a vindication of the
unity and superiority of revelation over against philosophy.
The prologue demonstrates the superiority of the revealed faith
over philosophy. The main body of the work demonstrates the
unity of revelation, which disagreements between Christians and
Jews may set into question. This concept of the purpose of the
Dialogue, says Goodenough, preferrably requires a pagan reader,
not a Jew.[53]

But could not a Jew be "a man interested in philosophy?"
And must the Dialogue's philosophical aspects exclude this document from being "a record of a controversy, or a text book for
controversy, against Judaism?" Justin himself portrays Trypho,
a Jew, as a man interested in philosophy. Trypho has studied
philosophy under one Corinthus of Argus and has cultivated a
positive appreciation of it (Dial. 1.2-3). It is on the basis
of his interest in philosophy that Trypho approaches Justin to
learn something of philosophical value (Dial. 1.1-3,6). On the
other hand, Justin, too, as a Christian is also interested in
"philosophy." He wears the philosopher's cloak (Dial. 1.2) and
claims to be a philosopher (οὕτως δὴ καὶ διὰ ταῦτα φιλόσοφος
ἐγώ, Dial. 8.2). The cultural assumptions behind Justin's portrayal of Trypho and his own self-understanding are significant.
They indicate that in the Graeco-Roman world both a Jew and a
Christian could be appreciative of the philosophical issues discussed in the prologue.[54] By the same token, interest in philosophy and the Jewish-Christian controversy need not be opposed
as they seem to be opposed by Goodenough. The Dialogue may well
arise out of the Jewish-Christian debate and still contain
philosophical interests nourished by the larger cultural cli-

---

[52]Ibid., p. 99.

[53]Ibid., p. 100.

[54]As far as the Jews are concerned, Philo is a notable
example. As far as the Christians are concerned, Athenagoras,
Aristeides, Origen, Clement of Alexandria and others, in addition to Justin, are examples of Christian thinkers who were
interested in philosophy.

mate.[55] Indeed, this seems to be the case.[56] Thus Goodenough's view of the intended reader of the Dialogue, and especially his contention that a Jewish addressee must be excluded, cannot be accepted.

In the instance of Hyldahl, the hypothesis of the addressees of the Dialogue being pagans finds most unequivocal support. The philosophical issues of the Dialogue's prologue, and especially the Apologist's view of Christianity as a philosophy,[57] lead Hyldahl to the uncompromising position that the intended readers of this work are neither Jews nor Christians, but only pagans.[58] His view is that the Dialogue is an exposition of Christian philosophy arising from the encounter of Christianity with Greek philosophy and that, therefore, the Dialogue is addressed exclusively to pagans. The only concession Hyldahl makes is to note that the readers of the Dialogue are pagans of a special kind, i.e., part of the wider Graeco-Roman public which, as he puts it, lively engaged itself with the question of Judaism along with philosophy and religion. In this he finds the only real difference between the addressees of the Dialogue and those of the Apology, the latter being for him a more official document directed to the Roman authorities.[59] Otherwise

---

[55]As far as Justin's concern for the "unity of revelation," whenever present in the Dialogue (e.g., Dial. 11.1; 23. 1-2), it has nothing to do with pagans but with Justin's gnostic opponents, a front which Goodenough does not at all consider. See above, pp. 27ff. and 157-63.

[56]See above, pp. 18ff. and 33ff.

[57]Philosophie und Christentum, p. 294.

[58]Hyldahl does not explicitly say that the Dialogue is not also addressed to Christians, but he does, p. 21, n. 5, call Harnack's suggestion that the Dialogue is also (for Harnack, mainly) written for Christians and Jews, along with receptive pagans, a compromise. For Hyldahl's views on the addressees and character of the Dialogue, see pp. 18-21 and 294-95 of his book.

[59]"Der Unterschied zwischen Apol.-App. und Dial. besteht nicht darin, dass sich die eine Schrift an das griechisch-römische Publikum und die andere an das jüdische wendet, sondern darin, dass Apol.-App. ein an die römischen Behörden gerichtetes offizielles Schreiben sein will . . . während Dial. für den Teil der griechisch-römischen Öffentlichkeit gedacht ist, welcher sich lebhaft mit Fragen über das Judentum samt Philosophie und Religion beschäftigt," Philosophie und Christentum, p. 20.

both of these writings of Justin are, according to Hyldahl, addressed to pagans.

But some fundamental distinctions are necessary. We
have already argued that philosophical interests in the Dialogue
do not necessarily imply pagan readers. In a similar way Justin's concept of the Christian faith as a philosophy does not
require that pagans be assumed as the addressees of this work.
Jews and Christians living in the Graeco-Roman world were also
interested in philosophy. Hyldahl seems to confuse the issue of
the cultural setting of the Dialogue with the issue of the addressees of this work. But these are separate questions. It is
true that Justin poses as a philosopher and that his thought
contains philosophical elements. It is true that pagans are
partly in view within the horizon of the Dialogue. The powerful
universalism with which Justin conceives of the Christian faith,
being for him the only true philosophy (Dial. 8.1), makes him an
advocate of the new faith to all men, including pagans. Nevertheless, it by no means follows that the Dialogue itself is a
writing addressed to pagans or much less that this document is
a point by point Christian answer to various philosophical issues of the pagan world, i.e., a direct and extensive refutation
of Greek philosophy implying pagan readership. Justin was no
doubt capable of such a task as his efforts in the Apology indicate. But in the Dialogue explicitly philosophical questions
receive no attention beyond the prologue,[60] the bulk of the
Dialogue dealing with the Mosaic Law, the Christology and the
theme of the true and false Israel (Dial. chaps. 7-142). Although the broader cultural setting of the Dialogue is that of
the Graeco-Roman world, the contents of the Dialogue arise for
the most part out of the Jewish-Christian debate, not out of
the encounter of Christianity with Greek philosophy, and are of
greater interest to Christians and Jews rather than to pagans.
The philosophical features of the Dialogue do not certainly

---

[60] And the intention of the prologue is to show that,
where all philosophy fails, because it is a merely human a-
chievement, divinely-inspired Scripture is the answer. Justin's first censure of Trypho is that he should not look to philosophy for benefit as much as to Moses and the Prophets (Dial.
1.3). This is more than a passing comment. The same idea is
also the connection between the prologue and the rest of the
Dialogue: Scripture is the only guarantee of the truth, whereas
philosophy has failed.

require pagans as the addressees of this document.[61] Hyldahl's view of the addressees of the Dialogue cannot also be maintained.

(4) The final argument for the case of pagans as the addressees of the Dialogue is provided by Voss.[62] Voss in a similar fashion supposes that the literary form of the Dialogue, which is, in his words, neither Jewish nor Christian, but pagan and Greek--probably a conscious imitation of the Platonic style--implies that this document has been written for cultured pagan readers.[63] But here we have the same identification of the question of the cultural setting of the Dialogue with that of the addressees of this work. The assumption is that a literary feature reflecting the cultural milieu of the Dialogue also indicates the actual addressees of this writing. Voss knows and supports Hyldahl's position. Yet this position cannot be sustained since, just as a Christian or a Jew living in the Graeco-Roman world, as well as a pagan, can be expected to share the philosophical concerns of the age, so also a Christian or a Jew, as well as a pagan, can equally be expected to find the literary form of the "dialogue" attractive. Justin himself who

---

[61] It may also be noted that Hyldahl advocates his hypothesis partly because of the modern scholarly conception of the Dialogue as a more or less free literary writing. At one point, p. 20, Hyldahl chides Zahn for his "historicism" in interpreting the setting of the Dialogue. This is the reason why most recent students of Justin seem to favor also Christians, rather than Jews, as the addressees of the Dialogue. See Barnard, p. 24, n. 1, and Chadwick, p. 278.

[62] Voss, p. 38.

[63] He writes: "Mit der Frage nach der äusseren Form seiner Traditionsbezogenheit, hängt die nach seinem Adressaten zusammen. . . . Bei Justin steht diese Form in einer Überlieferung, die weder jüdisch ist noch christlich, sondern heidnisch-griechisch. Also dürfte die Schrift in erster Linie nicht an die Juden und auch nicht so sehr an die Christen gerichtet sein, sondern an die--gebilden--Heiden" (ibid.). On the next page Voss even says that Justin, within certain limits, has thus refuted Celsus before the latter even takes pen in hand! But he at least grants, p. 39, that "wie jedoch die Apologien zwar an die--heidnischen--Herrscher adressiert waren, in Wirklichkeit aber hauptsächlich von Christen gelesen wurden, so wird auch der Dialogus vornehmlich unter den Glaubensgenossen seines Verfassers Leser gefunden haben."

writes the <u>Dialogue</u> is a Christian. In the case of Jews, it is common knowledge that Hellenistic Jews were not merely interested in, but also had already adopted Greek literary forms, including history, poetry and drama, centuries prior to Justin's <u>Dialogue</u>. Thus, as well, Voss' literary argument does not support the hypothesis of pagans as addressees of the <u>Dialogue</u>.

We have examined the evidence cited for the <u>Dialogue</u> as a writing to pagans. None of the above arguments provides adequate support for such a hypothesis. In some instances, the evidence is made to yield premises which do not follow. In other instances the evidence may be differently interpreted. The hypothesis of pagans as addressees of the <u>Dialogue</u> cannot be sustained. But there are also additional considerations which almost certainly exclude the possibility of pagans as the intended readers of the <u>Dialogue</u>. Three points may be offered:

(1) First of all, the <u>Dialogue</u> presupposes a familiarity with, even intimate knowledge of, both Judaism and Christianity which cannot be presupposed of a wider Graeco-Roman readership. It is true that, as Hyldahl notes, references to Jewish traditions and Jewish affairs, such as to the writings of the Old Testament Prophets, the Septuagint, the Bar Cochba war and to others, may be found in the <u>Apology</u>, which is undoubtedly addressed to pagans, just as they may be found in the <u>Dialogue</u>.[64] But it hardly follows that the <u>Dialogue</u> also is addressed to pagans. The crucial difference is that in the <u>Apology</u> Justin offers explanatory statements to his readers about matters which they could not be expected to know. Justin has to explain the origins, character and translation of the Old Testament (<u>Ap</u>. 31.1-5). He has to explain the composition of the Christian Church made up of gentiles, Jews and Samaritans (<u>Ap</u>. 53.3-12). He has to explain that the words of Jesus were brief and concise because Jesus was not a sophist (<u>Ap</u>. 14.5). The whole key in which the <u>Apology</u> is written is one of presenting Christianity to a wider public unfamiliar with the basic facts of the Christian faith.

In the <u>Dialogue</u>, however, one would in vain search for

---

[64]Hyldahl, <u>Philosophie und Christentum</u>, p. 20.

such explanations.[65] The Dialogue presupposes knowledge not
only of the Old Testament and the Mosaic Law, but also of the
Gospel(s)--all of which are introduced in the discussion between Trypho and Justin without explanatory comments (Dial. 8.4;
9.1; 10.2; cf. 1.3). Some passages of the Dialogue even presuppose knowledge of Old Testament contexts![66] Nor is the
length of the Scriptural citations necessarily indicative of pagan readership, as Goodenough suggests.[67] In the Apology, a do-
coment clearly addressed to pagans, the citations from the Old
Testament are much less extensive and, of course, the Old Testament itself is introduced very differently in the Apology (Ap.
31.1ff.) than in the Dialogue (Dial. 9.1; 10.3).

        (2) The extensive use of Scripture, as well as the con-
tents of the Dialogue, favor an immediate Jewish-Christian, not
a broader pagan, readership. Marcel Simon has pointed out that,
while the predictive proof from Scripture was to a certain degree effective with pagans, as the Apology shows, and as Harnack
had said, the use of the Old Testament suggests in the first
place recognition of its authority by the groups in controversy
and that, destined for pagans, Scriptural arguments tend to lose
their weight.[68] In the Dialogue, the interpretation of Scripture is the main issue and the authority of Scripture is the assumed court of appeals for both participants.[69]

---

[65]With the exception of Dial. 7.1 where, as part of Justin's conversion story, the old man by the sea introduces the
Prophets to Justin. Goodenough is not correct, pp. 98-99, in
thinking that this is also the case with Justin's qualification
"one of the twelve" when quoting the Minor Prophets (e.g. Dial.
19.5; 22.1; 109.1), for this would still remain cryptic to one
unfamiliar with the Old Testament Canon. Rather, this seems to
be a stylized reference to the Minor Prophets.

[66]For example in Dial. 10.3-4 where Gen. 17:14 is quoted.
The references to the purchased slaves and to circumcision as a
"covenant" presuppose the whole context of Gen. 17:2ff., 12-14,
27.

[67]Goodenough, p. 99.

[68]Simon, Verus Israel, pp. 169-70.

[69]Hyldahl makes the curious statement that Justin's emphasis on the authority of the Septuagint also points to pagans
as addressees of the Dialogue. But it points to nothing else
than to the Septuagint as the Christian Bible.

The bulk of the contents of the Dialogue also favors Christian and Jewish, rather than pagan, readers. The Dialogue deals mainly with the Mosaic Law (chaps. 10-30), the Christology (chaps. 31-118) and the true Israel (chaps. 119-142). These are the central issues of the Jewish-Christian debate. How are they relevant for pagan readers? In the instance of the Mosaic Law, which is a major issue in the Jewish-Christian debate, and one which occupies so much attention in the Dialogue, it is not mentioned even once in the Apology, a writing for pagans! The failure to raise the question of the relevance of the contents of the Dialogue, as they are presented in this document, for pagans, is the most obvious and perhaps most serious weakness of the scholars who have advocated the hypothesis of a pagan readership of the Dialogue.

(3) Finally, certain apologetic interests in connection with pagan culture which are evident in the Apology are absent from the Dialogue. Above all, Justin's theory of the Spermatikos Logos, so important in the Apology, is not at all invoked in the Dialogue, not even in the prologue where Justin momentarily looks to the intellectual horizon of paganism. This means that an argument constructed specifically with pagans and the pagan world in view, and the purpose of which is to link what is best in the pagan heritage with the Christian faith, is nowhere in evidence in the Dialogue! Such an omission would indeed be strange, if the Dialogue were written as a philosophical exposition for pagan readers.

On the contrary, in the Dialogue Justin concedes nothing to philosophy or to philosophers. Most philosophers are not true to their task (Dial. 1.4; 2.1ff.). They cannot have true knowledge of God unaided by the Holy Spirit (Dial. 3.7; 4.1; cf. 7.1ff.). They know nothing about how God can be known or what the soul truly is (Dial. 5.1). Justin has the old man even saying that he cares nothing about Plato and Pythagoras (Dial. 6.1). They are merely "reputed" philosophers (νομιζόμενοι φιλόσοφοι, Dial. 7.1). In the Apology, however, apologetic interests over against pagans whom Justin addresses lead the Apologist to declare that Socrates, Heraclitus, Plato and others are Christians prior to Christ who lived according to the true Logos.[70] The sharp contrast of attitude with respect to philosophy is inexplicable if the Dialogue was written for pagans, and pagans who are interested in philosophy at that!

The final conclusion is this: the Dialogue is not addressed to pagans. Neither direct nor indirect evidence shows that Justin's argumentation on the Mosaic Law, as well as the other themes of the Dialogue, should be read as formulated for pagan readers. On the contrary, between the Dialogue and the Apology there are differences which decisively favor Christians and Jews,[71] rather than pagans, as the readers of the Dialogue. The hypothesis of pagans as addressees of the Dialogue must be rejected.

---

[70]Ap. 46.3; App. 10.1ff.; 13.2ff. However, Holte's caveat regarding the role of apologetics behind these statements is well taken: "If we do not take due consideration to this fact, there is a decided risk of over-emphasizing the significance of the points of agreement between the teachings of Christianity and those of ancient philosophy . . . (and) of over-interpreting the theory of Logos Spermatikos," p. 10. Thus Merrill Young in his dissertation, "The Argument and Meaning of Justin Martyr's Conversion Story," pp. 2ff. and 202ff., is correct to insist that the Dialogue reflects Justin's true feelings about Greek philosophy.

[71]See above, pp. 32-44.

BIBLIOGRAPHY

A. Texts

Septuaginta, Vetus Testamentum Graece juxta LXX interpres. Edited by A. Rahlfs. 2 vols. 8th ed. Stuttgart, 1965.

The Old Testament in Greek. Edited by A. E. Brooke and N. McLean. 2 vols. Cambridge, 1917.

Novum Testamentum Graece. Edited by Eb. Nestle, Erw. Nestle, and K. Aland. 25th ed. Stuttgart, 1965.

Archambault, Georges. _Justin: Dialogue avec Tryphon._ 2 vols. Paris, 1909.

Bernhard, R. _Die Pseudoklementinen._ Vol. I: _Homilien._ GCS. Berlin, 1953.

Cohn, L. and Wendland, P. _Philonis Alexandrini Opera quae supersunt._ 7 vols. Berlin, 1896-1926.

Connolly, R. H. _Didascalia Apostolorum._ Oxford, 1929.

Cramer, J. A. _Catenae Graecorum Patrum in Novum Testamentum._ Vol. VIII. Oxford, 1844.

Danby, H. _The Mishnah._ London, 1964.

Funk, F. X. _Didaskalia et Constitutiones Apostolorum._ 2 vols. Paderborn, 1905 (reprinted 1960).

_____ and Bihlmeyer, K. _Die Apostolischen Väter._ Tübingen, 1956.

Goodspeed, E. J. _Die ältesten Apologeten._ Göttingen, 1914.

Harvey, W. W. _Sancti Irenaei Episcopi Lugdunensis: Libros Quinque adversus Haereses._ 2 vols. Cambridge, 1857 (Reprinted 1965).

Koetschau, P. _Origenes Werke._ 2 vols. GCS. Leipzig, 1899.

Migne, J. P. _Chrysostom: Adversus Judaeos._ Patrologia Graeca, XLVIII, 814-912.

Otto, Johannes Karl Theodor von. _Justini Philosophi et Martyris._ 3rd ed. Vol. I, Part 1. Jena, 1876-1881.

Quispel, G. _Ptolémée: Lettre à Flora._ SC 24. Paris, 1949.

198

Rehm, B. Die Pseudoklementinen. Vol. II: Rekognitionen. GCS. Berlin, 1965.

Schwartz, E. Eusebius' Kirchengeschichte. Berlin, 1952.

Stählin, O. Clemens Alexandrinus Opera. GCS. Berlin, 1909-1939.

Tränkle, H. Tertulliani Adversus Judaeos mit Einleitung und kritischen Kommentar. Wiesbaden, 1964.

Weber, R. Sancti Cypriani Episcopi Opera: Ad Quirinum. Corpus Christianorum, Series Latina III. Brepols, 1972.

Quinti Septimi Florentis Tertulliani Opera: Adversus Marcionem. Corpus Christianorum, Series Latina I. Brepols, 1954.

B. Works of Reference

Bauer, W., Arndt, W. F., and Gingrich, F. W. A Greek-English Lexicon of the New Testament. Chicago, 1957.

Encyclopaedia Judaica. Vol. XII. Jerusalem, 1972.

Goodspeed, E. J. Index Apologeticus sive Clavis Justini Martyris Operum aliorumque Apologetarum Pristinorum. Leipzig, 1912.

Kittel, G., and Friedrich, G. Theological Dictionary of the New Testament. Translated by G. W. Bromiley. Vols. I-VII (A-Σ). Grand Rapids, 1964-1971.

Kraft, H. Clavis Patrum Apostolicorum. Munich, 1963.

Lampe, G. W. H. A Patristic Greek Lexicon. Oxford, 1961-1968.

Liddell, H. G., Scott, R., and Jones, H. W. A Greek-English Lexicon. 9th ed. Oxford, 1940 (reprinted 1966).

Moulton, W. F., and Geden, A. S. A Concordance to the Greek Testament. Edinburgh, 1963.

Preisigke, F. Wörterbuch der griechischen Papyrusurkunden mit Einschluss der griechischen Inschriften, Aufschriften, Ostraka, Mumienschilder usw. aus Ägypten. Berlin, 1914-1927.

Sophocles, E. A. Greek Lexicon of the Roman and Byzantine Periods. Boston, 1870.

Stephanus, Henricus. Thesaurus Graecae Linguae. 8 vols. Paris, 1831-1865.

Hatch, E., and Redpath, H. A. A Concordance to the Septuagint. 3 vols. Graz, 1954.

C. Books and Articles

Amsler, S. L'Ancien Testament dans l'Eglise. Neuchâtel, 1960.

Andresen, C. "Justin und der mittlere Platonismus," ZNW 44 (1951-1953), 157-95.

_____. Logos und Nomos: Die Polemik des Kelsos wider das Christentum. Berlin, 1955.

Armstrong, G. T. Die Genesis in der alten Kirche: Die drei Kirchenväter (Justin, Irenaeus, Tertullian). Tübingen, 1962.

Aune, D. E. "Justin Martyr's Use of the Old Testament," Bulletin of the Evangelical Theological Society 9 (1966), 179-97.

Barnard, L. W. Justin Martyr: His Life and Thought. Cambridge, 1967.

_____. "The Old Testament and Judaism in the Writings of Justin Martyr," VT 19 (1965), 86-98.

Barnikol, E. "Verfasste oder benutzte Justin das um 140 entstandene, erste antimarcionitische Syntagma gegen die Häresien?" Theol. Jahrbücher 6 (1938), 17-19.

Barthélemy, D. "Redécouverte d'un chaînon manquant de l'histoire de la Septante," Revue Bibl. 60 (1953).

_____. "Les Devanciers d'Aquila," Supplements to VT. Vol. X. Leiden, 1963.

Bauer, W. Orthodoxy and Heresy in Earliest Christianity. Edited by R. A. Kraft and G. Krodel. Philadelphia, 1971.

Behm, J. Der Begriff ΔΙΑΘΗΚΗ im Neuen Testament. Leipzig, 1912.

Bellinzoni, A. J. The Sayings of Jesus in the Writings of Justin Martyr. Leiden, 1967.

Bergmann, J. Jüdische Apologetik im neutestamentlichen Zeitalter. Berlin, 1908.

Blackman, E. C. Marcion and His Influence. London, 1948.

Bousset, W. Jüdisch-christlicher Schulbetrieb in Alexandria und Rom: Literarische Untersuchungen zu Philo und Clemens von Alex., Justin und Irenaeus. Göttingen, 1915.

Bultmann, Rudolf. Theologie des Neuen Testaments. 5th ed. Tübingen, 1965.

Campenhausen, H. F. v. Die Entstehung der christlichen Bibel. Tübingen, 1968.

Chadwick, H. Early Christian Thought and the Classical Tradition. Oxford, 1966.

_____. "Justin Martyr's Defense of Christianity," Bull. John Ryl. Libr. 47 (1964-1965), 275-97.

200

Daniélou, J. From Shadows to Reality. Westminster, 1960.

_____. Message évangélique et culture hellénistique aux IIe et IIIe siècles. Tournai, 1961.

_____. "Saint Irénée et les origines de la théologie de l'histoire," RechSR 34 (1947), 227-31.

Davies, W. D. Torah in the Messianic Age. Philadelphia, 1952.

Engelhardt, M. v. Das Christentum Justins des Märtyrers. Erlangen, 1878.

Flesseman-Van Leer, E. Tradition and Scripture in the Early Church. Assen, 1954.

Franklin, C. F. "Justin's Concept of Deliberate Concealment in the Old Testament." Dissertation, Harvard, 1961.

Friedläender, M. Geschichte der jüdischen Apologetik als Vorgeschichte des Christentums. Zürich, 1903.

Gager, J. The Figure of Moses in Greek and Roman Pagan Literature. Dissertation, Harvard, 1967. Now published by Abingdon Press, 1972.

Geffcken, J. Zwei griechische Apologeten. Leipzig and Berlin, 1907.

Gerhardsson, Birger, Memory and Manuscript. Acta Seminarii Neotestamentici Upsaliensis. Vol. II. Uppsala, 1961.

Gill, D. "A Liturgical Fragment in Justin, Dialogue 29,1," HTR (1966), 98-100.

Goldfahn, A. H. "Justinus Martyr und die Agada," Monatshcrift für Geschichte und Wissenschaft des Judentums 22 (1873), 49-60, 104-15, 145-53, 192-202, 157-69.

Goodenough, E. R. The Theology of Justin Martyr. Jena, 1923.

Goppelt, Leonhard. Christentum und Judentum im ersten und zweiten Jahrhundert. BFChTh 55. Gütersloh, 1954.

Grant, R. M. The Letter and the Spirit. London, 1957.

Hanson, R. P. C. Allegory and Event. London, 1959.

Harnack, A. "Der Brief des Ptolemaeus an die Flora," SAB 25 (1902), 507-45.

_____. Judentum und Judenchristentum in Justins Dialog mit Tryphon. TU 39 (1913), 47-98.

_____. Marcion: Das Evangelium vom fremden Gott. TU 45. Leipzig, 1924.

Hasler, Victor Ernst. Gesetz und Evangelium in der Alten Kirche. Zürich, 1953.

Heinemann, I. Altjüdische Allegoristic. Breslau, 1935.

_____. *Philons griechische und jüdische Bildung*. Breslau, 1932.

Heinisch, P. *Der Einfluss Philos auf die älteste christliche Exegese: Barnabas, Justin, und Clemens von Alexandria*. Münster, 1908.

Hilgenfeld, A. "Der Brief des Valentinianers Ptolemaeus an die Flora," *ZWTh* 24 (1881), 214-30.

Hirzel, R. *Der Dialog: ein literarhistorischer Versuch*. Leipzig, 1895.

Holte, R. "Logos Spermatikos: Christianity and Ancient Philosophy according to St. Justin's Apologies," *StTh* 12 (1958), 109-68.

Hubik, K. *Die Apologien des H. Justinus des Philosophen und Märtyrers: Literarhistorische Untersuchungen*. Vienna, 1912.

Hulen, A. "The 'Dialogues with the Jews' as sources for the early Jewish argument against Christianity," *JBL* 51 (1932), 58-70.

Hyldahl, N. *Philosophie und Christentum: eine Interpretation der Einleitung zum Dialog Justins*. Copenhagen, 1966.

Jonas, H. *The Gnostic Religion*. Boston, 1963.

Klevinghaus, J. *Die theologische Stellung der apostolischen Väter zur alttestamentlichen Offenbarung*. *BFChTh* 44.

Koester, H. *Septuaginta und Synoptischer Erzählungsstoff im Schriftbeweis Justins des Märtyrers*. Heidelberg, 1956.

_____. "Νόμος Φύσεως: The Concept of Natural Law in Greek Thought," *Religions in Antiquity: Essays in Memory of E. R. Goodenough*. Edited by J. Neusner. Leiden, 1968. Pp. 521-41.

Kraft, R. A. *The Apostolic Fathers*. Vol. III: *Barnabas and the Didache*. Edited by F. M. Grant. New York, 1965.

_____. "The Epistle of Barnabas: Its Quotations and their Sources." Dissertation, Harvard, 1961.

Krüger, P. *Philo und Josephus als Apologeten des Judentums*. Leipzig, 1906.

Lindars, Barnabas. *New Testament Apologetic*. London, 1961.

Lohmeyer, E. *Diatheke*. Leipzig, 1912.

Lubac, Henri de. "Typologie et Allegorisme," *RechSR* 34 (1947), 180-226.

Marcus, R. A. "Pleroma and Fulfilment: The Significance of History in St. Irenaeus' Opposition to Gnosticism," *VigChr* 8 (1954), 193-224.

202

Moore, George Foot. _Judaism in the First Centuries of the Christian Era._ Cambridge, Mass., 1927.

Overbeck, Franz. "Über das Verhältniss Justins des Märtyrers zur Apostelgeschichte," _ZWTh_ 15 (1872), 305-49.

Pfättisch, J. M. "Christus und Sokrates bei Justin," _Theol. Quartalschrift_ 90 (1908), 503-23.

Prigent, P. _Les testimonia dans le christianisme primitif: l'Epître de Barnabée I-XVI et ses sources._ Paris, 1961.

_____. _Justin et l'Ancien Testament._ Paris, 1964.

Prümm, K. "Göttliche Plannung und menschliche Entwicklung nach Irenäus Adversus Haereses," _Scholastik_ 13 (1938), 206-24 and 342-66.

Pucke, Nestor. "Connaissance rationelle et connaissance de grâce chez Saint Justin," _EThL_ 37 (1961), 52-85.

Purves, George. _The Testimony of Justin Martyr to Early Christianity._ New York, 1889.

Richardson, P. _Israel in the Apostolic Church._ Cambridge, 1969.

Schmid, W. "Die Textüberlieferung der Apologie des Justins," _ZNW_ 40 (1941), 87-138.

Schoeps, H. J. _Die Tempelzerstörung des Jahres 70 in der jüdischen Religionsgeschichte._ Coniectanea Neotestamentica, Vol. VI. Uppsala, 1942.

_____. _Paul: The Theology of the Apostle in the Light of Jewish Religious History._ Translated by Harold Knight. Philadelphia, 1961.

_____. _The Jewish-Christian Argument._ New York, 1963.

_____. _Theologie und Geschichte des Judenchristentums._ Tübingen, 1949.

Semisch, C. _Justin der Märtyrer, Eine kirchen und dogmengeschichtliche Monographie._ 2 vols. Breslau, 1840-1842.

Shotwell, W. A. _The Biblical Exegesis of Justin Martyr._ London, 1965.

Sibinga, J. S. _The Old Testament Text of Justin Martyr._ Vol. I: _The Pentateuch._ Leiden, 1963.

Simon, M. "The Ancient Church in Rabbinic Tradition," in _Holy Book and Holy Tradition._ Edited by F. F. Bruce and E. G. Rupp. Grand Rapids, 1968. Pp. 94-112.

_____. _Verus Israel: Etude sur les relations entre Chrétiens et Juifs dans l'empire romain._ 2nd ed. Paris, 1964.

Smith, Morton. <u>Palestinian Parties and Politics that Shaped the Old Testament</u>. New York, 1971.

Stählin, Adolf. <u>Justin der Märtyrer und sein neuester Beurtheiler</u>. Leipzig, 1880.

Stendahl, Krister. <u>The School of St. Matthew and its Use of the Old Testament</u>. Philadelphia, 1968.

Story, C. I. K. <u>The Nature of Truth in "The Gospel of Truth" and in the Writings of Justin Martyr</u>. Leiden, 1970.

Strecker, G. <u>Das Judenchristentum in den Pseudoklementinen</u>. <u>TU</u> 70. Berlin, 1958.

_____. "The Kerygmata Petrou," in <u>New Testament Apocrypha</u>. Vol. II. Edited by E. Hennecke and W. Schneemelcher. Philadelphia, 1965. Pp. 102-27.

_____. Appendix on Jewish Christianity in Bauer, W. <u>Orthodoxy and Heresy in Earliest Christianity</u>. Edited by R. A. Kraft and G. Krodel. Philadelphia, 1971.

Stylianopoulos, T. "Shadow and Reality: Reflections on Heb. 10:1-18," <u>Greek Orthodox Theological Review</u> 17 (1972), 215-30.

Thieme, K. <u>Kirche und Synagoge</u>. Olten, 1945.

Thoma, A. "Justins literarisches Verhältniss zu Paulus und zum Johannes-Evangelium," <u>ZWTh</u> 18 (1875), 385-412 and 490-544.

Ungern-Sternberg, A. F. v. <u>Der traditionelle alttestamentliche Schriftbeweis 'de Christo' und 'de Evangelio' in der Alten Kirche</u>. Halle, 1913.

Van Ruler, A. A. <u>Die christliche Kirche und das Alte Testament</u>. BEvTh 23. Munich, 1955.

Van Unnik, W. C. "Ἡ Καινὴ Διαθήκη--A Problem in the Early History of the Canon," <u>TU</u> 79 (1961), 212-27.

Verweijs, P. G. <u>Evangelium und neues Gesetz in der ältesten Christenheit bis auf Marcion</u>. Utrecht, 1960.

Voss, Reiner. <u>Der Dialog in der frühchristlichen Literatur</u>. Munich, 1970.

Walzer, R. <u>Galen on Jews and Christians</u>. Oxford, 1949.

Weis, P. R. "Some Samaritanisms of Justin Martyr," <u>JThS</u> 45 (1944), 199-205.

Wiles, M. F. <u>The Divine Apostle</u>. Cambridge, 1967.

_____. "The Old Testament in Controversy with the Jews," <u>SJTh</u> 8 (1955), 113-26.

Williams, A. L. <u>Adversus Judaeos</u>. Cambridge, 1935.

_____. <u>Justin Martyr: The Dialogue with Trypho</u>. London, 1930.

9 2

Williams, George H. "Baptismal Theology and Practice in Rome as Reflected in Justin Martyr," Russia and Orthodoxy. Vol. III. Edited by Andrew Blane and Thomas Bird. The Hague, 1974. Pp. 9-34.

Windisch, H. L. Der Barnabasbrief. Tübingen, 1920.

Wolfson, H. A. Philo: Foundations of Religious Philosophy in Judaism, Christianity and Islam. 2 vols. 3rd ed. Cambridge, Mass., 1970.

Young, Merrill. "The Argument and Meaning of Justin Martyr's Conversion Story." Dissertation, Harvard, 1971.

Zahn, T. "Studien zu Justin III: Dichtung und Wahrheit in Justin's Dialog mit dem Juden Trypho," ZKG 8 (1885-1886), 56-61.